中国思想文化术语多语种对外翻译
标准化建设项目成果

CHINESE THINKING AND CULTURE
MULTILINGUAL TERMINOLOGY DATABASE

中华源·河南故事

CHINESE CIVILIZATION
Stories from Henan

# 中医
# TRADITIONAL CHINESE MEDICINE

主编　许二平
EDITOR-IN-CHIEF: XU ERPING

河南大学出版社
HENAN UNIVERSITY PRESS
·郑州·

**图书在版编目（CIP）数据**

中华源·河南故事．中医 / 许二平主编．—郑州：河南大学出版社，2019.3（2020.7 重印）

ISBN 978-7-5649-2664-9

Ⅰ．①中… Ⅱ．①许… Ⅲ．①地方文化－河南－通俗读物②中医学－通俗读物 Ⅳ．① G127.61-49 ② R2-49

中国版本图书馆 CIP 数据核字（2019）第 047363 号

责任编辑　纪庆芳
责任校对　任湘蕊
封面设计　翟淼淼
出版发行　河南大学出版社
　　　　　地址：郑州市郑东新区商务外环中华大厦2401号　邮编：450046
　　　　　电话：0371－86059701（营销部）　0371－86059753（大众读物分公司）
　　　　　网址：hupress.henu.edu.cn
排　　版　河南博雅彩印有限公司
印　　刷　河南博雅彩印有限公司
版　　次　2019年12月第1版　　印　次　2020年7月第2次印刷
开　　本　710 mm×1010 mm　1/16　　印　张　14.25
字　　数　204千字　　定　价　68.00元

## “中华源·河南故事”系列丛书编委会

顾　　问　黄友义　杨　平　范大祺
名誉主任　穆为民　何金平
主　　任　付　静
副 主 任　陈志伟　刁玉华　李向前　李　镇　梁留科　刘金锋
　　　　　孔留安　史永庆　许二平　万正峰　杨建伟　杨玮斌
　　　　　王建修　王自文　张改平　张松文　赵卫东

主　　编　付　静
执行主编　杨玮斌
编　　委　陈　玮　丁　锐　高　阳　徐恒振

## 中华源·河南故事·中医

主　　编　许二平
副 主 编　许敬生　朱剑飞（英文）
中文撰稿　许敬生　饶　洪　孟长海　许振国　尹笑丹
英文译者　朱剑飞　田开宇　赵俊卿　穆海博　李　蕾
英文审校　〔美〕Seto Pui

## The Editorial Committee
## *Chinese Civilization*
## *Stories from Henan*



## *Chinese Civilization*
## *Stories from Henan*
## *Traditional Chinese Medicine*

# 总 序

中国是世界四大文明古国之一，也是世界上唯一的古代文明传统未曾中断的国家。河南省地处中国中东部，是中华文明和中华民族的重要发祥地，在中国五千年的文明史上，河南作为国家政治、经济、文化的中心就长达三千多年。从某种意义上讲，一部河南史就是半部中国史。这里是中华人文始祖黄帝的故乡，是古丝绸之路的东方起点，是少林功夫和陈氏太极的发源地，这里创建了中国历史上最早的都城，镌刻了中国最古老的文字，诞生了中国最初的商业文明。

伴随着新时代的荣光，河南经济社会发展迅速，人民生活水平显著提升，这是自力更生、艰苦奋斗的历史结果，也是对外开放带来的益处。河南经济社会的发展、人民生活方式的改变都植根于深层次的文化积淀。为了让世界更多地了解河南，让河南更好地走向世界，2018年以来，河南省外事办认真研析了这片古老土地上的历史文化资源和时代风貌，组织各领域权威专家学者，编译了“中华源·河南故事”中外文系列丛书，选取少林功夫、太极拳、中医、汉字、文物、焦裕禄、红旗渠、丝绸之路、古都、农业、手工艺等多个主题，力图以故事的方式向世界展现一个立体、全面、真实的河南。

当今世界，人类文明无论在物质还是精神方面都取得了巨大进步，特别是物质的极大丰富是古代世界完全不能想象的。同时，当代人类也面临着许多突出的难题，比如，贫富差距持续扩大，物欲追求奢华无度，个人主义恶性膨胀，社会诚信不断消减，伦理道德每况愈下，人与自然关系日趋紧张，等等。要解决这些难题，不仅需要运用人类今天发现和发展的智慧和力量，而且需要运用人类历史上积累和储存的智慧和力量。河南历史文化底蕴深厚、包容性强，在今天仍极具现实意义。中原文化蕴含的思想智慧有助于修身养性，推动人类社会进步发展，焦裕禄精神、红旗渠精神所体现的为民爱民、艰苦奋斗的价值取向是构建人类命运共同体的力量源泉。我们期待与读者们一起从河南故事中汲取更多的智慧和力量，共同创造更加美好的未来。

# Series Foreword

China is one of the four ancient civilizations in the world, and is also the only country in the world where the ancient civilization has not been interrupted. Located in east-central China, Henan province is an important cradle for the Chinese nation and the Chinese civilization. In the course of the five thousand years of Chinese history, for more than three thousand years it served as the political, economic and cultural center of the country and therefore, as generally accepted, represents half of the history of China. Henan is the native place of Yellow Emperor, the cradle of Chinese culture, the starting point of the ancient Silk Road in the east, and the birthplace of Shaolin Kungfu and Chen-style Taijiquan—typical examples of the world-renowned Chinese martial arts. It was here that the earliest capital city in China was founded, the oldest Chinese characters engraved, and the earliest commerce took shape.

In the new era, Henan has witnessed rapid growth in its economy and remarkable improvement of people's living conditions, owing to the national reform and opening-up policy and unremitting endeavoring of the people. Modern economic achievements and social development as well as the changes of way of life could be traced back to its traditional values and cultural heritages. To enable people from other countries to understand Henan, and let the province integrate more efficiently into the world development, the Foreign Affairs Office of the People's Government of Henan Province, has organized teams of authoritative experts and scholars in relevant fields to compile this *Chinese Civilization: Stories from Henan* in Chinese and other foreign languages since 2018, by crystallizing the excellence of traditions and outstanding features of modern development. The book series include *Shaolin Kungfu, Taijiquan, Traditional Chinese Medicine, Chinese Characters, Cultural Heritage, A Model Official — Jiao Yulu, Man-made River — Hongqiqu Canal, the Silk*

*Road, Ancient Chinese Capitals, Handicraft* and *Feeding the People — Agriculture*, etc, attempting to present a panoramic picture of the province.

In today's world, human civilization has made great progress in both material accumulation and cultural and ethical advancement, and the great abundance of materials today, especially, is beyond the imagination of the ancient people. At the same time, however, modern people are also confronted with a lot of problems, such as the widening gap between the rich and the poor, the indulgence in pursuit of luxury and extravagance, the undesirable extension of individualism, the decline of social integrity, and the increasing tension between man and nature. To solve these problems, we need to draw on the wisdom and powers developed today as well as those accumulated in the past. Henan is endowed with a rich historical and cultural heritage characterized by its inclusiveness, and such a heritage remains significant today. The intelligence and wisdom in Henan culture are conducive to self-cultivation and to the promotion of social development. The spirit of serving the people and relentless struggle, as embodied in *Jiao Yulu* and *Hongqiqu Canal*, provides source of strength for building a community with a shared future for mankind. It is our hope that, wisdom and strength from Henan stories, could lead us to a shared brilliant future.

# 前言

河南文化的发展史，就是华夏文明史的缩影。河南地处中原腹地，在华夏古代文明发展的每个阶段，一直是核心区域。因河南位于华夏九州之中，境内多平原，故往往又被称为中原。中国最繁荣的史前文化多在河南：最早的国家政权在禹州；最早的成熟文字在安阳；玄妙幽深的道家文化以老子（河南鹿邑人）、庄子（河南民权人）为代表；对东亚地区影响深远的汉语佛教文化最先从洛阳传播，建于东汉明帝永平十一年（公元68年）的洛阳白马寺是中国最早的寺院，称“释源”“祖庭”。盘古开天、精卫填海、后羿射日、女娲造人、嫦娥奔月、伏羲画卦、神农尝草、仓颉造字、愚公移山等神话传说，均发生在河南。郑州商城、安阳殷墟、汉魏隋唐洛阳城、龙门石窟、大运河遗址、商丘华商始祖王亥故里、北宋东京城及少林寺等珍贵文化遗迹，均是河南古代文化发展的历史见证，处处闪耀着华夏文明之光。

早在1949年，德国哲学家卡尔·雅斯贝尔斯在他的《历史的起源与目标》一书中，提出了“轴心时代”的命题。他认为，公元前800年至公元前200年之间，是人类文明有重大突破的“轴心时代”。其间，各个文明都出现了伟大的精神导师：如古希腊有苏格拉底、柏拉图，以色列有犹太教的先知们，印度有释迦牟尼，中国有老子、孔子。这一观点已被学界的人广为接受，称这一“轴心时代”为东西方思想文化的大绽放。

处在“轴心时代”的春秋战国时期，正值社会大变革和大动荡时期，出现了诸子蜂起、百家争鸣的局面，促成了中国历史上第一次文化科学高峰。

而中国伟大的精神导师老子、孔子，后来分别成了道家和儒家的先师和代表。道家文化、儒家文化及诸子文化，这是中国传统文化的基础。而诸子文化的代表人物多为河南人。汉代以后，道家文化、儒家文化又同由印度传来的佛教文化相融合，形成了中国传统文化的核心。那些先哲们给我们留下了宝贵而丰富的精神财富，为我们构建了一座座宏伟的思想大厦。

因此，灿烂辉煌的中原文化对于中国历史进程的推动，对于中华民族精神的构建和传承，对于中国社会经济的发展，有着独特而重要的作用。这也正是河南中医药文化的深厚底蕴。

中医药学自诞生之日起，就融进了中华民族优秀传统文化的血脉之中，成为其中不可分割的一个重要组成部分，伴随着中华文明的发展历程而不断充实完善。在其发展演进的过程中，时时同博大精深的中国传统文化相交融，而最终成为我们中华民族的瑰宝。

医学大家们以开放兼容的姿态，不失时机地接受了诸家的先进思想，认真地吸收了先辈的智慧和灵光，以气血、阴阳、五行学说为根本方法论，整合古代文化多学科知识，总结人体生命现象及防治疾病的经验，形成了以《黄帝内经》为标志的中医学基本理论体系。

2010年6月20日，习近平出席皇家墨尔本理工大学中医孔子学院授牌仪式说：“中医学凝聚着深邃的哲学智慧和中华民族几千年健康养生理念和实践经验，是中国古代科学的瑰宝，也是打开中华文明宝库的钥匙。”这是对中医学非常精辟的论断和总结。

# Preface

Henan province is located in the hinterland of central China. The province is often called the Central Plains because it is located in the middle of nine regions of China classified in ancient times and has many plains within its territory.

At every stage of the development, Henan has always been the core region of the ancient Chinese civilization. Its cultural history is a microcosm of Chinese civilization.

Henan is the birthplace of Chinese civilization with the most prosperous prehistoric culture in China. The first state was established in Yuzhou. The earliest mature writing was in Anyang. Laozi and Zhuangzi, the two representative figures of Daoism, were born in Luyi and Minquan. The Chinese Buddhist culture, with a profound influence on the East Asia, first spread from Luoyang. The White Horse Temple in Luoyang, built during the reign of Emperor Ming of the Eastern Han dynasty (68 A.D.), was the earliest monastery in China. The temple is often named as "the origin of Buddhism", or "the Cradle of Buddhism". Many myths and legends took place in Henan province. From these myths come a lot of Chinese idioms such as Pangu Creating the Heaven and the Earth, Jingwei Trying to Fill up the Sea, Houyi Shooting the Sun, Nüwa Creating Human Beings, Chang E Rushing to the Moon, Fuxi Inventing the Eight Trigrams, Shennong Tasting Hundreds of Herbs, Cangjie Making Chinese Characters, and The Foolish Old Man Moving the Mountains.

Henan is also a home to a large number of heritage sites. The precious cultural relics include Zhengzhou City Ruins of the Shang dynasty, Anyang Yin Ruins, Luoyang City Ruins of Han and Wei dynasties; Luoyang City Ruins of Sui and Tang dynasties, Longmen Grottoes, the Grand Canal Ruins, Hometown of Wang Hai, the Ancestor of Chinese Businessmen in Shangqiu, Dongjing City Ruins of the

Northern Song dynasty and Shaolin Temple. All of them are historical witnesses to the development of ancient culture in Henan province.

The German philosopher, Karl Jaspers, introduced the concept of an Axial Age in his book *Origin and Goal of History* published in 1949. He argued that during the Axial Age, "the spiritual foundations of humanity were laid simultaneously and independently in China, India, Persia, Judea, and Greece. And these are the foundations upon which humanity still subsists today." Jaspers presented his first outline of the Axial Age by a series of examples:

"Confucius and Lao-Tse were living in China, all the schools of Chinese philosophy came into being, including those of Mo Ti, Chuang Tse, Lieh Tzu, and a host of others; India produced the Upanishads and Buddha and... in Palestine the prophets made their appearance from Elijah by way of Isaiah and Jeremiah to Deutero-Isaiah; Greece witnessed the appearance of Homer, of the philosophers-Parmenides, Heraclitus and Plato, - of the tragedians, of Thucydides and Archimedes. Everything implied by these names developed during these few centuries almost simultaneously in China, India and the West."

—Karl Jaspers, *Origin and Goal of History,* p. 2

During the Spring and Autumn period (770 B.C. - 476 B.C.) and the Warring States period, which are in the midst of the Axial Age (475 B.C. - 221B.C.), China was undergoing great changes and upheavals. Various schools of thought arose, and a hundred schools of thought contended, which contributed to the first cultural and scientific peak in Chinese history.

Confucius (c. 551 B.C. - 479B.C.), the founder of Confucianism, and Lao-Zi (c. 571 B.C. - 471B.C.), the founder of Daoism, were honored as the spiritual masters of China. Confucianism and Daoism, with other schools of thought, laid the foundation of ancient Chinese culture and most founders of various cultures were born in Henan. After the Han dynasty, Daoism and Confucianism were merged with Buddhism from India, forming the core of traditional Chinese culture. The philosophers have left us with rich and precious spiritual wealth, and built a magnificent ideological building for us.

The splendid Central Plains culture has promoted the Chinese historical process and built the Chinese national spirit. It has played a unique and important role in China's social and economic development, and thus formed the solid foundation for the development of Traditional Chinese Medicine (TCM) in Henan.

Since the day of its birth, TCM has been integrated into the blood of the excellent Chinese culture, and has become an inseparable part of it. It has been continuously enriched and perfected along with the development of Chinese civilization. In the process of its development and evolution, it always blends with the profound Chinese culture, and eventually becomes the treasure of China.

With open minds and all-embracing attitudes, the masters of TCM wasted no time to absorb the thoughts of the different schools. They combined the wisdom of the ancestors with the multidisciplinary knowledge of ancient cultures and adopted the theory of qi, yin and yang, and the Five Elements as the fundamental methodologies. On the basis of the experience of preventing and treating diseases, the basic theoretical system of TCM was established with the monumental work *Huangdi Neijing (Huangdi's Internal Classic)*.

On June 20, 2010, President Xi Jinping unveiled the plaque of Australia's first TCM Confucius Institute at the Royal Melbourne Institute of Technology. On the visit, Xi Jinping described TCM as a gem of ancient Chinese science, full of deep philosophical wisdom, representing thousands of years of the Chinese tradition of healthy lifestyle. He also described it as a key to open the treasure house of Chinese civilization. This is a very incisive conclusion and summary of TCM.

# 目录 Contents

## 第一章

# 中医药文化之主要根脉在河南

## Chapter I

# Henan: Major Roots of Chinese Medicine and Culture

## 一、火祖燧人氏点燃了华夏文明之火

在商丘有一个流传很广的传说。约一万年以前，商丘这个地方叫燧明国。燧明国有一种树，叫燧木，云雾在树枝间出没升腾。有种叫猫头鹰的鸟，常用嘴去啄击燧木，燧木就发出灿烂的火花。有位圣人从中受到启发，便折下燧木枝，用燧木枝钻燧木，终于生出了火。这位圣人把火种保存下来，并把这种取火方式传授给了大家。大家对他无比尊敬，便称他为燧人氏，后人尊称他为火祖。

据《韩非子·五蠹》记载："上古之世，人民少而禽兽众，人民不胜禽兽虫蛇……民食果蓏蚌蛤，腥臊恶臭，而伤害腹胃，民多疾病。有圣人作，钻燧取火，以化腥臊，而民说（悦）之，使王天下，号之曰燧人氏。" 这段话是说，上古时代，人类少，禽兽虫蛇多，人们受不了禽兽虫蛇的扰害。人们吃的是瓜果蚌蛤，又腥又臭，吃了伤害肠胃，常常生病。这时候出现了一个圣人，钻木取火，教民熟食，除去腥气。人们爱戴他，拥他做天下之王，称他做燧人氏。

燧人氏首创钻木取火，具体是在什么地方呢？2006年4月，中国首届火文化研讨会在商丘睢阳区召开，根据目前的史料和相关民俗，与会专家达成共识：燧皇陵在商丘，商丘是古黎丘，是燧人氏作为首领时，在瞿水、睢水流域的中心都邑。燧人氏首创钻木取火于商丘，商丘为火文化的源头。（见《燧人取火传天下　中华文明照神州》一文，2009年3月20日《中国艺术报》。）

火的发明和利用是人类社会发展史上的一个里程碑。燧人氏的钻木取火，是人类真正主动掌握火的时代的开始，燧人氏曾在商丘点燃起中华民族的神圣之火，并用这把圣火将中华民族带进了文明时代。

商丘也是火神阏伯司火的圣地。阏伯是中国有文字记载的第一位天文学家，是黄帝的第四代孙，帝喾高辛氏的儿子，曾辅佐大禹治水。北

## Ⅰ. Suirenshi: The "Father of Fire" Lighting the Flame of Chinese Civilization

An old legend has continued to echo widely in Shangqiu. About ten thousand years ago, Shangqiu was called Sui Ming. There were special trees in Sui Ming called "flint trees", and clouds and mist rose and fell among its branches. Owls often pecked at the "flint trees" which sparked at each peck. Inspired, an intelligent man cut some branches to make fire by rubbing them. He kept the kindling and imparted to everyone how to make fire. Thus he commanded great respect, and got the name "Suirenshi." He was later honored as the "Father of Fire".

As was recorded in the book *Hanfeizi,* "birds and beasts, insects and snakes outnumbered men in ancient times. Men could hardly stand the harassment of these animals...They had fruits, mussels and clams for food. Mussels and clams not only stank, but also impaired their body, often causing intestinal or stomach ailments. Then an intelligent man stood out, who drilled wood to make fire, taught people how to cook food to remove the unpleasant smell of raw food. He inspired great affection and respect from the people, and was made sovereign of the territory and called Suirenshi."

Where exactly did Suirenshi invent fire? In April 2006, China's first seminar on fire culture was held in Suiyang District, Shangqiu. Based on the historical data available and relevant folklore, experts reached a consensus: The Mausoleum of Suirenshi is located in Shangqiu, known as Liqiu in ancient times. It used to be the central city when Suirenshi ruled the Qü and Sui river basins. Shangqiu is exactly where Suirenshi first made fire by drilling wood and where fire culture originated. (Reference: "Suirenshi making fire & highlighting Chinese civilization", March 20, 2009, *Chinese Arts News*)

The invention and utilization of fire is a milestone in history. Drilling wood to make fire marks the era in which human beings started to make active use of fire. It was in here that Suirenshi ignited the sacred fire and ushered in a new era of Chinese civilization.

Shangqiu is also where E Bo governed fire. Credited as the Deity of Fire, E Bo is the first astronomer documented in China. He is the great-great-grandson of Huangdi (also

燧皇陵
The Mausoleum of Suirenshi

京收藏家协会研究员李福昌先生在《人类用火方式的研究与收藏》一文中说：“现今河南商丘仍矗立着35米高的火神台，是历代人民纪念火神阏伯的火神庙。四千多年前，阏伯在此一边守护火祖——燧人氏的陵墓，一边在台上照看保护火种，同时观察大火星的运动，研究历法，指导农耕。这里的火种代代相传，人称’中华第一火种’。”（见班琳丽《大商文化的强“商”之道》，2010年10月16日《京九晚报》。）

燧皇陵与阏伯台，燧人氏与阏伯，成为商丘独特的文化景观。商丘有“火都”“火墟”的称谓。商丘 “火神节”是商丘人生活中不可分割的一部分。“火”成了商丘的古代图腾。

2008年北京奥运会，商丘成为奥运圣火河南境内的传递城市之一。“燧人氏钻木取火”与“希腊普罗米修斯盗火解救人类”两个古老而美丽的传说，在 “华夏文明之火”的发祥地“相遇”。

由于火的发明，改变了先民的食性，熟食便是食养、食疗的开端，同时，火的应用也是灸法、焫法、熨法等疗法的起源。

known as the Yellow Emperor), and the son of Diku, who ssisted Dayu in harnessing the waters. Li Fuchang, a fellow of the Beijing Collectors Association, had similar descriptions in his article "Studies and Collection of the Use of Fire": "There is a 35-meter-high flat terrace in Shangqiu, Henan province, erected in memory of the Deity of Fire all through the ages. More than 4,000 years ago, E Bo watched and protected the kindling, observed the movement of Mars, and studied the calendar to guide farming while guarding the mausoleum of his ancestor, the Father of Fire". The kindling has been handed down from generation to generation and is called "the first Chinese kindling". (Reference: Ban Linli, October 16, 2010, *Jingjiu Evening News*)

The Mausoleum of Suirenshi and E Bo Tai, as well as Suirenshi and E Bo have been the cultural emblems distinctive to Shangqiu. "Fire" became an ancient totem in Shangqiu, which has thus got additional names like "the capital of fire" and "the remains of fire". And the Deity of Fire Festival has become part of the life indispensable to the citizens here.

At the 2008 Beijing Olympic Games, Shangqiu was one of the cities in Henan for the torch relay. The two ancient and beautiful legends of fire had a handshake in here, one in connection with Suirenshi and Chinese civilization and the other with Prometheus and Greek progress and civilization.

The invention of fire changed the eating habits of the ancestors. Having cooked food was the beginning of regimen and diet therapy. At the same time, the application of fire also gave rise to therapies such as moxibustion, cauterization and ironing.

Legend has it that Huangdi made "fu zeng" (steaming utensil) and taught people how to steam rice and make porridge with millet. Since then, our ancestors entered the cooking era.

## Ⅱ. Xinmi: The Origin of Qihuang Culture

Xinmi is a wonderful place being the core of Heluo Culture with rich historical resources. The Ruins of Gu Cheng Zhai excavated in 1997 round the border between Xinzheng and Xinmi reveal a complete outlook of an ancient city typical of the Longshan Culture. It was established by the experts to be the capital of Huangdi (also known as the Yellow Emperor), and the starting point of Chinese civilization as well.

阏伯台
E Bo Tai (Temple of the Deity of Fire)

传说黄帝轩辕氏制作釜甑，教百姓“蒸谷为饭”，“烹谷为粥”。从此，我们的祖先“火食之道始成”，我国才真正进入了烹饪时代。

## 二、新密是岐黄文化的发祥地

新密是一片神奇的土地，这里是河洛文化的核心区域，有着极其丰富的历史文化资源。1997年发现的位于新郑和新密交界处的古城寨遗址，保留了龙山文化时期完整的古城风貌，被专家确定为黄帝有熊氏之古都轩辕丘，同时也是中华民族进入文明时期的起始点。

《黄帝内经》是以黄帝与岐伯、雷公等对话的形式写成的。因此岐黄文化被认为是中医药文化的起源。《黄帝内经》虽是托名黄帝而作，但这个托名绝不是空穴来风，而是同黄帝确有关系。应该说是黄帝与岐伯、鬼臾区等臣子在一起讨论医道，经过口耳相传，一代又一代先贤们不断地补充完善，到了战国和秦汉之际，终于使《黄帝内经》成书，成

*Huangdi Neijing* (*Huangdi's Internal Classic*) was written in the form of discourses between Huangdi, Qi Bo, and Lei Gong. Therefore Qi (Qi Bo) Huang (Huangdi) culture is believed to be the source of Chinese Medicine culture. This book was compiled in the name of Huangdi. It recorded the discussions on medicine between Huangdi and his ministers such as Qi Bo and Gui Yuqu. These records were handed down orally, and replenished and polished from generation to generation till they made a classic of Chinese Medicine sometime between the Warring States and Qin or Han dynasty.

Evidences are available in books written in the Northern and Southern Song dynasties by Luo Mi and Zhang Junfang. Both tell the story of how Huangdi invited Qi Bo, master of herbal medicine, to take charge of medical work and compile the Internal Classic.

It can be inferred that Huangdi travelled westward to Qishan, Shaanxi province to invite Qi Bo to Xinmi, making him the master of medicine and having medical discussions there. Xinmi can be established as the major birthplace of *Huangdi Neijing* and Qi Huang culture.

Historical records and archaeological findings have proved that the ancient Zheng Kingdom, which covered the area of today's Xinzheng and Xinmi, used to be the major place of social activities of Huangdi and Qi Bo. A grand ceremony is held yearly in Xinzheng, hometown of Huangdi, on March 3 on the lunar calendar to commemorate the Chinese ancestor. There are over 60 Qi Huang cultural sites in Xinmi. These used to be where Huangdi and ancient medical celebrities lived, including Huangdi's Palace, Mount Qi Bo, Temple of Qi Bo, Mount Da Hong, Mount Da Wei, etc.

Press conference was held on December 24, 2010 to establish Xinmi as the origin of Qi Huang culture, based on investigation and researches done by over 20 medical literature specialists including Li Jingwei, a research fellow with China Academy of Chinese Medical Sciences.

## Ⅲ. Yi Yin (Prime Minister in Shang Tang's Reign): Progenitor of Herbal Decoctions

Yi Yin, who was born in the ancient Heluo region, is recognized as "father of

就了中医的经典之作。

据南宋罗泌的《路史》记载，当年黄帝曾西巡访贤，“至岐见岐伯，引载而归，访于治道”。又据北宋真宗天禧年间张君房编辑的《云笈七签·纪·轩辕本纪》所载：“时有仙伯出于岐山下，号岐伯，善说草木之药性味，为大医，帝请主方药，……作《内经》。”

可以推想，是黄帝西行把岐伯从陕西岐山一带，引载到自己的部落有熊氏所在地，拜为医学之师。而新密正是黄帝和岐伯等名臣讨论医学之道的主要活动场所之一，因此可以说新密是《黄帝内经》思想形成诞生的主要地区之一，是岐黄文化的主要诞生地。

史料记载与考古发现证明，古郑国是黄帝与岐伯等主要活动区域，而古郑国包括现在河南的新郑、新密等地区。每年农历三月三日，黄帝故里新郑都举行盛大的祭祖仪式。新密境内有关岐黄文化的遗址多达60余处，如黄帝宫、岐伯山、岐伯庙、大鸿山、大隗山等大量关于岐伯、黄帝与其他上古医家活动的遗迹。

中国中医科学院李经纬研究员等全国20多位医史文献专家经过考察论证，确定新密市为岐黄文化发祥地，并于2010年12月24日召开新闻发布会，举行了揭牌仪式。

## 三、商汤宰相伊尹发明了中药汤剂

出生在伊水之滨的河洛人伊尹被中国烹饪界尊为“烹饪之圣”“中华厨祖”，也是中药汤剂的首创者，在河南嵩县、伊川、开封、尉氏、虞城及相邻的山东单县等地均有伊尹祠、伊尹墓和大量相关传说，他还是商朝的开国元勋、著名的贤相。

关于伊尹对汤药的贡献，古籍多有记载。

晋朝大学者同时也是著名医家的皇甫谧，在他所著的《针灸甲乙经·序》中说：“伊芳尹以亚圣之才，撰用《神农本草》，以为《汤

Chinese cooking". He is also the pioneer of herbal decoctions, one of the founders of the Shang dynasty and famous prime minister as well. There are a legion of ancestral temples, tombs, and legends about Yi Yin in Songxian, Yichuan, Kaifeng, Weishi, Yucheng in Henan province, and in Shanxian, Shandong province as well.

Yi Yin's contribution to herbal medicine was documented frequently in ancient literature.

Huangfu Mi, a famous scholar and medical giant in the Jin dynasty, had the following description in the foreword to his works *Zhenjiu Jiayi Jing* (*A-B Classic of Acupuncture and Moxibustion*). Yi Yin was extremely talented and wrote a book entitled *Tangye Jing* (*Classic of Decoctions*) based on *Shennong Bencao Jing* (*Shennong's Classic of Materia Medica*). Zhang Zhongjing, the sage of Chinese Medicine in the late Han dynasty (206 B.C.–220 A.D.), compiled *Shanghan Zabing Lun* (*Treatise on Cold Damage and Miscellaneous Diseases*) after a lot consultation and studies had been done on this book. Formulas in this book had proved effective over the years.

*Tangye Jing* (*Classic of Decoctions*) was included in the Dunhuang manuscripts dating from late 4th to 11th centuries. Tao Hongjing of the Liang dynasty related in his book *Fuxing Jue* (*Essentials of Formulas for Zang-fu Ailments*) that anyone who had a complete command of the *Tangye Jing,* the essence of Yi Yin's *Tang Ye,* would definitely be a master of medicine. Yi Yin's *Tang Ye* was available in the populace of Song dynasty. The inheritance of *Fuxing Jue: Zangfu Yongyao Fayao was* recorded in a book edited by the contemporary scholars Zhang Dachang and Qian Chaochen and published in September, 2008.

Yi Yin's contribution to Chinese medicine is the invention of herbal decoctions inspired by cooking methods. He decocted mixture of herbs with different doses as he did when cooking dishes, and thus created compound formulas. This made it possible for different herbal ingredients to work together and improve the therapeutic effect dramatically. It has great significance both quantitatively and qualitatively in the change from the use of single herb to assorted ones. Yi Yin not only applied his theories about harmony of five flavors in cooking, but also interpreted to Shang Tang how to run a state in harmony. Shang Tang was greatly impressed by Yi Yin's brilliant elaboration of the relationship between making delicious food and governing a state, and made him the prime minister. Yi Yin is an outstanding cook, and more

液》。仲景论广伊芳尹《汤液》为数十卷，用之多验。”从中可知，伊尹凭借他的天才，在《神农本草经》的基础上，撰写了一本《汤液经》，到了汉朝末年，医圣张仲景参考研究这本《汤液经》，写出了他的《伤寒杂病论》，且用之多有效验。

敦煌遗卷中，梁代陶弘景所撰之《辅行诀·脏腑用药法要》中有《汤液经》图，据陶弘景云：“此图乃《汤液经法》尽要之妙，学者能谙于此，医道毕矣。”陶弘景提到的《汤液经法》，就是指伊尹的《汤液经》。伊尹的《汤液经》在宋代时民间还有残存。当代学者张大昌和钱超尘两位先生主编有《辅行诀·脏腑用药法要传承集》一书（2008年9月华夏出版社出版），记述了《辅行诀·脏腑用药法要》的传承经过。

伊尹对中医学的贡献在于他根据烹调的方法发明了中药汤液。伊尹按照烹调菜肴的方法把多种药物搭配进行煎煮，由此诞生了中药复方即方剂。汤液方剂的出现，使多味药物配合在一起相互协同作用，治疗效

伊川伊尹祠

Ancestral Temple of Yi Yin in Yichuan, Henan province

importantly a great doctor and statesman as well.

Back in the Shang dynasty 3000 years ago, most places on the earth were wild. Yi Yin assisted Shang Tang in defeating the tyrannical Xia Jie and completed the first revolution in Chinese history to change the regime by force. The Shang dynasty with its capital in Henan province had entered the Bronze Age, showing the world the splendid Central Plains civilization.

## Ⅳ. The Central Plains: Source of Food Therapy

A popular cure for common cold called "scallion-ginger porridge" was made into a doggerel, which goes like this:

A handful of rice is boiled with 7 scallion stem ends and 7 pieces of ginger; when the porridge is done, a half cup of vinegar is added to make it an effective remedy for cold.

Scallion stem ends and ginger are used both as food and medicinal with the functions of promoting perspiration and dispersing cold to relieve exterior syndrome. When boiled with rice to make porridge, and taken after vinegar is added to the porridge, they are very effective for common cold, especially applicable to senile and weak people.

The story of the "fairy porridge" has been spread among common people. One day, Lü Dongbin, one of the Eight Immortals, came down to earth and found a farmhouse where the family was eating scallion-ginger porridge. Greeted by the savory smell, he went over to ask for it. He had the porridge three times daily for three days continuously before leaving the farmhouse reluctantly. When he returned to heaven, the Jade Emperor heard about it and scolded him for greed and violation of the "heavenly rules." The Jade Emperor then ordered Lü Dongbin's life be reduced by 800 years. Because one meal of the scallion-ginger porridge could extend people's life by 100 years, Lü Dongbin's life was actually extended rather than reduced since he had 9 meals making 900 years. Hence the porridge later got the name of "fairy porridge".

Diet therapy is a part of food culture and an important part of Chinese Medicine as well. The idea that "medicine and food are like the two halves of the same whole" has been popular since ancient times. While people were looking for

果大大提高。从单味药物的应用发展成多味药物的复方，这不仅是量的变化，更是质的升华，意义重大。而且伊尹并没有把他的五味理论停留在饮食的烹调上，而是用五味调和的理论向汤王讲述为政的道理。伊尹以谈天下特产美味，联系治国之道的精彩论述，深深打动了成汤，后来被汤王任用为宰相，成为厨师中的人杰，此事更成为“上医医国”的典范。

早在3000多年前的商代，地球上大多数地方还蛮荒未开。河洛人伊尹辅佐商汤，打败暴虐的夏桀，完成了中国历史上第一次武力改朝换代的革命。建都在河南的商王朝已进入了青铜器时代，向世界展示了光辉灿烂的中原文明。

## 四、食疗之源在中原

民间流传一个治疗伤风感冒的验方“葱姜粥”，有四句顺口溜：

**一把粳米熬成汤，　七个葱头七片姜。**

**煮熟兑入半杯醋，　伤风感冒得健康。**

方中葱头、生姜，既是食物，又是发汗解表、发散风寒的中药，与粳米熬粥，并加入醋饮用，对治疗伤风感冒颇为有效，尤适于老年体弱之人。

民间曾流传“神仙粥”的故事。有一天，八仙之一的吕洞宾下凡来到人间，发现一户农家正在喝葱姜粥，香味扑鼻而来，于是上门讨吃。他一连在农家吃了三天九顿才恋恋不舍离去。后来回到天庭，玉皇大帝闻知此事，说他贪吃，冒犯天条，下令罚吕洞宾减寿800年。由于他吃了延年益寿的葱姜粥，一顿粥给他添寿100年，九顿共增寿900年，所以他的寿命反而有增无减。因此，后人就把葱姜粥改称“神仙粥”了。

食疗是饮食文化的一部分，也是中医学的一个重要组成部分。饮食文化实际上也包含着食疗的内容。自古常说“药食同源”，人们在寻找

food to relieve hunger, they gradually found some of them could also be used as medicine to cure diseases.

In the course of development, Traditional Chinese Medicine has always been closely related to daily diet. Very often, food can be used as medicine, and vice versa. Yi Yin, the father of Chinese cooking and inventor of herbal decoctions, prepared various kinds of soup and dishes for Shang Tang. He made soup out of different food (also medicinal) in different proportions within one formula to prevent or cure diseases. The soup he prepared was equivalent to a medicinal diet, from which Chinese herbal decoction has gradually evolved.

1. Origin of Chinese Food Culture

Henan occupies a very important position as the origin of Chinese food culture. The first Chinese banquet was held by Xia Qi at a place called Juntai in Yuzhou, Henan, historically known as "the Juntai Banquet." Henan cuisine originated from Xia and Shang dynasties and flourished in the Northern Song dynasty. It is the oldest cuisine in China. Later, it was spread to the south of China in the Southern Song dynasty and had a great influence on the formation of several major cuisines in the South. Henan cuisine once enjoyed glorious past until it faded in the first half of the 20th century.

One chapter of *Lüshi Chunqiu: Ben wei Pian* (*Master Lü's Spring and Autumn Annals*) describes the life of Yi Yin and the scene of Yi Yin discussing food related ideas with Shang Tang. To make it simple, the original ancient text was interpreted as follows in modern Chinese language.

Yi Yin said to Shang Tang, "What makes the most difference in the taste is water. The five flavors of sour, sweet, bitter, spicy, and salty, and the three materials of water, wood, and fire are all important in making good food. Good food need to be brought to boil several times in the tripod to ensure changes of the flavor by controlling fire, sometimes strong and others mild. By doing so can stink smells be eliminated. To make food tasty, subtle combination of flavors is the key. The five flavors (sweet, sour, bitter, spicy, and salty) should be used but in reasonable order and appropriate doses.It is ineffable how subtle and delicate the changes are although the chef is in their element, making food well-done yet not broken; mild yet tasty; sweet, sour, and spicy without being too much; rich but not greasy."

Yi Yin is the first outstanding cook who assisted the emperor by incorporating

充饥食物的同时，也渐渐找到了治病的药物。

在中医学发展的悠悠岁月中，一直就是与饮食紧密相关的。很多时候，食物即是药，药即是食物。中华厨祖、中药汤剂的发明者伊尹，为商汤烹制各种汤菜，将众多食物（也是药物）加以配方，制成汤饮来防治疾病。实际上他制作的这些汤饮就相当于药膳，中医的汤剂就从这里演变而来。

1. 中国饮食文化的滥觞

追溯中国饮食文化的滥觞，河南居十分重要的位置。中华第一宴是夏启在今河南禹州的钧台举办的，史称“钧台之享”。豫菜源于夏商，兴盛于北宋，是中国最古老的一种菜系。后来随南宋南下，对南方几个重要菜系的形成影响巨大。历史上，豫菜曾风光无限，直到20世纪前半叶，仍显示出其巨大魅力。

《吕氏春秋·本味篇》记述了伊尹的生平和同商汤论述饮食之道的情景。为了理解方便，我们用白话加以叙述：

伊尹对商汤说：“大凡味的根本，水是第一位的。依靠酸、甜、苦、辣、咸这五味和水、木、火这三材进行烹调，鼎中多次沸腾，多次变化，是依靠火来控制调节的。时儿武火，时儿文火。消灭腥味，去掉骚味，除却膻味，一定要发挥其长处，关键在于掌握火候，务必不要违背用火的规律。调味这件事，一定要用甘、酸、苦、辛、咸，但放调料的先后次序和用量的多寡，其组合是很微妙的，都有各自的道理。鼎中的变化，精妙而细微，语言难以表达，心里有数也不易说清楚。就好像射箭御马一样得心应手，如同阴阳二气配合一样化成万物，又仿佛四季推移一样主宰宇宙，所以才使菜肴做到久而不散，熟而不烂，甜而不过头，酸而不强烈，咸而不涩嘴，辛而不刺激，淡而不寡味，肥而不腻口。”

伊尹是第一个以调五味而辅佐天子治理国家的杰出庖人，他创立的“五味调和说”与“火候论”，至今仍是中国烹饪的不变之规。 正是

his ideas of making good food with five flavors into the governance of the state. He established the principles of "five flavors in harmony" and "control of fire" which are still observed in today's Chinese cooking. He has had a great influence in the Henan cuisine featuring salty, palatable with the use of broth, blended with five flavors, succulent, and acceptable by people from different places and regions.

2. Dieticians in the Zhou Dynasty

The earliest dieticians ever in Chinese history are the ones in the Zhou dynasty. As was recorded in the book *Zhou Li* (a classic on rituals and ceremonies in Chinese antiquity), imperial doctors were then classified into four categories including dietician, internal medicine doctor, surgeon, and veterinarian. Dieticians were designated professionals in charge of the healthy diet of the emperors and their wives.

3. Food Therapy in Chinese Medicine Classics

*Huangdi Neijing, Shanghan Zabing Lun*, and *Shennong Bencao Jing* are classics of Chinese Medicine, all born in Henan. Each of the classics gives equal importance to food therapy.

The concept of well-balanced dietary pattern with proportionally assorted cereals, meat, vegetables and fruit as well as the effects of food therapy were related systematically in *Huangdi Neijing*. It was explicitly written in the book that medicinals all have toxin or side effects, therefore they should not be taken in overdose or continued once the diseases have been cured; otherwise the vital energy will be impaired. The classics advocate that food therapy plays a vital part in regulating the body and restoring vital energy.

There are about 40 chapters on food therapy and 13 formulas, mostly combining food and herbs, in *Huangdi Neijing,* for example, *Ling Shu* (*the Miraculous Pivot*). It can be called a classic on the relationship between food and illnesses. There are quite a number of formulas in which food and herbs are combined in the treatment of diseases, including amenorrhea, insomnia, and distended stomach. It is the same case in externally applied formulas (e.g. horse fat ointment). In the formula for amenorrhea, Wuzei (cuttlefish) and Luru (Rubia cordifolia Linn.) are ground into fine power, made into balls with whipped egg, and then boiled with abalone soup for use. Banxia (Pinellia ternata) and sorghum are boiled together in the formula for insomnia.

A number of food therapy formulas, recorded in Zhang Zhongjing's masterpiece

受了伊尹的影响，长期形成了以盐定味、以汤提鲜、五味调和、追求时鲜、菜式规范、四方皆宜的烹调风格。这就是豫菜的传统特色。

2. 关于周代的食医

周朝的“食医”实际上就是食疗师，也我国最早的营养医生。据在中原成书的《周礼·天官·冢宰》记载，当时宫廷医生已有食医、疾医（内科医生）、疡医（外伤科医生）、兽医之分，食医排在首位，是负责周王及王后饮食的专职营养医生，可见周天子对饮食的重视。

3. 在中原成书的中医学经典均重视食疗

在中原成书的中医学经典《黄帝内经》《伤寒杂病论》《神农本草经》等均重视食疗。

《黄帝内经》不仅对膳食结构的综合平衡和谷肉果菜的合理搭配有系统的认识，还十分重视食疗的作用。《素问·五常政大论》说：“大毒治病，十去其六；常毒治病，十去其七；小毒治病，十去其八；无毒治病，十去其九。谷肉果菜，食养尽之，无使过之，伤其正也。”明确指出，不论服用什么药物，都有毒副作用，去病则止，不可多服。不能用药过度，而伤其正气。主张“谷肉果菜，食养尽之”，强调饮食调养，使正气恢复，邪气尽去。

在《黄帝内经》中，涉及饮食内容的有40多篇，像《灵枢·五味》篇专门论述饮食与疾病的关系，可以奉作食疗的经典。《黄帝内经》共载医方13个，其中多是食物与药物合用的方剂。例如治疗妇女闭经的“四乌贼一芦茹方”，要求将乌贼、芦茹舂成粉末后，用雀卵濡搓成丸，再与鲍鱼汤合煮食用。诸如治疗失眠的“半夏秫米汤”，调养方“稻米醪醴”，治疗臌胀的“鸡矢醴”及外用方“马膏（即马油）”“豕豪”等，都是采用灵活多变的形式，使药物食物合用以治疗疾病。

医圣张仲景在他的传世之作《金匮要略》中，为我们留下了多个食疗方，一直被广泛应用。如治血虚兼寒及胁痛里急的“当归生姜羊肉汤”，方中生姜、羊肉即是食物，正常人也可食用。而当归是常用的补血药，三

*Jingui Yaolue* (*Synopsis of the Golden Chamber*), have been applied down through the ages. One is a broth made of danggui (Chinese angelica), shengjiang (fresh ginger) and mutton. The first ingredient is a herb commonly used to replenish blood, and the last two are daily food. When combined they have the functions of warming the middle to replenish blood, and dispelling cold to relieve pain. Thus it is used to treat blood deficiency complicated with cold, hypochondriac pain and tenesmus. Another formula with three ingredients of gancao (liquorice), xiaomai (wheat), dazao (jujubae) is to treat hysteria in women because it has tranquilizing effect and is able to reinforce qi. Other examples include formulas for mental restlessness with baihe (Lilium) and yolk, pulmonary tuberculosis with gancao (liquorice) and ganjiang (dried ginger), vexation due to yin deficiency with baihe (Lilium) and dihuang (Rehmannia glutinosa), etc.

A good variety of common food materials can be found in Zhang Zhongjing's works. These include mainly five groups: cereals such as barley, wheat, rice, or red beans; meat and eggs such as egg yolk, egg white, or mutton; fructose such as jujubae, maltose, or honey; vegetables such as ginger, scallion stem ends; and alcoholic drinks such as liquor, rice wine, or bitter rice wine.

*Shennong Bencao Jing*, which was written in the East Han dynasty and a masterpiece of Chinese Materia Medica, covers 365 medicinal herbs. Among them, over 40 are common and natural plants and animals with both culinary and medicinal properties, such as tangerine, pomelo, grape, jujubae, clamshell, broomcorn millet, millet, honey, Chinese yam, lily, Chinese wolfberry fruit, black sesame, lotus seed, Nepeta cataria, longan, crab, red bean, etc.

It is evident that doctors down through the ages have all attached great importance to food therapy.

4. *Shiliao Bencao* (*Materia Medica for Dietotherapy*): The oldest extant monograph on food therapy

In the Tang dynasty, food therapies had been widely spread and applied. The oldest extant monograph on food therapy is *Shiliao Bencao,* completed by Meng Shen, a native of Ruzhou, Henan. This book is a summary of theories and practices of food therapy before the Tang dynasty. It provides detailed illustration of the properties and functions of over 200 kinds of food or medicinal. Also discussed in the book are culinary skills, effects of these foods, and their compatibilies. Meng Shen

张仲景
Zhang Zhongjing

者结合起来，具有温中补血、祛寒止痛的作用，是药食两用的食补佳品。还有治妇人脏燥，宁心补气的甘麦大枣汤，由甘草、小麦、大枣三味组成。又如治心神不宁、清热除躁的“百合鸡子黄汤”，治肺痿的“甘草干姜汤”，治阴虚烦热的“百合地黄汤”等。

在张仲景的著作中，涉及的食物非常广泛，有粮食类，如大麦、小麦、粳米、赤小豆等；有肉蛋类，如鸡子黄、鸡子白、羊肉；有果糖类，如大枣、饴糖、蜂蜜等；有蔬菜类，如生姜、葱白等；有酒类，如白酒、清酒、苦酒等。这些均为常见的食用之物。

在成书于东汉的中药祖典《神农本草经》中，共收药 365 种，其中至少有 40 多种常见食物。如橘、柚、葡萄、大枣、海蛤、黍米、粟米、蜂蜜、山药、百合、枸杞子、黑芝麻、莲子、荆芥、龙眼、蟹、赤小豆等。均是来自大自然的药食两用的植物和动物。

因此历代医家都重视食疗。

was a disciple of Sun Simiao, "Father of Chinese Herbal Medicine". His monograph has an epoch-making significance in the history of food therapy because it is the oldest extant book on the medicinal properties of food.

Articles and monographs on food therapy have come into being ever since then.

## Ⅴ. Wine and Its Medical Application

There was an anecdote in the book *Bo Wu Zhi* (*Records of Diverse Matters*) written by Zhang Hua in the Jin dynasty. Three people were traveling in the morning mist. One of them had porridge for breakfast, one nothing, and the other some wine. The one who had porridge later had a serious illness. The one with an empty stomach died of miasma related disease. The one who had wine was healthy.

This story shows that wine was better than food, able to promote blood flow and reinforce vital qi to expel pathogenic factors. It prevented the person from being hurt by the unpleasant miasma. This story is frequently quoted by later generations.

1. Henan: Home of Wine

The earliest wine makers were recorded in *Zhanguo Ce* (*Strategies of the Warring States*) and Volume 14 of *Shuowen Jiezi* (*Explanation of Script and Elucidation of Characters*). There were two different legends associated with the father of wine. One had Yi Di, the minister of emperor Yu in the Xia dynasty, while the other was Du Kang, the emperor revitalizing the Xia dynasty. Du Kang once served, so the story goes, as a senior official in charge of cooking. He kept the leftovers in the hollow of a tree for some time, which got fermented and smelt fragrant. This inspired him to make wine. Although people disagree on the original wine maker, where wine was made was decided by consensus in the Heluo area.

Archaeological findings have proved that special wine vessels had been found in the unearthed pottery of the Neolithic Age. This indicates that wine-making was prevalent in primitive Chinese society. The production of drinking utensils continued unabated since the Xia and Shang dynasties. To this day, all kinds of wine related articles unearthed across China are mostly in the Heluo area, including those excavated in the site of Peiligang, Yangshao and Longshan.

Guo Moruo's *Chinese Historiography* says, "Yi Di was said to be the first to make wine, much more tasty than the primitive one." This seems to be authentic

4. 现存第一部食疗专著《食疗本草》

到了唐代，“食治”“食疗”的概念得到广泛传播和应用。我国现存第一部食疗专著是河南汝州人孟诜编撰的《食疗本草》。该书总结了我国唐代以前有关食疗的理论和经验，对 200 多种食物（当然也是药物）的性味和保健作用进行了详细的描述，并论述了一些食物搭配及烹调加工的方法和效用。孟诜是药王孙思邈的弟子，他充分运用从老师那里学来的中药知识，首次以专著的形式介绍食物的药性，在食疗史上有着划时代的意义。

此后，讲食疗保健的专章和专著相继问世，都有各自独特的贡献。

## 五、酒在中原的问世及其在医学上的应用

晋代学者张华在《博物志》中，记述了一个有趣的故事。曾有三个人早起在大雾中赶路，一个人早晨喝了粥，一个人空着肚子，一个人饮了点酒。他们三人，其中吃粥的人患了重病；那空腹的人因患雾瘴，得病死去；那个饮酒的人没有生病，而且身体还很健康。

从这个例子就可以看出，酒能活血益气，辟除秽恶，有优于食物的效用，故能避免大雾对机体的侵袭和危害而不得雾瘴之患。后人曾多次引述这则故事。

1. 酒之源在河南

关于最早的造酒者，在《战国策·魏策》和《说文解字·卷十四下》均有记载。一说是夏禹之臣仪狄，一说是夏代的中兴之主杜康。据说杜康曾担任“庖正”，专司做饭，他把剩饭放进树洞里，久而发酵，气味芬芳，他受此启发，发明酿酒。总之，不论是仪狄造酒还是杜康造酒，都是在河洛一带完成的。

考古证明，在出土的新石器时代的陶器制品中，已有了专用的酒器，说明在原始社会，我国酿酒已经盛行。以后经过夏、商两代，饮酒的器具也越来越多。迄今为止，全国各地考古发掘的有关酒的实物也以河洛为最

account of the origin of wine making.

One of the major archeological findings in Henan back in the late 20th century was in the Neolithic village of Jiahu in Wuyang county. It revealed that eight or nine thousand years ago, natives of Jiahu had had fermented beverage, which was four thousand years earlier before Du Kang reigned in the Xia dynasty. An article entitled "Skilled Craftsmen in the Village of Jiahu" was published in the *Dahe Daily* on April 29, 2014. It says Zhang Juzhong, the person in charge of the excavation, and some other people found some traces of wine-like sediments on sixteen broken pieces of pottery jars. To prove it, some samples were sent to Patrick McGovern, a professor and molecular archaeologist of the University of Pennsylvania. Analysis of the sediments, combining gas and liquid chromatography, has revealed that a mixed fermented beverage of rice, honey and fruit was preserved in these jars.

Ancient Chinese believed medicine and wine were inseparable from each other, and wine was the best medicine. The ancient Chinese character "醫" (medicine) comprises two parts, the upper referring to the state of being unwell and the lower wine jar. This pictogram signifies that wine was used to treat diseases.

The above interpretation of the character was made by Xu Shen in his *Shuowen Jiezi*. He believed the meaning of that character was that doctors used wine to treat patients. Medicine and wine are like a couple, and wine has played a significant role in Chinese medicine ever since it was born.

2. Application of Wine in Chinese Medicine

Countless examples have proved that wine has been used frequently in the treatment of diseases through ages. Medicine could be immersed in wine, or taken with wine, or made with wine as an additional ingredient. Wine could also be applied externally.

The earliest ever Chinese book on formulas was *Wushier Bingfang* (*Fifty-Two Medical Formulas*), which was written on silk and unearthed in the Mawangdui Han dynasty tombs. There were a few formulas in this book about how wine was used to treat illnesses. For instance, a cupful wine was added and mixed well with herbs before administered to the patient to treat knife or spear injury so that it would not cause much pain. Another formula recorded in the book was to reduce pain and to promote healing in patient who was bit by a dog. The patient was asked to lie in bed when the doctor cleansed the wounds with appropriate amount of wine. It is clear

多。从裴李岗文化、仰韶文化到龙山文化，河洛地区均出土了大量与酒有关的实物。

郭沫若先生在《中国史稿》中说："相传禹臣仪狄开始造酒，这是指比原始社会时代的酒更甘美浓型的旨酒。"此说似乎可信。

20世纪末，河南重大考古发现之一的舞阳贾湖新石器时代遗址提供的资料显示：在八九千年前，贾湖人已在享用酿造酒，比夏代杜康早4000多年。据《大河报》2014年4月29日《能工巧匠出贾湖》一文记载：贾湖遗址发掘主持者张居中等人，在16个贾湖陶器皿碎片上，发现了疑似酒类沉淀物。为了弄清真相，他们将部分陶片样本提供给美国人麦克戈文——一位从事世界酒史研究的宾夕法尼亚大学教授。麦克戈文把这些沉淀物进行了气象色谱、液酱色谱等化学分析，结果显示，这些陶器曾经盛放过酒，是以稻米、蜂蜜和水果为原料混合发酵而成。

古代早有"医酒同源""药酒同源"的说法。《汉书·食货志》说："酒，百药之长。"考繁体字"醫"字，其部首为"酉"，酉，本为酒器，此指酒。表示用酒以治病。我们不妨查看一下许慎的解释，《说文·卷十四下》云："醫，治病工也。殹，恶姿也。醫之性然，得酒而使。从酉。王育说：一曰殹，病声，酒所以治病也。"许慎在强调醫是治病工（即为人治病的人）之后，指出上部分"殹"是"恶姿"，即人患病时萎靡不振、痛苦不堪的病态。而医生多爱用酒，得到酒用来治病。所以此字的义符从"酉"（"酉"即酒）。接着又引用前人王育的另一说，上部分"殹"表示病声，即人患病时发出的呻吟声。下部分"酉"表示酒是用来治病的。

通过以上的分析，可以看出许慎认为"醫"字的含义是人患了病，或是病态而卧，或是痛苦呻吟，医生用酒来治疗。医从"酉"而来，医和酒溶为一体，说明了自古以来酒在医药中的地位和重要性。

2. 酒在中医学上的广泛应用

事实上，自古以来，治病每多用酒。或者用酒浸制药物制成酒剂，或者服药时用酒送服，或者制药时加入酒的成分，或者以酒为外用药物。

that wine was for external use in this case.

Other records are available in *Shiji* (*Records of the Historian*). It records how Bianque used wine to cure illnesses and Chunyuyi (a well-known doctor in the Western Han dynasty) applied wine effectively to a pregnant woman by using a handful of *Semen Hyoscyami* with wine to treat difficult labour.

*Lie Zi* includes a story of Bianque about the exchange of hearts between two men with contradictory characters, using wine for aneasthesic purpose.

It should be noted that the invention and development of medicinal wine is China's great contribution to wine making industry of the world and also a great contribution from our Chinese culture to the world. Medicinal wine is an integrated product of herbs and wine, Chinese Medicine and diet, and a treasure of food therapy. It has been popular with the Chinese people through ages.

As is written in one chapter of *Huangdi Neijing*, there are two essential requirements in the making of medicinal wine: good quality rice and rice straws as fuel in the process of distillation. "Jishili" was a well-known medicinal wine mentioned in *Su Wen* (*Plain Questions*), used for distending stomach at that time.

A good number of formulas are recorded in Zhang Zhongjing's *Shanghan Zabing Lun*. Among them over twenty include the use of wine. Some are medicinal wine, for instance, "Honglanhua Jiu" for gynecological disease; others are a mixture of wine and herbal decoction, such as "Fangji Dihuang Tang" (Decoction of *Fourstamen Stephania Root & Rehmannia Root*). In the latter formula, herbal ingredients were immersed in wine the day before the concentrated liquid was taken.

Shen Kuo (1031-1095), a famous scientist in the Northern Song dynasty (960-1127), tells a story about "Su He Xiang Wan" (Storax Pills) in Volume IX of his encyclopedia-like memo *Mengxi Bitan* (*Dream Creek Essays*). A senior official named Wang Dan (957-1017) was weak and often came down with illnesses. Emperor Zhen Zong of the North Song dynasty sent him a jar of medicinal wine and asked him to take it regularly before meal. The emperor told him it could regulate qi and blood flow to dispel exogenous pathogens. So Wang Dan took the wine and recovered. He extended his sincere gratitude to the emperor at the court. "This was made of Su He Xiang Wan with wine, extremely good to regulate the body and eliminate many pathogens if you have a cup in cold mornings," the emperor said. Then each official close to the emperor was granted several cups. Later, all the

如此等等，不胜枚举。

我国现存最早的方书，马王堆汉墓出土的帛书《五十二病方》中，就多处记载有以酒治病的方法。如"令金伤毋痛……，醇酒盈一衷（通"中"）桮（杯），入药中，挠饮"。意思是治疗刀枪伤疼痛，用中等杯子一满杯醇酒放入药中，以酒搅匀调服。再如，治狗咬伤："犬所啮，令毋痛及易瘳方，令啮者卧，而令人以酒财沃其伤。"意思是能让被狗咬伤后不痛，而且易痊愈的方法，是令被咬伤的人卧床，然后用适量的酒冲洗伤口。这显然是以酒做外用药。

《史记·扁鹊仓公列传》中说："其在肠胃，酒醪之所及也。"记录了扁鹊用酒剂治病的论述。文中记载有西汉名医仓公淳于意用酒治病的验案。如以莨菪药一撮，用酒冲服，治疗菑川王美人"怀子而不乳（难产）"。

《列子》中记载有扁鹊为"志强而气弱"的鲁公扈和"志弱而气强"的赵齐婴两位病人醉酒换心的故事。

值得一提的是，药酒的创制与发展，是我国对酿酒业的一个巨大贡献，也是中国文化对世界的贡献之一。药酒是中药与酒相结合的产物，它是我国中医药文化与饮食文化巧妙融合的结晶，也是我国食疗文化的瑰宝。自古以来一直受到人们的青睐。

中医的经典《黄帝内经素问》中的《汤液醪醴论》，曾对药酒做了专门的论述，并强调要以禀受天地之和气的稻米作原料，以稻杆作燃料，来制作药酒。《素问·腹中论》中治疗臌胀病的"鸡矢醴"，就是当时的药酒名。

医圣张仲景在《伤寒杂病论》和《金匮要略》中记载的诸多药方中，有 20 多个方剂中配用了酒，其中有的是药酒，如治疗妇科病的"红兰花酒"；有的是水酒合剂，如防己地黄汤，"以酒一杯，浸之一宿，绞取汁"，然后同地黄汁混合服饮等等。

北宋大科学家沈括在《梦溪笔谈·卷九·人事》中，记载了苏合香丸药酒的故事。太尉王旦身体虚弱多病，宋真宗送他一满瓶药酒，叫他空

ministerial and official households began to duplicate it, and Su He Xiang Wan has been popular ever since.

Formulas of medicinal wine roughly amount to one hundred in Li Shizhen's *Bencao Gangmu* (*Compendium of Materia Medica*) of the Ming dynasty (1368-1644). A famous one "Medicinal Wine with Tiger Bone" was his invention. To this day, a total of 1622 formulas were collected in the *Compendium of Chinese Medicinal Wine*.

It is self-evident that wine has medical effect. However an overdose is harmful to the body. This was noted by ancient Chinese, especially in the legend about Xia Yu and Yi Di. Xia Yu started to estrange himself from Yi Di after trying the wonderful wine made by Yi Di because he had recognized the potential harm of wine and asserted that some state would decline and perish if wine became increasingly prevalent without any control.

According to *Shang Shu: Jiu Gao* (*Decree on Wine of the Classic of History*), the first king of Zhou issued an order for abstinence from wine in the territory of Wei after he defeated the rebel Wu Geng. The area of Wei (equivalent to areas around Anyang, Henan) used to be inhabited by Yin people, who were greatly disorganized and lost their virtue because of their indulgence in spirits. The King of Zhou issued such abstinence for fear of disorders caused by drunkenness. This was probably the earliest of its kind in China.

## Ⅵ. *Yi Jing* (*The Book of Changes*) Culture and Its Influence on TCM

There are quite a number of the *Yi Jing* (*the Book of Changes*) related cultural and historical sites in Henan, including Mengjin, Gongyi, Luoning where the *He Tu* (*The Yellow River Map*) and *Luo Shu* (*Lo Shu Square*) Diagrams (Numerology in Chinese Antiquity) were generated, Huaiyang where Fuxi drew bagua (Eight Trigrams), and Tangyin where King Wen devised the sixty-four hexagrams. Since yarrow stalks were used in Chinese antiquity for cleromancy, there are also yarrow plant yards in Shangcai, Huaiyang, and Tangyin.

*Yi Jing* was grounded in the *He Tu* and *Luo Shu* Diagrams, which illustrated the philosophy of correspondence between man and universe, images and random

腹时喝下，说可以调气理血，排除外邪。王旦喝了这药，深感安定康健多了，于是乘上朝拜见真宗时表示感谢。真宗说："这是用苏合香丸与酒合制而成的药酒。最能调理人体的内脏，驱除腹中的多种毛病。每当寒天早起，就喝上一杯。"于是对左右亲近的大臣各赐数杯。从这以后，群臣百官之家都仿造这种药酒，而苏合香丸也流行起来。

明代李时珍的《本草纲目》记载药酒方约百首，其中著名的虎骨酒就是他发明的。时至今日，多达 110 万字的《中国药酒大典》，收录了 1622 种药酒方。

酒的重要功用自不待言，但是过量饮酒则伤害身体，以致造成祸害，古人早就认识到这一点。如夏禹品尝了仪狄所造的美酒，却疏远了仪狄而"绝旨酒"，并断言"后世必有以酒亡其国者"，正是基于这一认识。

据《尚书·酒诰》记载，约三千年前，周王室曾在中原大地的卫国郑重地发布了戒酒令。当年周公旦平定武庚的叛乱以后，把年幼的弟弟康叔封为卫君，统治殷民。卫国处在黄河和湛水之间（今河南安阳一带），是殷商的故居。殷人酗酒乱德，周公害怕这种恶习会酿成大乱，所以命令康叔在卫国宣布戒酒令，不许酗酒。这大概是中国最早的戒酒令了。

## 六、源于河南的易学文化对中医学产生了重要影响

河南有孟津"河出图"处、巩义"河出图"处、洛宁"洛出书"处、淮阳太昊陵、淮阳伏羲画卦圣地、汤阴文王推演六十四卦处、淮阳龙湖白龟出水处、上蔡蓍草园、太昊陵蓍草园、汤阴羑里城蓍草园等多处易学文化遗迹。

作为"易学"源头的河图洛书，其阐发的天人相因相应模式、象数思维模式以及气运法则，对中医天人思想、脏象学说、脏气升降学说都有深刻影响。

人们常说"医易同源"，因为易学阐述事物阴阳动静变化的道理，

numbers as well as the five circuits and six qi theory. These had a strong impact on the philosophy of Chinese Medicine, including the unity of the heaven and humanity, viscera and its manifestations, and qi's ascending and descending.

Chinese Medicine and the theory of *Yi Jing* are inseparable from each other because they are both grounded in the understanding of the changes of yin and yang within the same whole and their inter-transformations, the former interpreting the mechanism of wane and wax of bodily yin and yang, while the latter the dynamic changes of yin and yang in the universe. "One who knows nothing about the *Yi Jing* would never make a great doctor," said Sun Simiao in his *Qianjin Yaofang* (*Important Prescriptions Worth a Thousand Gold Pieces*). This tells exactly how one interacts with the other. It is believed that medicine, divination and astrology are all sub-divisions of the *Yi Jing* theory, so it is evident that *Yi Jing* has been a primary guideline in the formation and development of Chinese Medicine. That is why great ancient Chinese doctors invariably valued the study of *Yi Jing*.

*Yi Jing* expounded the dynamic changes of yin and yang in the universe, considered the unity of yin and yang was a general and essential rule of the universe and life. Based on the text of *Yi Jing*, Chinese Medicine has gradually developed a unique way of understanding bodily changes by incorporating these changes into a macro unity and specific context. There are quite a few such examples in *Huangdi Neijing*. It is written in the *Yi Jing* that "Vast is the 'great and originating (power)' indicated by Qian! All things owe to it their beginning. It contains all the meaning belonging to (the name) heaven." Similar lines were available in the *Huangdi Neijing*. For instance, "The vast universe, full of material energy, is where all things generate." Both interrelate to each other and include descriptions like "Yin and yang are interdependent forming the Tao, the Heaven and the Earth, and humans."

So many *Yi Jing* related cultural sites and relics now existent in Henan, as was previously listed, have proved that Henan is the home to this culture, which in turn is instrumental to the birth and growth of Chinese Medicine.

中医学阐明人体阴阳盛衰消长的机制，两者同源于对事物阴阳变化的认识，故称“医易同源”。隋唐名医孙思邈在《千金要方》中说：“不知易，不足以言大医”，更是强调了医易关系的重要性。方术家所谓“医卜星相”，皆易之支流，直接表明了易学对于中医学理论形成、发展的指导作用。所以中国古代许多著名医家都非常重视对于易学的研究。

易学阐述天地万物阴阳动静变化之理，强调阴阳的对立统一是宇宙的一般规律，同时也是生命运动的规律。在易理的影响下，中医学始终是在一个宏观的整体的时空条件下来认识人身所发生的一切，形成了自己独有的特色。我们可以从中医的经典《黄帝内经》中找到诸多例证。如：《周易·乾卦》说：“大哉乾元，万物资始，乃统天。”《黄帝内经·素问·天元纪大论》则说：“太虚寥廓，肇基化元，万物资始，五运终天。”《周易》说：“一阴一阳之谓道。夫易开物成务，昌天下之道。乾称父，坤称母。”《素问·阴阳应象大论》则说：“阴阳者，天地之道也，万物之纲纪，变化之父母。”可以看出，《内经》与《周易》两者关系密切，互为体用。

从伏羲画八卦到文王推演六十四卦，从孟津河出图到洛宁洛出书，从上蔡的蓍草龟池到淮阳的蓍草龟池，从殷墟的甲骨到羑里城的蓍草园，这一切均发生在中原的河南大地。充分说明河南是易学文化的发祥地。而博大精深的易学文化对中医药文化的产生和发展，起到了积极的推动作用。

## 七、道家和杂家的著作催生了中医养生学

在扎根于中原的先秦诸子文化中，道家和杂家对中医的养生学影响最大，可以说催生了中医养生学。特别是《黄帝内经》中的养生思想，也是深受道家和杂家的著作影响。

1. 崇尚自然，顺乎自然，是道家养生的基本原则

道家学说以自然天道观为主，他们追求精神的安宁，尤其强调精神

# Ⅶ. Chinese Regimen (Disease Prevention) Born out of Daoism and Miscellaneous Schools of Philosophy

Of all different pre-Qin dynasty cultures, works of Daoism and miscellaneous schools of philosophy had the greatest influence on Chinese Regimen, especially on the disease prevention theories in *Huangdi Neijing*.

1. Love for and Compliance with the Nature: An Essential Principle of Daoist Regimen

Daoism focuses on compliance with the nature, namely the "naturalness." Daoists are in a constant pursuit of mental peace, especially the state beyond spiritual limits, integrity, and freedom. Therefore, Daoism doctrines embody more practices for achieving longevity.

Laozi (571-471 B.C.) said, "Man takes his law from the Earth; the Earth takes its law from Heaven; Heaven takes its law from the Dao. The law of the Dao is its being what it is." Man should align himself to the law of the natural world and "the way" of the elements. The primordial state of human beings was parallel with that of the Nature. That was why Laozi had advocated returning to the original nature, freeing oneself from selfishness and desire, and appreciating simplicity. Freed from material desires one could cultivate the physique and attain spiritual peace. Only when both physical and spiritual integrities were accomplished could man achieve longevity. This has a significant influence on the later generations.

Zhuangzi (roughly 369-286) made it plain, "To be guileless and pure, and free from all admixture; to be still and uniform, without undergoing any change; to be indifferent and do nothing; to move and yet to act like Heaven: this is the way to nourish the spirit."(Cited from *Zhuangzi*) He regarded indifference to worldly gain, solitude, humbleness, and wu wei (action without intention) as the baseline for balancing Heaven and the Earth, and the ultimate state of moral and spiritual cultivation. He emphasized all things in line with the natural laws in the attainment of peaceful spirit.

Apart from spiritual cultivation, Zhuangzi also advocated physical exercises featuring tuna (Taoist breathing techniques) and daoyin (physical movements with controlled inhalation and exhalation). The following was cited from *Zhuangzi* "Blowing and breathing with open mouth; inhaling and exhaling the breath;

的超然与人格的独立，渴望人生的自由。因此他们的学说包含更多的养生内容。

老子说：“人法地，地法天，天法道，道法自然。”人的一切都应该顺应自然规律，不悖天地之理。而人最初的状态最接近自然，因此他提出返朴归真，恬淡清静，顺乎自然。去物欲以养形，致虚静以养神，形神不亏，便可长生。这一养生理论对后世产生了深远的影响。

庄子说得更明白：“故曰：纯粹而不杂，静一而不变，淡而无为，动而以天行，此养神之道也。”（《庄子·刻意》）他把“恬淡、寂寞、虚心、无为”看成是天地赖以均衡的基准，而且是道德修养的最高境界。因而主张清静无为，一切活动都顺应自然而行，即所谓“动而以天行”，这就是养神之道。

庄子在强调养神的同时，还提出吐纳导引之法的养形健身作用。在《刻意》篇中说：“吹呴呼吸，吐故纳新，熊经鸟申，为寿而已矣。”认识到人通过吸纳新鲜空气，吐出废浊之气，实行导引之术，模仿熊直立肢体、鸟伸展翅膀的动作来锻炼身体，可以加强新陈代谢而延年益寿。这些都是非常可取的，对中医养生学的发展产生了重要影响。

马王堆汉墓出土的《导引图》，是现存最早的关于保健运动的彩绘帛画，它为古代文献中失散不全的导引健身运动资料，找到了最早的图形例证，也为研究导引健身运动的历史发展提供了具体线索。

在其后两千多年的历史中，它不仅一直被医家和养生家所采用，而且也被道家和佛家广泛用作修炼身心之法。东汉末年，神医华佗吸取了《导引图》的精华，创造了“五禽戏”，一直流传至今，成为中国传统保健体育的著名项目。此后的八段锦、太极拳等运动方法更是一脉相承。

先秦诸子特别是道家的养生思想与实践，在经典著作《黄帝内经》中得到了集中的体现，并作了全面的总结。唐朝王冰注《黄帝内经·素问》，即引了许多道家语。如《上古天真论篇·第一》竟引老子、庄子之语数十句。一篇文章，不过数百字，而注解引用了这么多道家语来诠析文本，

expelling the old breath and taking in new; passing their time like the (dormant) bear, and stretching and twisting (the body) like a bird— all this simply shows the desire for longevity."These are all practical techniques to improve metabolism and for longevity, serving as a precursor to Chinese Regimen.

A painted scroll known as the *Daoyintu* found in the Han dynasty tomb at Mawangdui is the earliest extant coloured silk chart about physical exercise. The coloured figures are solid proof of illustrated Tao Yin exercises in history. It also provides clues to study the historical development of Tao Yin exercises.

This chart has been adopted by medical and regimen practitioners in over 2000 years of history. It has also been practiced by the Taoist and Buddhist followers for physical and spiritual cultivation. In the late East Han dynasty, Huatuo known as a medical deity created Wu Qin Xi (Five-Animal Exercise) by absorbing the essence displayed in the chart. The Five-Animal Exercise has been handed down over the years till today, and become a well-known exercise in traditional health sports. Ba Duan Jin (Eight-Section Movements), and Taijiquan are all similar exercises originated from the same precursor.

Life-nurturing wisdom and practices of the philosophers, and authors in the pre-Qin dynasty period, especially of the Taoist philosophy are embodied and summarized in the Chinese Medicine classic of *Huangdi Neijing*. Quite a number of Taoist lines of wisdom were cited in Wang Bing's interpretation of *Suwen* (*Plain Questions*). It is a short article of a few hundred words, but with quite a few quotations. This is not surprising, though, because the attitude advocated in *Su Wen* is parallel to that of the Taoist philosophy.

Born in the Central Plains, it has a complete interpretation of life nurturing and disease prevention, and is a theoretical foundation for Chinese Regimen. It includes a summary of the growth of human body as well as pathological changes at different phases. This provides the theoretical basis for the adoption of varied nurturing methods for different age groups. It has a profound understanding of the aging mechanism, physical activities, and pathological manifestations in the elderly. It also explains varied factors affecting the life span. It is clearly stated in the book that great doctors are not the ones who were good at treating diseases, but the ones who excelled in disease prevention. It also discusses the principle and methods for mental and physical cultivation.

并不令人感到奇怪，因为整体《黄帝内经·素问》所表现的人生态度，确实近于道家。

诞生于中原的《黄帝内经》，从医学理论的高度全面地阐述了养生防病的一系列原则，为中医养生学奠定了系统的理论基础。《黄帝内经》对人的生长发育过程以及各个阶段的病理变化作了精妙的观察和概括，为各种不同年龄的人采用不同的养生方法提供了理论根据；对人衰老、变老的机理以及老年人的生理活动和病理表现有着深刻的认识，对各种影响寿命的因素都作了论述；明确提出“不治已病治未病”的观点和形神兼养的原则和方法。

《黄帝内经》的养生思想奠定了中医养生学的基础。《黄帝内经》既是中医理论体系形成的产物，也是中医养生学理论体系形成的标志。其后，历代有大批有关养生的论著相继问世，但大多是在《黄帝内经》的基础上发展起来的。

2. 杂家的代表著作《吕氏春秋》保留了大量的养生内容

在杂家的代表著作吕不韦（河南濮阳人）的《吕氏春秋》中，保留

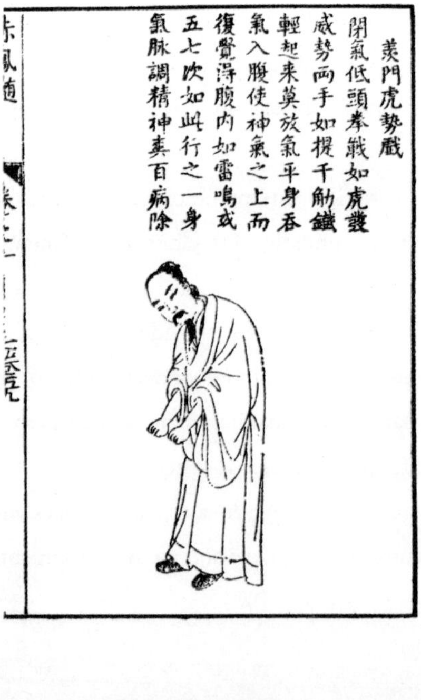


五禽戏·虎戏图
Tiger-Like Exercise Chart

The life nurturing thought in *Huangdi Neijing* laid a foundation for disease prevention. It was born out of Chinese Medicine theories and was a milestone, marking the completion of theoretical system of disease prevention. A legion of works on regimen came into being down the ages, mostly based on this classic.

2. Regimen in *Lüshi Chunqiu*, Masterpiece of Miscellaneous Schools of Philosophy

*Lü Buwei* was a native of Puyang, Henan. A substantial number of medical texts were recorded in his *Lüshi Chunqiu*, of which quite a few were about disease prevention.

The chapter "Jin Shu" is dedicated to disease prevention. It says without preamble that "Nature has generated yin and yang, cold and summer heat, dryness and dampness," and that "seasonal changes and transformation of all things invariably bring about both benefits and harms at the same time." This was the precursor of "liu qi (six pathogenic factors)" theory in Chinese Medicine. Later, the six pathogenic factors refer to wind, cold, summer heat, dampness, dryness, and fire.

The idea of life nurturing through exercises was put forward in the article. It says, "The reason why running water never gets stale, and a door-hinge never gets worms is that they constantly move." This has also given rise to a Chinese idiom.

It also states that the water people regularly drink affects the body remarkably. People in places with light water are more likely to be bald or have cervical tumor, while those in places with heavy water more to be lame or have swollen feet. In places where water is sweet, people are more likely to be good-looking, while in places where water is acrid, people are more likely to have carbuncles or festering sores. In places where water is bitter, people are more likely to have pigeon chest (pectus carinatum) or hump. This indicates that ancient Chinese were aware how living surroundings affected people's health, and considered it greatly important to protect environment and nurture life.

It also advocates life nurturing through regular diet. It says, "People with regular meals are unlikely to get sick. It is healthy to have meals without having hunger pangs nor feeling full, which is beneficial for the viscera."

These ideas have all influenced the growth of Chinese Medicine, and are still enlightening today.

Also expounded in one chapter of the book were "The Three Warnings" in life

了大量的医学内容，其中有多篇文章专论养生。

如《尽数》篇系统地论述了养生长寿之道。开门见山指出：“天生阴阳、寒暑、燥湿，四时之化，万物之变，莫不为利，莫不为害。”这里提到的“阴阳、寒暑、燥湿”，就是早期的“六气”之说，后来中医称“风、寒、暑、湿、燥、火”为六气。从中可以看出“六气”学说的演变痕迹。

文中提出了著名的运动养生思想。指出：“流水不腐，户枢不蝼，动也。形气亦然。”成语“流水不腐，户枢不蠹”即源于此。

文中还提出，不同的居处饮水环境对人的身体会产生重大影响。指出：“轻水所，多秃与瘿人；重水所，多尰与躄人；甘水所，多好与美人；辛水所，多疽与痤人；苦水所，多尪与伛人。”告诉人们，水质轻的地方，多秃发和颈部长肿瘤的人；水质重的地方，多脚肿和瘸腿的人；水甘甜的地方，多容貌美好漂亮的人；水辛辣的地方，多患痈疮和脓疮的人；水苦的地方，多鸡胸和驼背的人。充分说明古人对居处环境的重视，显示了先贤的环境保护意识，体现了古人的养生智慧。

文中还提出了饮食养生之道：“食能以时，身必无灾。凡食之道，无饥无饱，是之谓五脏之葆。”

这些论述对中医学的发展产生了深远的影响，直到今天，对我们仍然有着深刻的启示。

在《本生》篇中，提出了有名的养生“三患”：“富贵而不知道，适足以为患……出则以车，入则以辇，务以自佚，命之曰招蹷之机；肥肉厚酒，务以自强，命之曰烂肠之食；靡曼皓齿，郑、卫之音，务以自乐，命之曰伐性之斧。三患者，富贵之所致也。”告诫人们，富贵却不懂得养生之道，恰好能带来疾患。出门就乘车，回家就坐辇，一味追求骄逸，这是招致痿躄的关键；对肥肉美酒，一味暴食暴饮，这是使肠胃生病的食品；对美貌女子，淫靡之音，一贯沉溺享乐，这是砍伐生命的斧头。《吕氏春秋》养生“三患”的告诫对后世颇有影响，汉代的枚乘和宋代的苏轼等名家都曾引述过。

nurturing. It warned rich people of the potential health risks if they were not aware of proper ways of disease prevention. For example, people were likely to become weak or lame if they often took carriage or sedan chair; excessive drinking or consumption of meat was harmful to the stomach and intestines; lechery or indulgence in provocative music was like a killing axe hanging over the body. "The Three Warnings" were quite influential, and were quoted by celebrities, such as Mei Sheng in the Han dynasty, and Su Shi in the Song dynasty.

The origin of music and dance is available in the chapter *Gu Yue* (*Music in Antiquity*). When Zhuxiangshi was in reign, due to gross wind and excess yang qi, all things were scattered, and hardly any fruit could ripen. Therefore, Shi Da devised a five-string musical instrument and played it to collect yin qi, thus balancing yin and yang so that the world was restored to a normal state.

Another similar story goes like this. When Taotang Shi was in reign, excess of yin qi caused the riverbed to silt up and water flow was stagnated. Consequently local people had contracted muscles due to stagnated yin qi in the body. Dance was then created to free the body from stagnant qi.

The two chapters suggested the birth of music and dance was so closely related to medicine. Music was to balance yin and yang to attain harmony, while dance was to release stagnant qi to attain unrestrained muscle movements.

## Ⅷ. The Unique Contributions of Oracle Bone Inscriptions and *Shuowen Jiezi* to TCM

1. The Medical Literature Recorded in Oracle Bone Inscriptions

The vast majority of the oracle bone inscriptions, with a history of 3,000 years, were unearthed at the village of Xiaotun in Anyang, Henan province. The ancient name of Anyang was called Yin when Pan Geng, the 20th king of the Shang dynasty established his capital in the north part of the city, and it had been the last capital until the last King Zhou was wiped out along with the dynasty by the King Wu of the Zhou dynasty in 1046 BC. During that period, the Chinese written characters had evolved into what we find in the inscriptions and became the prevailing form of written characters of that time.

Legend has it that Wang Yirong, director of the Chinese Imperial Academy,

导引图
Daoyintu (Tao Yin chart)

在《古乐》篇中有两段关于音乐和舞蹈起源的论述。一段说："昔古朱襄氏（炎帝的别号）之治天下也，多风而阳气畜积，万物散解，果实不成。故士达（炎帝之臣）作为五弦瑟，以来阴气，以定群生。"意思说，从前朱襄氏治理天下时，经常刮风，阳气过多，万物散落，果实不成熟，所以士达制作弹奏五弦琴瑟，用来招阴气，协调阴阳，以安定众生。

另一段是："昔陶唐氏（传说中古代帝王称号）之始，阴多滞伏而湛积，水道壅塞，不行其原，民气郁阏而滞著，筋骨瑟缩不达，故作为舞以宣导之。"意思说：从前陶唐氏开始治理天下的时候，阴气过多，凝聚不散而积聚，河道壅塞，源流不通。人民受其影响，阴气郁结，阻滞不畅，筋骨收缩而不舒展，所以创作舞蹈，使郁结之气散发出来，以求舒畅。

这两段记载给我们提供了一个重要信息，原来音乐和舞蹈的发明与医学息息相关。音乐用来协调阴阳之气，以定群生；舞蹈用来宣发郁结之气，使瑟缩不达的筋骨伸展舒畅。

was the first person to discover the oracle bone inscriptions, which coincided with ingredients of a formula. In summer of 1899, he was prescribed a remedy containing "dragon bones" for his illness. "Dragon bones" were widely used in TCM as fossils of dead animals at that time. To his surprise, he noticed some unusual carvings that looked like some kind of writing on the bones. Based on his study on the ancient bronze ware and tablet scripts, he concluded that these bones were used as divination and the scripts engraved on them were the early form of Chinese writings of the Shang dynasty. It turned out that the so-called dragon bones were turtle shells and animal bones, and mistaken as ingredients of formulas by the people in the village of Xiaotun of Anyang. Through this, he became the first person to discover, name and collect oracle bones in China.

There are many records about diseases in oracle bone inscriptions. Among them, more than 30 kinds of diseases can be identified, involving such human organs and functions as head, eye, ear, nose, mouth, teeth, tongue, speech, chest, hand, elbow, shin, foot and bone. Many records are about dental diseases in the divination inscriptions. For example, there is such a record in the scripts that "there are worms in the dental disease," which indicates the teeth were sick because venomous worms were in the teeth. This is what people call "decayed teeth," which in medicine, is named dental caries. It can be seen that doctors in the Shang dynasty have already had a systematic understanding of various diseases of human body. This is the earliest literature available about TCM, which is of great value to the study of TCM history.

2.The First Chinese Dictionary *Shuowen Jiezi* and Its Value to TCM

*Shuowen Jiezi*, the first Chinese dictionary and often shorten for *Shuowen* (*Explanation of Script*), was written by Xu Shen in the Eastern Han dynasty in about 100A.D. Xu Shen was born in the Zhaoling district of Ru'nan prefecture, today known as Luohe in Henan province. The dictionary included 9,353 characters which were categorized into 540 sections with shared components, called radicals, and hence he was the first person to use the principle of organization by radicals. "The Six Categories of Characters" were established by his creative application of explaining characters in the book. The dictionary recorded the writing system of seal scripts, the ancient semantic explanation and pronunciation before the Han dynasty. This dictionary provided us with important references for paleography, Chinese etymology, and ancient phonology, and thus was considered to be the important

# 八、甲骨文和《说文解字》对中医学的独特贡献

1. 甲骨文中的医学文献

河南安阳小屯是甲骨文的圣地，它是商朝盘庚迁都于殷（即安阳）至纣王亡国这段时期通行的字体，距今已有 3000 多年的历史。

关于甲骨文的发现，有一个传奇故事，机缘巧合竟与一味中药有关。光绪二十五年（1899 年）夏天，国子监祭酒王懿荣因患病差人去药店抓中药，在煎药时发现，有一味“龙骨”药上面有类似商代青铜器铭文模样的刻画。王懿荣凭他多年对金石文字学的研究，敏感地意识到这龙骨上的刻画非同寻常，经细心研究，断定这些龙骨是商代卜骨，刻在龟甲和兽骨上的文字就是商代文字。经查实，原来是安阳小屯一带的村民，把在地里挖取的龟甲和兽骨，当作龙骨卖给了药店。王懿荣于 1899 年从中药“龙骨”中发现甲骨文，从而成为我国发现、命名及收集甲骨的第一人。

甲骨文·疾鼻

Oracle Bone · Nose Diseases

reference for ancient books and ancient Chinese characters in the pre-Qin periods.

*Shuowen* is not a medical book but is of great value to the study of TCM. There are 9353 characters in the dictionary, of which 1163 are variants. A preliminary statistic show that nearly 1,300 are directly related to medicine which accounted for one sixth of all the characters with the variants removed.

The statistic shows: 674 characters are in physiology, 427 in pathology, 150 in medicinal materials, and 42 in acupuncture, meridians and collateral. Among them, there are 359 words indicating the names of diseases and as many as 102 characters with the "疒" (indicating disease) as the radical. Below are some examples.

Some Chinese characters describe human body parts and physiological phenomena. For example, "the character 题 refers to the forehead." "The character 脚 refers to the shank." Some Chinese characters describe symptoms and syndromes. For example, "the character 眇 refers to being blind." "The character 眚 refers to nebula." Some Chinese characters describe etiology and pathogenesis. For example, "the character 痱 refers to hemiplegia." "The character 瘀 refers to blood stasis." Some Chinese characters describe the disease names. For example, "the character 瘿 refers to neck tumor. " It is now commonly known as a big neck, goiter." "The character 痔 refers to the disease on the anus," which indicates that hemorrhoid had been recognized at that time. Some Chinese characters describe the diagnosis. For example, "the character 妊 refers to being pregnant." "The character 娠 refers to fetal movement." Some Chinese characters describe the medicinal materials. For example, "the character 药 referred to herbs," which indicates that all herbs for curing diseases belonged to the category of medicine and Chinese herbal medicinal materials were mainly based on grass plants. "The Chinese character 丹 refers to red stones in the Bashu area", today known as the area to the south of the Yangtze River and Sichuan basin, which indicates that cinnabar was a mineral for Chinese herbs produced in the place mentioned above. Some Chinese characters describe the acupuncture and moxibustion therapy. For example, "the character 砭 refers to treating diseases with flints", which indicates that stone needles were used to treat diseases. "The character 灸 refers to cauterization", which indicated moxibustion was a therapy in which moxa cones were used to cauterize the acupoints of human body. There is a

在甲骨文中，有不少关于疾病的记载。其中能够辨识出疾病名称的有疾首、疾目、疾耳、疾自（鼻）、疾口、疾齿、疾舌、疾言、疾胸、疾手、疾肘、疾胫、疾止、疾骨等 30 多种。如疾齿，是指牙齿的疾病，这种病在卜辞的记载比较多。例如："有疾齿住蛊"，意思是牙齿得了病，是因为有虫在作怪。这就是人们所说的"虫牙"，在医学上叫龋齿。可以看出，商代医生们对人体各部分疾病已有了系统的认识。这是最早的中医文献，对研究中国医学史有着非常重要的价值。

2. 中国第一部字典《说文解字》及其对中医学的价值

中国第一部字典是东汉时许慎所著的《说文解字》（简称《说文》），大约成书于公元 100 年。许慎是东汉汝南郡召陵人，即今河南省漯河市郾城人。《说文》按汉字的形体和偏旁结构，将全书所收的 9353 个字，"据形系联"，分为 540 部，首创部首编排法；用"六书"的理论解释文字，确立了六书的体系；保存了篆文的写法系统和汉以前的古训古音，为古文字学、汉语词源学和古音学提供了重要参考资料，是研究先秦古籍和古文字学的典籍。

《说文解字·心》
*Shuo Wen Jie Zi (Explanation of Script and Elucidation of Characters)·Heart*

record on the theory of yin-yang and the five-element, which is used to explain the numerology, the ten Heavenly Stems and twelve Earthly Branches. For example, "the number four belongs to yin." "The Chinese character 甲, the Heavenly Stem One, is similar to appearance of seeds generated by the most abundant yang-qi in the east." The five-element theory was used exclusively to explain the five-zang organs. For example, "Lung is for storing metal"; "Liver for storing wood"; "Kidney for storing water"; "Heart for storing fire"; "Spleen for storing earth".

A wealth of systematic medical literature has been recorded in the dictionary. As we all know, the Han dynasty is the first peak in the development history of TCM. The book *Shuowen*, compiled in the Eastern Han dynasty, is a glimpse of the brilliant medical achievements of that period from the perspective of philology and has become the basis and norm to interpret medical terms for later generations. It has enlightened us to study TCM. It is essential for us to read *Shuowen Jiezi* carefully in order to obtain a correct interpretation of Chinese medical classics and excavate the great treasure house of TCM.

Seen from the oracle bone inscriptions in Yin Ruins, the main stages of the development of Chinese characters have been completed in Henan province from their formation: establishment to standardization. For example, under the order of the First Emperor of the Qin dynasty, Li Si systematized and unified the written Chinese characters by simplifying the large-seal script and promulgating the small-seal script as the imperial standard. He was a native of Shangcai county of Henan province. The emergence of clerical script marked the beginning of today's scripts, which made the form of Chinese characters evolve into a new stage. Cai Yong, a native of Qixian county of Henan province and a great scholar in the late Eastern Han dynasty, was a great master of calligraphy for the clerical script. The regular script had been evolved into a matured form in the end of the Eastern Han dynasty. Zhong Yao was the first famous calligrapher for the regular script in the Three Kingdoms period. He was born in Changge county of Henan province. Since Wei and Jin dynasties, regular script had become the main form of Chinese characters, and also the standard form of Chinese writing. The Song style character was established in Kaifeng and has been popular. With the advent of the computer age, Chinese characters faced a possibility of death. At that critical moment, Wang Yongmin, a native of Henan province, solved the computer input problem of Chinese

《说文》虽然不是医学著作，但是它对中医学的研究有着重要的价值。《说文》共收字 9353 个，其中重文（即异体字）1163 个，经初步统计，其中与医药学直接相关的文字将近 1300 个，如果去掉重文 1163 个，实际将近占全书收字的六分之一。

其大体分布是：生理方面的有 674 字，病理方面的有 427 字，药物方面的有 150 字，经络及针灸方面的有 42 字。其中表示病名的有 359 字，仅“疒”字旁的字就有 102 个。

我们举一些实例以做简要介绍。

有对人体部位和生理现象的描述，如：“题，额也”；“脚，胫（小腿）也”。有对症状证候的描述，如：“眇，一目小也”；“眚，目病生翳也”。有对病因病机的描述，如：“痱，风病也”；“瘀，积血也”。有对病名的记述，如：“瘿，颈瘤（俗称大脖子病，即甲状腺肿大一类的病）也”；“痔，后病也”。“后”指肛门。说明此时已认识了痔疮病。有对诊断的记述，如：“妊，孕也”；“娠，女妊身动也”。有关于药物的记述，如：“药，治病草也。”说明凡是治病的草均属药的范畴。同时也说明中药基本上是以草木植物为主。“丹，巴越之赤石也。”说明朱砂是产于巴蜀和越地的矿物药。有对针灸疗法的记述，如：“砭，以石刺病也。”说明用石针治病。“灸，灼也。”说明是用艾炷烧灼或熏熨人体穴位的一种疗法。有关于阴阳五行学说的记述，对于数、天干、地支用阴阳解释，如“四，阴数也”；“甲，东方之孟阳气萌动”。关于五脏，完全用五行学说作解释，如“肺，金藏也”；“肝，木藏也”；“肾，水藏也”；“心，火藏也”；“脾，土藏也”；等等。

全书保存了丰富而系统的医药文字资料。众所周知，两汉时期是中医药发展史上的第一个高峰，而成书于东汉时期的《说文》一书，正从一个侧面展示了那个时期辉煌的医学成就，而且成为后世解释医学词语的依据和规范。对今人研究中医药学有着深刻的启迪意义。我们要想正确地阅读中医药古籍，发掘中医药这座伟大的宝库，就必须认真阅读《说文解字》。

characters, and inaugurated a new information era for Chinese characters.

## Ⅸ. The Treatment Principle Established by the Medical Sage Zhang Zhongjing: the Core Idea, the Diagnosis and Treatment Mode of TCM

Zhang Zhongjing, born in Nanyang city at the end of the Eastern Han dynasty, left his government official position to become a doctor when the epidemic caused many death. "Diligently seeking for the ancient maxim and collecting various formulas," he applied the theory of *Huangdi Neijing* to the clinical practice, wrote the classic Chinese medical book *Shanghan Zabing Lun*, and established a system of "syndrome differentiation and treatment".

According to the various syndromes displayed by the complicated conditions, Zhongjing used ancient dialectical thoughts to analyze and study, to find out the attributes, parts, waning and waxing of the vital and pathogenic qi, and morbid manifestations. He summarized and distinguished diseases and syndromes with yin, yang, exterior, interior, cold, heat, which are summarized as the eight principles by the later generations, taken as an outline for the differentiation of diseases and used to understand the universal laws at all stages of the disease development process. Zhongjing also summed up different types of diseases with three yin and three yang, comprehensively grasping the general laws and special phenomena of the development and change of diseases through the syndrome differentiation of "six meridians", so as to make a correct diagnosis of diseases. On the basis of careful differentiations of symptoms and signs according to the location, sequence and severity of the diseases, Zhongjing formulated various treatment methods such as sweating, vomiting, purging, harmonizing, warming, clearing, tonifying and eliminating, which were summed up as the eight methods by Cheng Zhongling in the Qing dynasty, making the system of syndrome differentiation and treatment more systematic and complete. This system provides not only a programmatic rule for the diagnosis and treatment of all exogenous diseases, but also a clear demonstration for TCM diagnosis and treatment rules, which is taken as the diagnosis and treatment method in TCM culture. This mode of diagnosis has been followed by other physicians. In the next two thousand years, the accomplished doctors of all ages

自殷墟甲骨文以来，汉字从形成、确立到规范，其发展过程中的主要阶段都是在河南完成的。如小篆是秦朝李斯（河南上蔡县人）受秦始皇之命取大篆整理简化而成的，也称“秦篆”，统一了天下的文字。隶书的产生，标志着今文字的起始，使汉字的形体演变到了一个崭新的阶段。东汉末年的大学者河南杞县人蔡邕就是书写隶书的圣手和大师。楷书到东汉末年渐趋成熟。三国时代的钟繇是第一个著名的楷书书法家。他是河南长葛县人。自魏晋以来，楷书便成了应用汉字主要的形体，也是我们书写汉字的规范形体。宋体字是在开封创立的，沿用至今。当世界进入到计算机时代，汉字面临“生死劫难”的时候，又是一位河南人解决了汉字进入电脑的世界性难题，开创了汉字信息化的新纪元。这位河南人叫王永民。

## 九、医圣张仲景确立的论治法则是中医学术的核心思想和诊疗模式

生于东汉末年的南阳人张仲景，在当时瘟疫大流行、人民死亡惨重的背景之下，弃官从医，“勤求古训，博采众方”，将《黄帝内经》的理论用于临床实践之中，写出了中医的经典之作《伤寒杂病论》，创立了“辨证论治”体系。

张仲景根据错综复杂的病情所表现出的各种证侯，运用古代辩证法思想，加以分析研究，找出其中的属性、部位、邪正消长和病态表现，用阴阳、表里、寒热、虚实概括并区分病证（后人总结为“八纲”），作为辨识疾病的大纲，去认识疾病发展过程中各个阶段的普遍规律。仲景又以三阴和三阳来归纳疾病所呈现的不同类型，通过“六经”辨证，全面地把握疾病发展变化的普遍规律和特殊现象，以对疾病做出正确诊断。仲景在认真辨证的基础上，根据病变的表里先后和轻重缓急，随证施治，相应地制定出汗、吐、下、和、温、清、补、消等多种治疗方法（清人程钟龄总结为“八法”），从而使辨证论治体系更加系统完备。这一体系不

have inherited the diagnosis and treatment method of the TCM culture.

Moreover, Zhang Zhongjing created a series of corresponding prescriptions based on syndrome differentiation. These prescriptions are well matched, profound in medical principles and remarkable in curative effects, which are revered as "classic formulas" by later generations. After being developed for generations, these formulas are not limited to the treatment of the diseases described by Zhongjing, but far exceeding the scope of their application, widely used to treat various diseases. In the process of using classical formulas, doctors of all ages have derived many effective prescriptions according to different formulation methods and the condition of illnesses by adding and subtracting medicines and changing the dosage. These formulas have played an important role clinically and also made a great contribution to the well being of humanity.

In short, Zhang Zhongjing, with his academic system and noble medical ethics, has become a model of TCM and the best representative of TCM culture in all previous dynasties, and is naturally regarded as the "medical sage". Zhongjing's study has always been the mainstream of TCM. He has provided a broad platform for future generations to read, use, and update, from which new values are generated and vitality is maintained. All previous generations of doctors gathered under the banner of Zhongjing's study and continued to inherit and develop, forming the largest academic school of TCM. As the Japanese scholar Mototane Tanpa says in *Zhongguo Yiji Kao* (*Textual Research of Chinese Medical Records*): "It is always bright like the brilliance of the sun and moon, whether it is daytime or night."

## X. The Medical Achievements of the Northern Song Dynasty: A Monument to the History of TCM

A particularly noteworthy phenomenon is that many places in the ancient Central Plains were designated as capitals. Thousands of years of the ancient capital culture have taken root in the Central Plains and have made the greatest influence there. After the capital was built in the central plains, it has stimulated the prosperity and development of the Central Plains and formed the unique style of the Central Plains culture. However, the importance attached to medicine by dynasties that have occupied the Central Plains has promoted the development of TCM culture to

仅为诊疗一切外感病提供了纲领性的法则，同时也为中医诊疗规律做出了明确的示范，成为中医药文化的诊疗模式。这一诊疗模式，一直为后代医家所遵循。在此后近两千年的岁月里，历代有成就的医家无不继承了这种中医药文化的诊疗模式。

不仅如此，张仲景与辨证论治相配合，还创制了一系列相应的方剂。这些方剂配伍精当，医理深奥，疗效显著，被后世尊为“经方”。经过历代医家的发扬光大，这些经方已不局限于治疗仲景所述之疾病，而是远远超过其应用范围，广泛用以治疗各种疾病。历代医家在运用经方的过程中，根据其组方思路及病情需要，通过加减药味和改变药量等方法，又衍化派生出了许多有效方剂，在临床上发挥了重要作用，为人类的健康做出了巨大贡献。

总之，张仲景以其创建的学术体系和高尚的医德，成为历代中医的楷模和中医药文化的最优秀代表，理所当然地被尊为“医圣”。仲景之学一直是中医的主流之学，他为后代学者提供了一个常读常新、常用常新的广阔平台，从中不断地生发出新的价值，始终保持着旺盛的生命活力。历代医家聚集在仲景之学的旗帜下，不断地继承和发展，形成最大的中医学术流派。正如日本学者丹波元胤在《中国医籍考》中所说：“如日月之光华，旦而复旦，万古常明。”

## 十、北宋的医学成就树立了中国医学史上的丰碑

一个值得注意的现象是，在古代，国都多定在中原。几千年的古都文化在中原地区扎根最深、影响最大，一次次在中原建都后更激发了中原的繁荣发展，形成了中原文化的独特风采。而历代入主中原的王朝对医药的重视，则不同程度地促进了中医药文化的发展。

建都在河南开封的大宋王朝所取得的辉煌医学成就，是中国医学发展史上一座不朽的丰碑。千百年来，对中医药文化的发展一直起着引领和

varying degrees.

The Song dynasty, which built its capital in Kaifeng city of Henan province, has made brilliant medical achievements, regarded as an immortal monument in the history of TCM development. For thousands of years, it has always played a leading and demonstrating role in the development of TCM.

Since the Qin and Han dynasties, after thousands of years of cultural accumulation, the culture of the Song dynasty has experienced the unprecedented prosperity and reached the peak of ancient Chinese culture. With the policy of "promoting culture, education and suppressing martial arts," the Northern Song dynasty government attached great importance to medicine and formulated a series of correct measures to promote the development of medicine, which made the medical culture thrive in the Song dynasty.

1. An Extensive Collection of Medical Documents

The emperor of the Northern Song dynasty fully recognized the value of medical documents and paid special attention to the collection of medical documents. According to the records of *Song Shi* (*History of the Song dynasty*)", in the third year of Taiping Xingguo reign (978 A.D), Emperor of the Song dynasty Zhao Guangyi issued a letter saying: "The Hanlin Medical Officers' Academy has presented ten thousand pieces of formulas, which were handed down according to individual family experiences". Emperor Taizong not only ordered the collection of medical books, but also practiced "receiving thousands of wonderful prescriptions after personal trials". [Recorded in *Song Dazhaoling Ji* (*The Collection of Emperor's Orders in the Song dynasty*), revised by Si Yizu] The speech and behavior of Emperor Taizong set a good example for later emperors. The Five Emperors of the Song dynasty made the book purchase orders for more than ten times, making the collection work unprecedented and providing an important basis for the compilation of medical records.

2. The Establishment of Various National Medical Institutions

Various national medical institutions have been set up, including Taiyi Bureau, Huimin Pharmaceutical Bureau and Medical Records Correction Bureau (specialized in sorting out medical books), etc. The Correction Medical Book Bureau established by Renzong emperor was unique in the entire feudal era. Here, many top-ranking scholars assembled, including Zhang Yuxi, Gao Baoheng, Lin Yi and Sun Zhao. They

示范作用。

自秦汉以来，经过千百年的文化积淀，宋代文化出现了空前的繁荣，达到了中国古代文化的高峰。在“兴文教，抑武事”的政策背景下，北宋政府对医药学高度重视，制定了一系列促进医药学发展的正确措施，使宋代的医药文化呈现一派生机勃勃的景象。

1. 广泛征集医药文献

北宋皇帝充分认识到图籍的价值，特别重视医药文献的征集。据《宋史》记载，太平兴国三年（978 年），宋太宗赵光义诏：“翰林医官院各具家传经验方以献，又万余首。”太宗不仅下令征集医书，而且还身体力行“收得妙方千余首，无非亲验”（见司义祖校订《宋大诏令集》）。太宗的言行为以后的皇帝树立了榜样。宋代五帝先后十多次颁布求购书诏令，使征集工作出现了空前局面，为医书的整理编纂提供了重要条件。

2. 建立各种国家医疗机构

先后建有太医局、惠民和剂局（制药）和校正医书局（专门整理医书）等机构。仁宗时设立的校正医书局，在整个封建时代是绝无仅有的。在这里集中了一流的学者，掌禹锡、高保衡、林亿和孙兆四人为校正医书官，整理了《素问》《伤寒杂病论》《金匮要略》《千金方》《脉经》《外台秘要》《甲乙经》《诸病源候论》等十多部重要医籍，使其成为指导临床应用的范本。

3. 多次修订本草并编撰多部大型方书

宋代是修订本草最多的。政府 4 次修订本草，为历朝之冠。

早在开宝六年（973 年），宋太祖赵匡胤命刘翰等人整理，后又命李昉刊定，修成了《开宝重定本草》，收药 984 种，较前增药 100 多种。宋仁宗嘉祐二年（1057 年），又命掌禹锡、林仁、苏颂等人编著《嘉祐补注本草》，增药 82 种。公元 1061 年，又命各地将所产药物绘图呈上，由苏颂编辑成《图经本草》。北宋末年，通仕郎艾晟将唐慎微编的《经史

worked as medical book correction officers, and sorted out more than ten important medical books, such as *Su Wen Shanghan Lun* (*Treatise on Cold Damage*), *Jingui Yaolüe* (*Synopsis of the Golden Chamber*), *Qianjin Fang* (*Prescriptions Worth a Thousand Gold Pieces*), *Mai Jing* (*Pulse Classic*), *Waitai Miyao* (*Arcane Essentials from the Imperial Library*), *Jiayi Jing* (*A-B Classic of Acupuncture and Moxibustion*), and *Zhubing Yuanhou Lun* (*Treatise on Causes and Manifestations of Various Diseases*), which were taken as models for guiding clinical application.

3. Revising the *Materia Medica* for Many Times and Compiling Many Large-scale Formula Books

*Materia Medica* was mostly frequently revised in the Song dynasty. The government revised the *Materia Medica* for four times, which was more frequent than any dynasty in the history.

As early as the sixth year of Kaibao reign (973A.D.), Zhao Kuangyin, Emperor of the Song dynasty, ordered Liu Han and others to sort out, and later ordered Li Fang to compile *Kaibao Chongding Bencao* (*Revised Materia Medica of the Kaibao Reign*), including 984 medicinals, with 100 medicinals more than before. In the second year of Jiayou reign of the Ren emperor of the Song dynasty (1057A.D.), he also ordered Zhang Yuxi,Li Ren and Su Song to compile *Jiayou Bencao* (*Materia Medica of the Jiayou Reign*) and added 82 medicinals. In 1061A.D., the government ordered all medicinal producing places to present the medicinals, which were compiled into *Tujing Bencao* (*Illustrated Classic of Materia Medica*) by Su Song. At the end of the Northern Song dynasty, Ai Sheng, with an official rank of Tong Shilang, slightly revised the *Jingshi Zhenglei Beiji Bencao* (*Classified Materia Medica from Historical Classics for Emergency*) edited by Tang Shenwei and renamed it *Daguan Jingshi Zhenglei Beiji Bencao* (*Overview of the Classified Materia Medica from Historical Classics for Emergency*). It was published by the government. Before the appearance of *Bencao Gangmu*, this book had always been regarded as the template.

Organizing and Compiling a Number of Large-scale Formula Books

From 978A.D. to 992A.D., after 14 years of hard work, Hanlin medical officer Wang Huaiyin (born in Shangqiu) followed the emperor's order to compile *Taiping Shenghui Fang* (*Taiping Holy Prescriptions for Universal Relief*), prefaced by Tai emperor of the Song dynasty in person. In 1046A.D., He Xipeng was ordered to

证类备急本草》略加修订，改名为《大观经史证类备急本草》，由国家刊行。在《本草纲目》之前，此书一直被奉为范本。

组织编撰多部大型方书。公元 978 ~ 992 年，经过 14 年努力，翰林医官王怀隐（商丘人）奉诏编成《太平圣惠方》，宋太宗亲笔作序。公元 1046 年令何希彭将此书缩编成《圣惠选方》60 卷，作为教科书。

宋太宗晚年还下昭创办了御药院，其职责是专门掌管帝王用药及保管国内外进献的珍贵药材，并且整理出了我国第一部宫廷内的成方制剂规范——《御药院方》，计 11 卷。宋真宗在位时，高相国有疾，他针对病情，亲自查阅《御药院方》，选“生犀丸”赐给高相国，以祛痰清目而进饮食。

公元 1102 ~ 1106 年，宋徽宗崇宁年间，政府药局编制了《和剂局方》作为制剂规范的手册，南宋时更名为《太平惠民和剂局方》，这是我国历史上第一部政府颁发的成药药典。今天方剂书中讲授的许多方剂都出自此方书，如二陈汤、十全大补汤、牛黄清心丸、四君子汤、至宝丹、八正散、附子理中丸、逍遥散、藿香正气丸、平胃散、人参养荣汤等。

北宋末年，徽宗赵佶诏集海内名医编写《圣济总录》，收方 2 万多首。是当时方剂的集大成者。

4. 发展针灸并规范针灸穴位

公元 1023 ~ 1032 年，宋仁宗赵祯接受王惟一的建议，命其创铸针灸铜人两尊，并著成《铜人腧穴针灸图经》3 卷，使针灸穴位得以统一和规范。1027 年 10 月铜人铸成，1030 年又把《铜人腧穴针灸图经》范刻于石板上，陈列于东京的大相国寺内，供人自由参观学习。这是一项伟大的历史创举，对针灸知识的普及有极大的促进作用。石刻的题篆为宋仁宗亲笔御书，并指令大学士夏竦为《铜人腧穴针灸图经》作序。

另外，政府还大力兴办医学教育并实行禁巫兴医等政策。

北宋政府的这一系列政策，对后世产生了深远的影响。由于大宋统治者对医学的重视与提倡，文人知医、通医成为风尚。文人士大夫广泛涉猎医学领域，通晓医学、养生学，积极编撰方书，或者参与政府组织的修

condense the book into 60 volumes of *Shenghui Xuanfang* (*Holy Prescriptions for Universal Relief*), which was used as a textbook.

In his late years, Taizong emperor of the Song dynasty founded the Royal Medicine Academy, whose responsibility was to take charge of the imperial medicine to keep precious medicinal materials offered domestically and abroad, and to sort out the first imperial prescription standard in China, namely *Yuyao Yuanfang* (*Formulas collected by the Royal Medical Academy*), including 11 volumes. When Zhen Emperor was in reign, Gao Xiangguo, a senior official, had a disease. The emperor personally consulted *Yuyao Yuanfang* and chose Shengxi Wan (Raw Rhino Horn Pill) for his illness, which was used to eliminate phlegm, clear eyes, and promote appetite.

From 1102A.D. to 1106A.D., during the Chongning reign of Hui emperor of the Song dynasty, the Pharmacy Bureau compiled *Hejiju Fang* (*Formulary of the Bureau of Pharmacy*) as a manual for the formulation specification and renamed it *Taiping Huiminju Fang* (*Formulary of the Taiping People's Welfare Bureau*) in the Southern Song dynasty. This is the first pharmacopoeia issued by the government in the history of China. Many of the prescriptions taught today come from this formula book, such as Erchen Tang (Decoction of Two Old Ingredients), Shiquan Dabu Tang (Ten Major Tonics Decoction), Niuhuang Qingxin Wan (Heart-clearing Bovine Bezoar Pill), Sijunzi Tang (Four Gentlemen Decoction), Zhibao Dan (Supreme Treasured Pill), Bazheng San (Eight-ingredient Rectification Powder), Fuzi Lizhong Wan (Middle-regulating Aconite Pill), Xiaoyao San (Peripatetic Powder), Huoxiang Zhengqi Wan (Qi-righting Patchouli Pill), Pingwei San (Stomach-calming Powder), and Renshen Yangrong Tang (Nutrient-nourishing Ginseng Decoction).

At the end of the Northern Song dynasty, Hui emperor Zhao Ji ordered famous doctors throughout the country to compile *Shengji Zonglu* (*Comprehensive Recording of Sage-like Benefit*), which included more than 20,000 formulas. It was the master of the formulas at the time.

4. Developing Acupuncture and Standardizing Acupuncture Points

From 1023A.D. to 1032A.D., Zhao Zhen, Ren emperor of the Song dynasty, accepted Wang Weiyi's suggestion and ordered him to creat two bronze figures of acupuncture and moxibustion and compile a three-volume *Tongren Shuxue Zhenjiu Tujing* (*Canon of Acupoints Illustrated Manual of Acupoints of the Bronze Figure*),

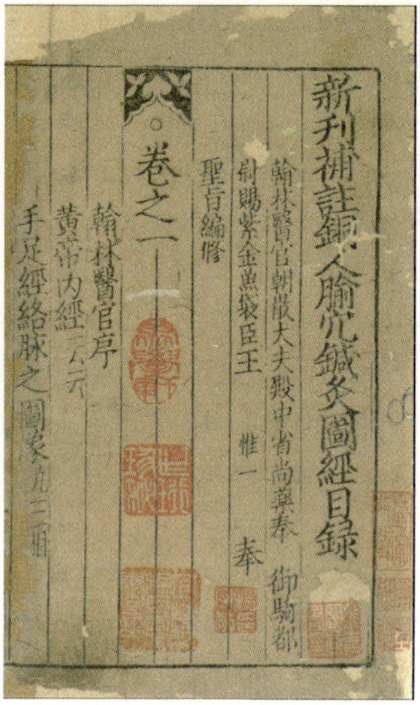


《新刊补注铜人腧穴针灸图经》

*A Newly Revised Tongren Shuxue Zhengjiu Tujing (Canon of Acupoints Illustrated Manual of Acupoints of the Bronze Figure)*

订医学典籍工作。如苏轼、沈括、陆游、朱熹、欧阳修、王安石、范仲淹、辛弃疾、司马光、黄庭坚、范成大、苏颂、洪迈、郑樵、蔡襄、文天祥、张载、文彦博等，几乎到了“无儒不通医”的地步。“儒医”现象成为大宋一道独特亮丽的风景。人们认为医为仁术，“医国医人，其理一也”，“不为良相，则为良医”。大批儒士渗入医学领域，一代又一代儒医的涌现，使医学队伍的素质明显得到提高，促进了从医人员知识结构的更新和医学研究的进展。无论对医药理论的发展还是对临床经验的总结提高，都起到重要的作用。

从火祖燧人氏点燃华夏文明之火，到酒圣杜康发明酿酒，从伏羲制九针、神农尝百草、岐黄论医道、伊尹创汤液，到道圣老子尚修身养性、庄子倡导引养生、神医华佗妙用麻沸散、医圣仲景论六经辨证而创经方，从殷墟甲骨文到许慎的《说文解字》，中医的经典著作《黄帝内经》《伤寒杂病论》《神农本草经》等纷纷在中原问世，饮食之学、食疗之学、养生之学及汤剂方药之学均在中原形成并发展起来。从佛教于汉代传入

which unified and standardized the acupuncture points. The bronze statue was cast in October, 1027A.D., and *Tu Jing* (*Illustrated Classic*) was carved on a stone slab in 1030A.D. and displayed in the city center of Daxiangguo Temple for people to freely visit and study. This is a great historical initiative that has greatly promoted the popularization of acupuncture knowledge. The stone inscription was written by Ren emperor of the Song dynasty, who also asked Daxueshi (a senior official) Xia Song to preface for *Tu Jing*.

In addition, the government has also vigorously set up medical education and implemented policies such as banning witchcraft and promoting medicine.

This series of government policies in the Northern Song dynasty had a greater impact on later generations. Due to the emphasis and advocacy of the rulers of the Song dynasty on medicine, mastering medical knowledge and skills became a fashion among intellectuals. The literati and high officials were widely involved in the medical field. They became familiar with medicine and health preservation, actively participating in compiling formula books, or participating in government-organized compilation of medical books. Su Shi, Shen Kuo, Lu You, Zhu Xi, Ouyang Xiu, Wang Anshi, Fan Zhongyan, Xin Qiji, Sima Guang, Huang Tingjian, Fan Chengda, Su Song, Hong Mai, Zheng Qiao, Cai Xiang, Wen Tianxiang, Zhang Zai and Wen Yanbo were all good examples. There was a phenomenon of "All scholars knew something about medicine." The appearance of "scholar-physician" has become a unique and beautiful phenomenon in the Song dynasty. People thought that medicine was a benevolent technique, thus creating concepts of "governing the country is like governing people" and "either being a high official or being a good doctor". A large number of scholars went into the medical field. With the emergence of generations of scholars, the quality of the medical staff was obviously improved, which promoted the advancement of the knowledge structure of medical workers and the progress of medical research. Whether for the development of medical theory or the improvement of clinical experience, it all played an important role.

The ancestor of Suiren Shi ignited the fire of the Chinese civilization; the wine sage Du Kang invented wine; Fu Xi created nine needles; Shen Nong tasted one hundred herbs; Qi Bo and Huang Di discussed the medical doctrine; Yi Yin invented the decoction; the Taoist saint Laozi worshipped self-cultivation; Zhuangzi advocated the Daoyin skills for health preservation; skilled doctor Hua

中国，直到禅宗祖庭少林寺融禅、武、医于一体而形成的禅医文化及温县太极拳等武术文化，这一切均发生在中原大地。几千年的中原古都文化促进了中原中医药文化的发达，并在全国起到示范和引领作用，极大地彰显了中医药文化。徐光春同志在《中原文化与中原崛起》中说：“中医药文化起源于中原，中医药大师荟萃于中原，中医药文化发达于中原，中医药巨著诞生于中原。”（《中原文化与中原崛起》，2007 年 4 月由河南人民出版社出版。）

寻根溯源，是光辉灿烂的中原文明孕育了中华瑰宝中医药文化。经过几千年的历史积淀，中医药文化在中原文明的沃土中生根开花、发展壮大，并从儒、道、释及华夏文明的多个领域中吸取精华和营养，逐渐在九州大地兴旺发达，一直传到五湖四海，为华夏文明增添了绚丽的色彩，为人类的健康做出了杰出的贡献。不能忘记，这是我们的历史，这是我们的根脉。

Tuo magically used Mafei Powder; the medical sage Zhang Zhongjing discussed six-meridian syndrome differentiation and created formulas. From the oracle bones of the Yin Ruins to Xu Shen's *Shuowen Jiezi*, the classics of TCM, such as *Huangdi Neijing, Shanghan Zabing Lun*, and *Shennong Bencao Jing,* have all appeared in the Central Plains. The study of diet, dietary therapy, health preservation, decoctions and formulas have all been formed and developed in the Central Plains. The introduction of Buddhism into China in the Han dynasty, the combination of Zen, martial arts and medicine in the ancestral Shaolin temple, and Zen Buddhism and martial arts culture, such as Taijiquan in Wen county, all took place in the Central Plains. The ancient capital culture of the Central Plains for thousands of years promoted the development of TCM in the Central Plains, and played a demonstration and leading role in the country, greatly demonstrating the culture of TCM. Xu Guangchun said in *The Culture and the Rise of the Central Plains:* "TCM culture originated in the Central Plains. TCM masters gathered in the Central Plains. TCM culture developed in the Central Plains. TCM masterpieces were created in the Central Plains." (*The Culture and the Rise of the Central Plains*, published by Henan People's Publishing House in April, 2007)

Tracing back to the origin, it was the brilliant civilization of the Central Plains that bred the Chinese treasure——TCM culture. After thousands of years of historical accumulation, TCM culture has taken its root and blossomed in the fertile soil of the Central Plains culture. It has absorbed essence and nutrition from many fields, such as Confucianism, Taoism, Buddhism and various fields of Chinese civilization, gradually flourishing in China and being passed to all corners of the country. It has added brilliant colors to the Chinese civilization and made outstanding contributions to human health. We must not forget that this is our history and this is our root.

第二章

# 博大精深的中国医学和智慧

Chapter Ⅱ

# Profound Chinese Medicine and Wisdom

中医药学是中华民族的瑰宝，是带有浓厚中国传统文化基因的医学体系，与现代西方医学、其他民族医学一样，是人类与疾病做斗争的经验和智慧的结晶，表达着中国人对人体生命、生理病理的独特认识，展示着中国人的智慧和创造。

## 一、独特的思维方式与中国智慧

中医学的思维方式与中国文化一脉相承，中国传统文化发源于中原大地，如果从其出现的年代而言，可以大致分为伏羲文化、炎黄文化、诸子文化三个阶段，这正是中医学逐渐形成和系统完善的时期。

（一）伏羲文化影响下的中医学

晋代学者皇甫谧在《帝王世纪》中说："伏羲画八卦，所以六气、六腑、五脏、五行、阴阳、四时、水火升降，得以有象；百病之理，得以有类；乃尝百药而制九针，以拯夭枉焉。"具体记述了伏羲文化对中医学的重大影响。

中国文化根源集中体现在《易经》中，《易经》也被称为群经之首。"河出图，洛出书"，伏羲作八卦，文王演周易。后经不同时代圣贤的解说，逐渐形成一种思维、一种文化的体系，与医学结合形成了"易医文化"。"易医文化"主要表现在以下几个方面。

一是天人合一的整体观念。人与自然是一个统一体，人体是一个不可分割的整体。人生活在自然当中，自然界的变化直接或者间接地影响到人体，从而发生一系列或好或坏的反应。当人体不能适应，就会出现病理性反应。

中医十分注重自然天气变化的影响，发现了五运六气与人类生理病理的关系，发现了季节变化对疾病发生的影响，从一天太阳的起落和月亮的圆缺而发现了人体气血变化的规律，发现了因地域、环境、饮食等的不同而造成某些疾病的现象，从而形成了中医因人而宜、因时而宜、因地而

Traditional Chinese Medicine (TCM), a treasure of Chinese nation, is a medical system with thick imprint of Chinese traditional culture. Similar to modern western medicine and other ethnic medicines, TCM is also the crystallization of experience and wisdom of humans in fighting against diseases. It demonstrates the unique understanding of Chinese people towards human life, physiology and pathology, and shows Chinese wisdom and innovation as well.

## Ⅰ. Chinese Wisdom and Unique Mindset

The mindset of TCM is in accordance with Chinese traditional culture, which originates from the Central Plains. In chronological order, Chinese culture may be roughly divided into three stages: Fuxi Culture, Yan-Huang Culture and The Philosophers Culture. These stages were exactly the periods when TCM was gradually established and systematically perfected.

1. TCM under the Influence of Fuxi Culture

Huangfu Mi, a scholar in the Jin dynasty, says in his book *Diwang Shiji* (*The Ages of Emperors*) that "Fuxi draws the Eight Trigrams; hence there are corresponding images for six climatic factors, six Fu-organs, five Zang-organs, five elements, yin and yang, four seasons, water and fire, ascending and descending; the pathogenesis of various diseases can be classified accordingly. He tasted hundreds of herbs and made nine kinds of needles in order to rescue the life." The record indicates the great influence of Fuxi Culture on TCM.

The origin of Chinese culture is intensively embodied in *Yi Jing,* which is regarded as the greatest one among all classics. The book writes that *He Tu* (*The Yellow River Map*) is carried out from the Yellow River, and *Luo Shu* (*Lo Shu Square*) from the Luo River. Deriving from them afterwards, Fuxi drew the Eight Trigrams and King Wen later composed the *Zhouyi* (*The Book of Changes*). Interpreted by scholars of later generations, a system of thought and culture was gradually established. It combines with medicine, and then the Yi-medicine Culture was formed. Its characteristics are as follows:

(1) The Holistic Concept of Heaven-Man Unity

Humans and the natural world are in unity. The human body is an inseparable whole. Living in the nature, human body is directly or indirectly influenced by the

宜的养生保健和治病原则。

二是运动变化的辩证观。中医学受到易学的影响，认为世界是阴阳二气相互作用的结果。气又是孕育生命的本源，也是维持生命活动的物质基础，因此中医善于从变化运动的角度看待生命的变化，这就从根本上与巫术、神学划清了界限。

中医的特点集中体现在“三因制宜”（因人制宜、因时制宜、因地制宜）与“辨证论治”上面，天下无有不变，万物皆自不同。所以，考虑事物特别是所面对的人的独特性，就成为中医思维的一大特点。

随着时间的推移，医者的治疗，病者的生命状态不断地变化，饮食、情绪等等不断地施加影响，证也在发生着不断的变化。医者需要随证变化，调整医方，加减药味，以保证药证相符，药方更加贴合所有的变化状态。

因此，天时不同，治疗不同；方域不同，治疗不同；男女不同，治疗不同；病证不同，治疗不同。这样灵动的医学，真可谓是“圆机活法，存乎一心”。

三是阴阳、五行学说。阴阳、五行学说是中国古人用来认识自然和解释自然的世界观和方法论，也是中医重要的说理工具和核心理论体系。

阴阳理论发端于《易经》，通过阴阳学说解释世界本源。这个思维与西方哲学崇尚上帝创造世界发源形成鲜明的对比。

《周易·系辞上》说：“一阴一阳之谓道。”是说一阴一阳的变化叫作道。

《庄子·天下篇》所谓“易以道阴阳”，说明所有的易理都是建立在阴阳之道的基础之上。阴阳学说认为世界在阴阳二气的相互作用中发生、发展、变化，最初就是指日光的向背，向日为阳，背日为阴，后来引申为上下、左右、内外等状态。一般将运动的、外向的、上升的、温热的、明亮的、光明的归属于阳，把静止的、内守的、下降的、寒冷的、晦暗的归属于阴。中医将阴阳学说作为重要的生理病理解释工具，动态把握机体各脏腑以及气血变化、消长平衡、相互转化的关系，进而诊治疾病。

changes of the natural world, thus the positive or negative response may occur. When human body fails to adapt to the changes, the pathological reaction will take place.

TCM pays high attention to the influence of the climatic changes, and finds out the relationship between Five-Circuits-and-Six-Qi and human physiology-pathology, as well as the impact of seasonal changes on the occurrence of diseases. By observing sunrise to sunset, and moon's wane to wax, TCM understood the rule of changes of qi and blood in human body. It also discovers that certain diseases are caused by the changes of location, environment and diet. As a result, it forms the principles of health preservation and treatment by the three considerations of individual time and location.

(2) Dialectical View of Motion and Variation

Influenced by Yi-ology, TCM regards the world as a result of the interaction of yin and yang. Qi is the source of life and the material basis to maintain life activities. Therefore, TCM tends to view the change of life with motion and variation. On this point, it is fundamentally different from sorcery and theology.

TCM is mainly characterized by "Three considerations" (individual, time and location) and "Treatment according to pattern differentiation." Everything in the world is changing and is different from each other. As a result, considering the uniqueness of everything (especially the human being) has become a special characteristic of TCM thinking.

The pattern changes accordingly to the passage of time, treatment by doctors, and changes of diet, emotion and condition of the patient. The doctor needs to adjust the prescription formula and modify herbs to make sure that the treatment is in accordance with the pattern. The therapeutic effect will be thus achieved. Therefore, treatment may differ from the changes of the time, location, gender, and pattern. What a smart medical science! No wonder there is a saying that "flexibility and skillful therapies are always in a doctor's mind."

(3) Yin-yang Theory and Five Elements Theory

Yin-yang theory and Five Elements theory are the world view and methodology of ancient Chinese to understand and explain the nature. They are also the core theoretical system of TCM.

Originated in *Yi Jing*, yin-yang theory explains the origin of the world by yin-yang doctrine. This thinking is completely different from that of the west, which

黄帝轩辕氏像

Emperor Huangdi AKA Xuan Yuan Shi

五行学说是中国哲学的重要思想，五行的概念形成于夏商之初，发展于春秋战国，在《尚书·洪范》中做了较完整的记载。

古代中国哲人将世界的物质分成金木水火土五种，而这五种物质都是农业社会中百姓生活所不能缺少的，进而又发挥引申，将世界上所有的物质归属于五行当中。中医学将心肝脾肺肾五脏功能按五行统一归属，即心归火，肝属木，脾属土，肺属金，肾属水。并将喜怒忧思悲恐惊七情、自然现象的风寒暑湿燥火，以及颜色、气味、方位、季节等物质世界，全部纳入了五行当中。根据五脏之间的相互关系以及五行相生、相克、相乘、相侮的理论，进行演绎推论，进而有效地指导临床诊疗。

（二）炎黄文化影响下的中医学

在炎黄时代，炎黄二帝更是直接参与了中医学的创建工作。《淮南子·修务训》记载："神农乃始教民尝百草之滋味，当时一日而遇七十毒，由此医方兴焉。"而黄帝与岐伯、伯高、鬼臾区等臣子在一起讨论医道，

believes that God creates the world.

It is written in *Zhouyi* that "Alternating between yin and yang is called Tao."

The book *Zhuang Zi* (*Chuang Tzu*) notices that "Yi is to explain the action of yin and yang." It means that all the theories of Yi are built on the basis of yin and yang. Yin-yang theory holds that the world is growing, developing, and changing by the interactions of yin and yang. In the beginning, yin and yang referred to the sunshine and the shadow. Afterwards, they were extended to represent the up and down, left and right, interior and exterior, etc. Normally, things with nature of activeness, outgoing, ascending, warmth, and brightness are classified into yang category; while quietness, descending, cold, and gloominess are classified into yin category. By using yin-yang theory as an important tool, TCM explains dynamically the physiological functions and pathological changes of the human body to understand the changes, balance, and mutual transformation among the *Zangfu* organs, qi, and blood, in order to correctly diagnose and treat diseases.

Five Elements theory is another important thought of Chinese philosophy. The concept of Five Elements was formed at the early period of Xia and Shang dynasties, and developed in the Spring and Autumn and the Warring States period. It was quite completely recorded in *Shang Shu* (*The Book of History*).

Ancient Chinese philosophers sorted all things into five categories: metal, wood, water, fire and earth, which were indispensable in the daily life of agricultural society. Furthermore, they categorized all the other substances into these five elements. According to TCM theory, heart pertains to fire, liver to wood, spleen to earth, lung to metal and kidney to water. The seven emotions (joy, anger, grief, thought, sorrow, fear and fright), natural phenomenon (wind, cold, summer-heat, dampness, dryness, and fire), colors, flavors, location, and seasons are all categorized into the five elements. TCM deduces and reasons according to the relationship of *Zangfu* organs, and the theory of inter-promotion, inter-restraint, subjugation and counter-restriction, in order to effectively guide the clinical diagnosis and treatment.

2. TCM under the Influence of Yan-Huang Culture

The Emperor Yan and Emperor Huang, legendary Chinese rulers in pre-dynastic times, directly participated in the establishment of TCM. There is the record in the book *Huainanzi* "Emperor Yan taught his people to grow crops and tasted the herbs himself. He got poisoned 70 times in a single day. As a result,

经过口耳相传，一代又一代先贤补充完善，终于成就了中医的经典之作《黄帝内经》，早已传为佳话。伏羲、神农、黄帝都是上古时代中原大地上的英雄人物，他们在医学创始阶段的贡献，以各种形式记载下来，给我们留下了宝贵的财富。

作为华夏始祖的炎黄二帝，两者结合是和谐包容思想的体现。黄帝伟大的贡献之一，是在部族征战的过程中，不再杀掉战争中的俘虏，而是与战败者融合，成为一个更大的部族。炎黄部族的合并，为中国文化兼容并包、吸纳化用的特性奠定了基础。

炎黄文化对中医学的影响，直接体现在以人为本的伦理观和医德的形成。中医学历来推重医德，具有尊重生命、珍惜生命、顾护生命的特征，中医认为天地之间人为重，医学的本质围绕着人而开展，在治病救人中要体现对人的尊重，体现出医务人员的人文情怀。

《黄帝内经·素问·宝命全形论》中说：“天覆地载，万物悉备，

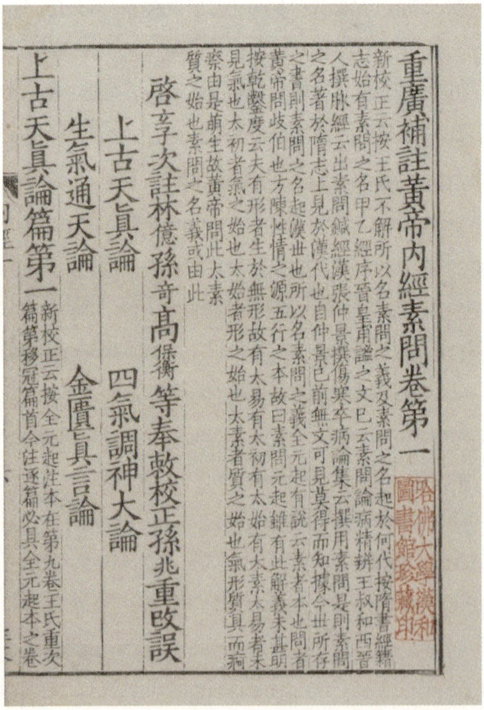
重廣補註黃帝內經素問卷第一

新校正云按王氏不解所以名素問之義及素問之名起於何代按隋書經籍志始有素問之名甲乙經序晉皇甫謐之文已云素問論病精辨王叔和西晉人撰脈經云出素問鍼經漢張仲景撰傷寒卒病論集云撰用素問是則素問之名著於隋志上見於漢代也自仲景已前無文可見莫得而知據今世所存之書則素問之名起漢世也所以名素問之義全元起有說云素者本也問者黃帝問岐伯也方陳性情之源五行之本故曰素問元起雖有此解義未甚明按乾鑿度云夫有形者生於無形故有太易有太初有太始有太素太易者未見氣也太初者氣之始也太始者形之始也太素者質之始也氣形質具而痾瘵由是萌生故黃帝問此太素質之始也素問之名義或由此
啓玄子次註林億孫奇高保衡等奉敕校正孫兆重改誤
上古天真論　四氣調神大論
生氣通天論　金匱真言論
上古天真論篇第一　新校正云按全元起注本在第九卷王氏重次篇第移冠篇首今注逐篇必具全元起本之卷

《重广补注黄帝内经·素问》

*Annotation of Huangdi's Internal Classic-plain · Question*

medicine originated and developed greatly." Emperor Huang discussed the art of medicine with his ministers Qi Bo, Bo Gao and Wei Yuqu. Their dialogues were passed down by word of mouth, and supplemented by scholars of later generations, thus TCM classic *Huangdi Neijing* was finally compiled. Emperor Fuxi, Emperor Huang and Emperor Yan were all heroes living in the Central Plains in ancient times. In the early stages of Chinese medicine, their contributions are recorded in different forms as a precious treasure.

The Emperor Yan and Emperor Huang are the ancestors of Chinese nation. Their coalition represents the thought of harmony and inclusiveness. One of the greatest contributions of Emperor Huang is that, instead of killing the prisoners during the tribe battles, he aligned with the defeated and established a larger tribe. In the meantime, the coalition of the tribes under Emperor Yan and Emperor Huang laid a foundation for the characteristics of Chinese culture on inclusiveness and absorption.

The influence of Yan-Huang Culture on TCM is directly reflected by the establishment of human-oriented medical ethics, which is characterized by respecting, cherishing and guarding life. TCM believes that humans are supreme of the world, and the nature of medical science should be human-oriented. During the treatment, humans need to be respected, and medical staff must show their humanistic feelings to their patients.

In *Huangdi Neijing*, there is a sentence, "Among the creatures covered by Heaven and carried by Earth, humans are superior to all other things."

In the article *Dayi Jingcheng* (*On the Absolute Sincerity of Great Doctors*), Sun Simiao said, "While treating diseases, the distinguished doctors must tranquilize the mind and abandon the selfish thought, be compassionate to the patients and determine to relieve their sufferings." "Whether rich or poor, aged or young, beautiful or ugly, friend or enemy, compatriot or alien, dull or intelligent, they are all the same and should be treated like close relatives." Humans are animals with emotions and thoughts. From the view of psychology, some "incurable diseases" may still be cured without administration of medication, only if enough care and attention are given to the patient. The human-oriented thought has been passed down and has become an important part of the national moral construction.

"Prevention is better than cure" is the core idea of *Huangdi Neijing* as well as

莫贵于人。”就是说，苍天覆盖着大地，大地托载着万物，自然界万物齐备，没有什么比人更宝贵的了。

孙思邈在《大医精诚》中说：“凡大医治病，必当安神定志，无欲无求，先发大慈恻隐之心，誓愿普救含灵之苦。”众生平等，在医者的眼中，一切有情众生别无二致，对他们“不得问其贵贱贫富，长幼妍蚩，怨亲善友，华夷愚智，普同一等，皆如至亲之想”。人是有血有肉、有情感、有思想的动物。从心理学的角度来看，人们如果能够得到足够的关爱与关注，有时候“不治之症”一样可以治愈，甚至于不药而愈。以人为本的思想传承至今，成为今天国家道德建设的重要组成部分。

不治已病治未病，这是《黄帝内经》的核心思想，也成为中医的核心思想内容。中医之道，是治未病之道，即人们常说的“上工治未病”。于疾病未发之时，将疾病阻截于中道，从而达到健康长寿的生命状态。

早在战国时代，曾有一个人问名医扁鹊：你们三兄弟之中，谁的名气最大？谁的医术最高？扁鹊说：我大哥善治病之未发，所以默默无闻；我二哥善治病之初起，所以闻名乡里；我治的多是病之已成，因此名传天下。最高明的医术是什么，就是在病之未发时已得到防治，而让人不得病。

《黄帝内经·素问·上古天真论》中说：“上古之人，其知道者，法于阴阳，和于术数，食饮有节，起居有常，不妄作劳，故能形与神俱，而尽终其天年，度百岁乃去。”饮食、起居、劳作、情绪等日常的调养，都是为了不得病，养形神。《淮南子》中有句名言：“良医者，常治无病之病，故无病；圣人常治无患之患，故无患也。”

（三）诸子文化影响下的中医学

先秦时期，百家争鸣的诸子文化对中医发展产生了深刻的影响，其中以儒学、道学等影响最为明显。

1. 儒学对中医药学的影响

儒学自孔子创立，后经孟子、荀子的继承和发展，奠定了儒家思

TCM. Prevention is the principle of TCM, which can be seen in the saying "A well-skilled doctor treats the undiseased." Doctors should prevent the diseases from the onset or recurrence, in order to maintain a good living condition of healthiness and longevity.

In the Warring States Period, someone asked the famous doctor Bianque, "Among your three brothers, who has the best fame and skill"? Bian answered, "My elder brother prevents diseases from occurring, so he is unknown. My second brother treats diseases at very early stages, so he is known locally; while what I mostly treat are the diseases which have already occurred, so I am well-known in the country. The best doctor should be the one who prevents diseases from occurring."

*Plain Questions* states that "Wise people in ancient times followed the rule of yin-yang theory, harmonized with the law of nature, and regulated their diet, emotion and daily life without overexertion or indulgence. Thus, they were healthy physically and spiritually, and enjoyed their longevity till 100 years old." There is another famous sentence in *Huainanzi*, "Great doctors treat diseases prior to, so no disease happens. Wise men prevent prior to troubles, therefore no trouble bothers."

3. Influence on TCM by the Philosophers Culture

In the pre-Qin period, the flourishing Philosophers culture, especially Confucianism and Taoism, had profound influence on the development of TCM.

(1) Influence on TCM by Confucianism

Confucianism was created by Confucius, inherited and developed by Mencius and Xuncius. Then the theoretical foundation had been established. In Han dynasty, the philosopher Dong Zhongshu improved it and made it orthodox school of feudal society. In the past 2000 years, Confucianism had deeply influenced the development of Chinese culture, especially TCM.

First, Golden Mean of Confucianism promotes the formation of the concept of "balance and harmony"in TCM. "Balance" means being in neutral, and "harmony"means cherishing good atmosphere. For TCM, "Golden Mean" is reflected in the balance of yin-yang, the unification of Five Elements, the coordination of *Zangfu* organs, and medication reconciliation. "Harmony" is the essence of the thought of "Heaven-Man Unity" in *Huangdi Neijing*.

"Harmony" here refers to harmony in human life, harmony between man and society, and harmony between man and the nature. The basis of these three

想的理论根基。汉武帝时期经董仲舒改造作为封建社会的正统学派，近2000年，深刻地影响了中国文化特别是中医药学的发展。

一是儒家中庸思想促进了中医“致中和”理念的形成。“中”就是不偏不倚，以和为贵，对于中医来讲，阴阳平衡、五行统一、脏腑协调以及用药和解都体现了中庸之道。《黄帝内经》所蕴含的“天人合一”思想，其精髓就是“和谐”。

和谐包含三个层次：人自身生命的和谐、人与社会的和谐、人与自然的和谐，但在这三个和谐中，基础是人的自身和谐，也就是一个人心、身、脑之间的协调统一。和谐是生命的最佳状态，是生命的极致追求，也是形神一体的完全表述。

二是以仁学为核心，促进了中医医德的形成。仁学是儒家道德修养的最高境界，儒家“穷则独善其身，达则兼济天下”的思想，为历代知识分子所信奉，对中医学的医德形成和医学人文思想的发扬起到了重要作用。特别是宋代儒医现象的形成，使医学与人学达到了良性的结合。范仲淹提出“不为良相，愿为良医”，许多儒家把医疗行善作为实现自我价值和社会价值的途径，与儒家积极入世思想相切合。

三是儒学促进了中医独特的思维方法。儒家重形象思维，重思辨，促使中医从宏观的功能出发来认识人体，逐渐形成了天人相应、取类比象的思维方法。

2. 道家对中医药学的影响

道家的几位先师老子、庄子、列子是河南人。道家主张清静无为、心灵虚寂、返璞归真，对中医学产生了深刻影响。中国古代历来有十道九医之说。

中医的经典《黄帝内经》即明显有道家思想的痕迹。《黄帝内经》所表现的人生态度，近于道家，其所用术语有不少与道家相同，其恬淡守朴、去世离俗、积精全神之主张，也正是道家所强调的。

道家对中医影响主要表现在：一是精气神学说和元气学说。这也是

"harmonies" is the harmony in human life, i.e. the coordination and unity of one's heart, body and brain. Harmony is the best state and ultimate pursuit of life. It is also the perfect manifestation of the integrity of body and spirit.

Second, Doctrine of Benevolence as a core promotes the formation of TCM ethics. Doctrine of Benevolence is the supreme virtue of Confucianism. Confucianism advocates that you "behave yourself when you are in poverty; benefit the society when you succeed." This thought has always been followed by the scholars of generations, and played an important role in establishing the TCM ethics and promoting medical humanities. It is worth mentioning that the appearance of the Confucian Medicine in the Song dynasty enabled the perfect integrity of medicine and humanology. Fan Zhongyan of the Song dynasty once said, "If you can't be a good minister, you must be a great doctor." Many Confucian scholars started practicing benevolence and medicine as an approach to realize self-value and social value. It is also in line with Confucianism's active participating in social activities.

Third, Confucianism promotes the unique thinking method of TCM. Confucianism emphasizes imagery thinking and critical thinking. It guides TCM to understand the human body from the macroscopic function, and gradually to form the thinking methods of "Man corresponding to nature" and "Analogy by classification."

(2) Influence on TCM by Taoism

The great founders of Taoism such as Laozi, Zhuangzi and Liezi are all Henan natives. Taoism advocates quietism, silent soul, and returning original simplicity, and has profound influence on TCM. Therefore, there was a saying in ancient China that "nine tenths of Taoists are doctors."

The TCM classic *Huangdi Neijing* is obviously related to Taoism. The attitude toward life, as is manifested in the book, is the same as that in Taoism. They even share many terminologies. Quiet mind, meditation and reclusion in TCM are emphasized in Taoism as well.

The influence of Taoism on TCM is manifested in three aspects. The first ones are Essence-Qi-Spirit Theory and Original-Qi Theory, which are also the description of TCM on the origin of life. The second one is Health-preservation Theory. Taoism pays high attention to health preservation, and calls for "following the nature." Along with the rising of Taoism afterwards, more health-preservation methods came up,

中医药学描述生命发源的表达方式。二是养生修身学说。道家十分注重养生，主张“道法自然”。后来随着道教的兴起，养生方法则更多，包括服食、辟谷、外丹、内丹、导引等。道教在炼丹过程中也产生了早期的化学药物，如朱砂、信石等的发现，丰富了中医药学。三是对医德的影响。道家崇尚淡泊名利、知足常乐等思想，对医学医德的形成有重要的影响。

可以看出，受到以上三个不同时期中原文化的影响，中医学形成了自身极其独特的思维方式和诊疗系统。心理学中说，人的生命早期的经验对他未来的人格及思维模式、行为方式有着无与伦比的影响。这就是原生家庭对一个人的影响。而秦汉之前的中国文化，对于中医学的发展而言与原生家庭的影响并无二致。

中医学的发展过程，是一个不断包容、不断创新和进取的过程。东汉明帝时印度佛教传入中国，之后，佛经中的有关医药知识，逐步融入中医，成为中医防病治病的组成部分。这充分体现了中华文化（也包括中医文化）的包容精神。

汉末张仲景的《伤寒杂病论》，发展自《伊尹汤液经法》，肇端于先秦的医方学派，演化为伤寒学派；后世有温病学派，则源于伤寒，别出机杼，至近代发扬光大。正是经历这样的发展历程，中医学才形成完整系统的理论和应用体系，为中华民族屹立于世界民族之林作出了不可磨灭的贡献。

## 二、系统完整的中医理论体系

1.《黄帝内经》等经典的诞生标志中医系统理论的形成

中医的经典《黄帝内经》《伤寒杂病论》《神农本草经》等著作，相继于秦汉之际在河南诞生，标志着中医系统理论的形成。

以《黄帝内经》为基础的中医学，充分吸收借鉴了古代科学技术的成果，形成了阴阳学说、五行学说、脏腑学说、经络学说、五运六气学说

i.e. elixir taking, inedia, external alchemy, internal elixir and guiding technique. In the process of alchemy, the early chemical medications like cinnabar and arsenic sublimate were produced, and enriched the TCM medications. Third, Taoism has influence on medical ethics. It advocates indifference of fame and fortune, and satisfaction with a contented mind. These thoughts had important influence on the formation of medical ethics.

We can see that TCM, influenced by the Central Plains culture mentioned above, formed its unique thinking mode and diagnostic-therapeutic system. Psychology theory believes that the experiences at the early stage of human life have the incomparable impact on his life-long personality, thinking mode and behavior. Therefore, Chinese culture before the Qin and Han dynasties has the great influence on the development of TCM in the same way.

The development of TCM is a process of tolerating, innovating and advancing. In the Eastern Han dynasty, Indian Buddhism was introduced into China. After that, some medical knowledge in the Buddhist scriptures was absorbed into TCM. It fully reflects the inclusiveness of Chinese culture, including TCM culture.

Derived from *Yiyin Tangye Jingfa* (*Canon of Yi Yin's Decoction*), Zhang Zhongjing wrote *Shanghan Zabing Lun*. He inherited the Medical Formula School of pre-Qin period, and transformed it into School of Cold-damage. School of Warm Disease by later generations originated from School of Cold-damage and became well-known in modern times. With the continuous development, TCM formed its complete theoretical and practical system, and made remarkable contribution to China's status in the world.

## Ⅱ. Systematic and Complete TCM Theoretical System

1. Completion of Classics Such as *Huangdi Neijing* Marks the Establishment of TCM Systematic Theory

TCM classics such as *Huangdi Neijing, Shanghan Zabing Lun, and Shennong Bencao Jing* (*Shennong's Classic of Materia Medica*), were completed in Henan during Qin and Han dynasties, symbolizing the establishment of TCM systematic theory.

Based on *Huangdi Neijing*, TCM fully absorbed the achievements of ancient

等理论。

从运动变化的角度看待生命的变化，对人体生理的认识，建立于阴阳气血的平衡和人精气神的功能状态，从人与自然、人与社会的整体角度，把握疾病发生变化的规律。主张未病先防、已病防变。

医圣张仲景的《伤寒杂病论》开启了辨证论治的先河。《伤寒杂病论》由《伤寒论》《金匮要略》组成，通过对外感热病的发生和发展，以六经论伤寒，以脏腑论杂病，融合理、法、方、药为一体，开启了辨证论治的先河。长期以来指导着历代医家的临床实践，因临床疗效确切，组方简单实用，而受到历代医家推崇，被尊为经方。

约成书于东汉的《神农本草经》为中药学祖典。《神农本草经》托名华夏始祖神农帝而作，内容涉及药性、采集、配伍、剂型、服法、用药原则、适应病症等，开创了本草学之先河。书中所述的"七情和合""四气五味""有毒无毒""君臣佐使"等理念，奠基了中国药学理论，一直影响至今。

2. 中医的藏象学说

"藏"就是藏在体内的脏器，可分为五脏、六腑、奇恒之腑。五脏就是心、肝、脾、肺、肾，六腑为胆、胃、大肠、小肠、膀胱、三焦，奇恒之腑为脑、髓、骨、脉、胆、女子胞。"象"就是表现在外的生理、病理现象。

藏象学说就是通过对人体生理病理的观察，研究人体各个脏器的生理功能、病理变化和相互存在的关系，形成的对疾病进行认知的思维模式。

如中医认为肝开窍于目，很多眼疾从肝论治，才能收良效。而根据眼睛不同部位发生的不适现象，又可以与其他脏腑功能失调结合起来诊治，如眼睛水肿，可考虑从疏散表邪入手或从肾论治。

在《黄帝内经·素问·灵兰秘典论》中有形象的描述。认为心是君主之官，主宰全身，人的精神意识思维活动都由此而出。肺是相傅之官，犹如相傅辅佐君主，因主一身之气而调节全身的活动。肝是将军之官，像

science and technology, and formed such important theories as yin and yang, the Five Elements, *Zang Xiang* (Visceral manifestations), Meridian and Collateral, and Five-Circuits-and-Six-Qi.

TCM observes the change of life from the view of development and variation, and understands human physiology on the basis of the equilibrium of yin-yang and qi-blood, as well as the functional status of essence-qi-spirit. TCM judges the rules of occurrence and changing of diseases from a holistic perspective including integration of human and nature, integration of human and society. Therefore, TCM advocates the idea of prevention prior to the occurrence, exacerbation and recurrence of diseases.

*Shanghan Zabing Lun* by Zhang Zhongjing, the Medical Sage, opened up Treatment According to Pattern Differentiation. The book is composed of *Shanghan Lun* (*Treatise on Cold Damage*) *and Jingui Yaolue* (*Synopsis of the Golden Chamber*). It discusses cold-damage diseases by Six-meridian Pattern Differentiation, and miscellaneous diseases by *Zangfu* Pattern Differentiation, and integrates principles, methods, formulas, and medicinals. It has long been used to guide the medical doctors of the later generations in their clinical practice. Owing to its simplified formulas and remarkable clinical effects, the formulas of herbal prescription are called "Classical Formulas."

*Shennong Bencao Jing,* completed around the Eastern Han dynasty, is the classic of TCM Herbology. The book is named after Shen Nong, an ancestor of Chinese nation. It records the property, collecting, compatibility, dosage and form, administration, and indications of natural medicinals. It is regarded as the origin of books on herbal medicinals. The concept in the book has laid the foundation of Chinese medicinal pharmacological theory. These concepts include "Seven relations of medicinal compatibility", "Four natures and Five Flavors", "Toxic or nontoxic", "Formulating principle of chief, deputy, assistant and envoy".

2. *Zang Xiang* (Visceral Manifestation) theory of TCM

*Zang* refers to the internal viscera, including five *Zang*-organs (heart, liver, spleen, lung, kidney), six *Fu*-organs (gallbladder, stomach, large intestine, small intestine, bladder, triple energizer), and Extraordinary *Fu*-organs (brain, marrow, bone, vessel, gallbladder and uterus). *Xiang* means the physiological and pathological manifestations in the exterior.

将军一样勇武，谋略由此而出。脾和胃是仓廪之官，主司饮食的受纳和布化，五味的营养靠它们得以消化、吸收和运输。肾是作强之官，它能够使人发挥强力而产生各种技巧。

这就是中医学中的“取类比象”的思维方法的具体体现。古代哲人在科学技术有限的条件下，通过观物取象、取类比象等象思维方法来认识人体生命现象。

人体的各个组织器官具有各自的独特功能，但这些功能的发挥不是独立地作用而是和谐地统一。各器官组织密不可分，在功能上相互协调，在病理上相互影响。机体统一性的形成，建立于以脏腑为核心的体系。

在中国传统文化的影响下，心、肝、脾、肺、肾五个脏器的功能处于系统统领的地位，以五脏为中心，通过经络，把六腑、五体、五官、四肢百骸等全身的器官组织有机地联系在一起，再通过气血津液的作用发挥正常的生理功能。又吸收了儒家伦理观念，以五脏与国家运行机器职位对

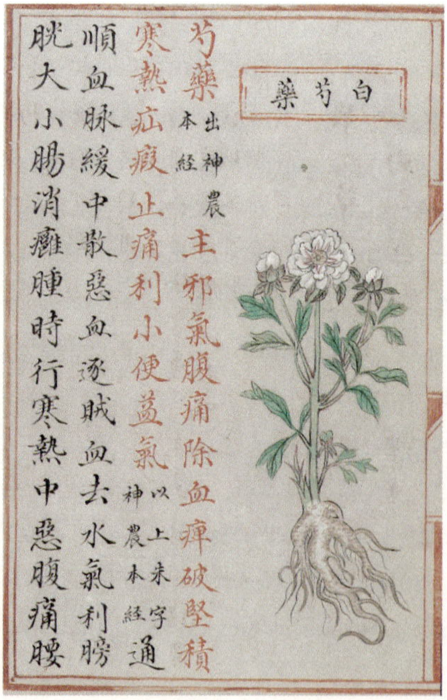


芍药图

Old Picture of Shaoyao

(Paeonia lactifora)

Through the observation of physiology and pathology, visceral manifestation theory studies the physiological functions, pathological changes and their relationship of internal organs, forming the thinking mode toward diseases.

For example, TCM holds that liver opens into the eyes. Therefore, eye dieases maybe cured by treating the liver. Disorders on different parts of the eyes are related to the dysfunction of the certain internal organs. For example, edema around the eye may be treated by dispersing exterior pathogenic factors or from the kidney.

In *Su Wen*, there is a vivid personified description about the internal organs. For example, heart is personified as a "monarch" organ governing the whole body and thinking activities; lung as a "minister" organ governing qi of the whole body to regulate all the activities; liver as a brave "commander" organ making tactics and strategy; stomach and spleen as "granary storekeeper"organ in charge of ingestion and digestion of food, absorption and transformation of nutrients; kidney as a "power" organ, giving a person power and skills.

These are embodiments of the analogical thinking method of TCM. Ancient philosophers, with limited science and technology, tried to discover human body by observing the world and taking analogy.

Every organ has its specific functions, but any single organ cannot work alone without coordinating with others. All organs are closely related to each other, and coordinate in function and influence each other in pathology. The thought of human integrity depends on the *Zangfu* organs-centered theory.

Influenced by Chinese traditional culture, TCM holds that five *Zang*-organs (heart, liver, spleen, lung, and kidney) are the centre and at the leading position of the body. Through the meridian system, all parts of the body (six *Fu*-organs, five body constituents, five sense organs, four limbs and hundreds of bones) are organically linked and function properly with the assistance of qi, blood and body fluid.

In addition, by absorbing Confucian ethics, five *Zang*-organs were personified by the positions of a state administration (monarch, minister, assistant and envoy), which is also applied to the compatibility and combination of medicinals and formulas.

3. Collaboration of Four Diagnostic Methods in TCM

Modern natural science emphasizes the observation and perception on tangible objects. TCM uses four diagnostic methods (inspection, listening and

应起来，形成了君、臣、佐、使的脏腑关系，并指导了中药的使用和方剂的配伍。

3. 中医的四诊合参

现代自然科学认识世界的方法，主要强调的是对看得见、摸得着的物质实体的观察和认知。中医观察和获取人体信息的方法是望、闻、问、切，称为“四诊合参”。

望、闻、问、切作为四种收集病人资料的有效手段，一直在临床上应用,并成为中医的特色,而脉诊、舌诊是其中最具有特色的中医诊断技术。通过外在的信息，去了解、推测和分析内在的、看不见的机体的变化状态。中医用肉眼观察患者舌质、舌苔的颜色以及变化，来判断脏腑功能以及气血津液运行情况；同时重视寸口诊脉，一方面将患者的各种变化与脉象对应来描述脉象，另一方面依据不同脉位与内脏对应来判断气血运行状态。

《难经》说：“望而知之谓之神，闻而知之谓之圣，问而知之谓之工，切而知之谓之巧。”“神、圣、工、巧”，充分体现了中医诊疗运用四诊的熟练程度。

4. 中医的辨证论治

辨证论治是中医认识疾病和治疗疾病的基本原则。中医治病既要辨病又要辨证，核心在于辨证。证是机体在疾病发展过程中某一阶段的病理概括，包括病变的部位、原因、性质以及邪正关系，反映出疾病发展过程中某一阶段病理变化的本质。

医生通过四诊合参将收集的资料、症状、体征分析综合，辨清疾病的病因、性质、部位、转归，概括为某种性质的证，从而采取有效的手段进行治疗。辨证论治的过程就是认识疾病的过程，辨证是治疗的前提和依据，论治是治疗疾病的手段和方法，通过效果检验辨证论治的正确与否。而围绕证这一核心形成的同病异治、异病同治理论，又丰富了中医治疗手段。

smelling, inquiry, and palpation and pulse-taking) to observe the patients and obtain information.

The four diagnostic methods, as the effective means to collect the information of patients, have always been used in the clinical practice and become a feature of TCM. Among the four methods, pulse-taking and tongue-observing are the most characteristic diagnostic techniques. Doctors can recognize, speculate and analyze the interior and invisible conditions by exterior manifestations. By observing the color and change of tongue nature and tongue coating, a TCM doctor is able to tell the functions of *Zangfu* organs and the flowing conditions of qi, blood and body fluid. Pulse-taking at *Cunkou* is another important diagnostic method. TCM describes the pulse according to the corresponding changes of a patient, and judges the flowing condition of qi and blood according to the pulse locations of corresponding *Zangfu* organs.

As written in the book *Nanjing* (*Classic of Difficulties*), "A saint can make a diagnosis only by inspection, a sage by listening and smelling, a master by inquiry, and a craftsman by palpation and pulse-taking." The four levels indicate the proficiency of the doctors in using the four diagnostic methods.

4. Treatment According to Pattern Differentiation

Pattern differentiation is the basic principle of TCM to understand and treat diseases. Treatment with TCM needs not only disease differentiation, but also pattern differentiation. The core is the latter. Pattern is the summarization of the pathologic changes during the progression of a disease at a certain stage, including the location, cause, nature, and relationship between the healthy qi and pathogenic factors.

After summarizing and analyzing the data, symptoms and signs collected by four diagnostic methods, doctors make clear the cause, nature, location and prognosis of the disease, and then generalize into a certain pattern in order to give the effective treatment. Treatment According to Pattern Differentiation is a process to understand the disease. Pattern differentiation is the prerequisite and evidence for treatment, while treatment is the means and methods to deal with diseases so as to verify whether the pattern differentiation is correct or not. On the basis of the above, the theories "treating same diseases with different methods" and "treating different diseases with the same method" are formed and broaden the therapeutic thought of

5. 中药的四气五味

中药包括植物药、矿物质药、动物药，其发挥作用在于本身具有的物质成分，但有效成分的提取并不能很好地解释中药的作用。中医认为药物具有升、降、沉、浮四种性质和酸、苦、甘、辛、咸五种味道，而这些性质和味道，与相应的脏腑有对应关系，对于治疗疾病具有指导意义。这种理论也是对自然界药物性质与脏器功能对应的取类比象。

在《黄帝内经》《伤寒杂病论》《神农本草经》等经典著作的指引下，中国医学逐步形成了完整的医学体系，彰显了中医学的博大精深和中国人的高超智慧。

21 世纪的时代，是中华文化昌盛的时代，而中医学将因其“天人合一”“形与神俱”的特点，高踞于时代的潮头，不断融合其他的生命文化，以其更大的视野，更加包容的精神，开创出全新的医学理论体系，以适应新时代的要求。

TCM.

5. Four Natures and Five Flavors of Chinese Medicinals

Chinese medicinals include botanicals, minerals and animal products. It is the material ingredients of the medicinals that work. However, the extraction of ingredients cannot explain the effects of medicinals very well.

TCM believes that Chinese medicinals have four natures (ascending, descending, floating, and sinking) and five flavors (sour, bitter, sweet, acrid and salty), which correspond to the *Zangfu* organs. This theory shows another analogy between the nature of medicinals and the function of internal organs.

Under the guidance of such classics as *Huangdi Neijing, Shanghan Zabing Lun* and *Shennong Bencao Jing*, TCM gradually developed into a complete medical system, which demonstrates the charm of TCM and the wisdom of Chinese people.

The 21st century is an era for Chinese culture to flourish. With the characteristics of "Heaven-Man Unity" and "Body-Spirit Inseparability", TCM will continue adopting other life science and cultures. In addition, with wider perspective and more inclusive mind, TCM will create a brand new medical theory system to adapt to the new era.

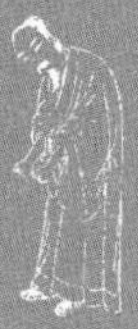

第三章

# 灿若群星的河南名医

Chapter Ⅲ

# Henan Famous Doctors Like Bright Shining Stars

# 一、河南自古多名医

灿烂的中原古代文化造就了一大批著名医家，他们的医疗实践及其留下的宝贵著作，构建了中原中医药文化大厦，极大地彰显了中医药文化。

医者，仁术也。在古人看来，做官与行医，为良相与做良医，都是济世利天下，其本质是一致的。正是基于这一点，张仲景弃高官而不做，潜心于医学，“勤求古训，博采众方”，写出了不朽的《伤寒杂病论》，实现了他“上以疗君亲之疾，下以救贫贱之厄，中以保身长全，以养其生”（《伤寒杂病论序》）的愿望。

河南自古多名医。在这块土地上，除了伟大的医圣张仲景之外，还有许多杰出的医学家。早在商代初期，就有商汤的宰相伊尹著《汤液经》，发明了汤剂。早期的医方大家，晋朝的范汪是南阳顺阳（今河南淅川县）人，他著有《范汪方》。南朝的褚澄是阳翟（今河南禹州）人。他著的《褚氏遗书》，是继《黄帝内经》之后，较早的中医基础理论著作。

唐代的针灸和中药名家甄权是许州扶沟（今河南扶沟）人。唐代名医张文仲为高宗时御医，是治疗风病专家，曾著《疗风气诸方》，为洛州洛阳（今河南洛阳）人。唐代的崔知悌对痨病（结核病）提出独到见解，著有《骨蒸病灸方》一卷，他是许州鄢陵（今河南鄢陵）人。中国现存最早的食疗专著《食疗本草》的作者，唐代的孟诜是汝州（今河南汝州）人。

北宋著名的医方类书《太平圣惠方》的作者王怀隐是宋州睢阳（今河南商丘）人。宋代著名的儿科专家阎孝忠是许昌（今河南许昌）人，他为恩师编写《小儿药证直诀》一书，使儿科大师钱乙的学说得以传世。北宋仁宗时，“校正医书局”中整理古医书的高手有好几位河南人。如撰《嘉祐本草》的掌禹锡为许州郾城（今河南漯河市郾城区）人，完成《重广补注黄帝内经素问》的孙兆、孙奇，均为河阳（今河南孟州）人。特别是校正医书局的重要人物林亿，他是开封人，校勘医籍成就尤为突出。

# Ⅰ. Henan Famous Doctors since Ancient Times

The splendid ancient culture of the Central Plains has brought up a large number of famous doctors. Their medical practice and valuable works left behind have constructed and highlighted TCM culture.

Being a doctor is a noble profession, and a doctor should have benevolence. In the view of the ancients, serving either as an official or as a medical worker, serving either as a good minister or as a good doctor, they all are beneficial to the world, and their essence is just the same. It is precisely why Zhang Zhongjing left the high-ranking government official position and devoted himself to medicine. By diligently seeking ancient training, discovering, and making use of the strong points of all others, he wrote *Shanghan Zabing Lun* and realized his wish to " treat the illness of parents, save the lives of the poor, prevent disease and have longevity" which comes from preface to *Shanghan Zabing Lun*.

Henan has been producing many famous doctors since ancient times. In this land, besides Zhang Zhongjing, the great medical sage, there are many other outstanding physicians. As early as in the Shang dynasty, decoction was invented by Yi Yin, Prime Minister of Emperor Shang Tang, who wrote *Tangye Jing*. Fan Wang of the Jin dynasty came from Shunyang of Nanyang (today's Xichuan county of Henan province) who wrote *Fan Wang Fang* (*Fan Wang's Prescriptions*). Chu Cheng in the Southern dynasty came from Yang Zhai (today's Yuzhou city of Henan province). He compiled *Chushi Yishu* (*Fragmentary Book of Master Chu*), which was an earlier theoretical work of TCM after *Huangdi Neijing*.

Zhen Quan was a famous doctor of acupuncture and moxibustion and TCM in the Tang dynasty. He was born in Fugou of Xuzhou (today's Fugou county of Henan province) and passed away at the age of 103. Zhang Wenzhong, a famous doctor of the Tang dynasty, was the imperial doctor of the reign of Emperor Gaozong, and an expert in treating wind diseases. He wrote *Liao Fengqi Zhufang* (*The Prescriptions for Treating Wind Diseases*) .He was born in Luoyang of Luozhou (today's Luoyang city of Henan province). Cui Zhiti of the Tang dynasty put forward his original opinion on tuberculosis. He was from Yanling of Xuzhou (today's Yanling city of Henan province) and wrote *Guzhengbing Jiufang* (*Moxibustion Prescriptions for*

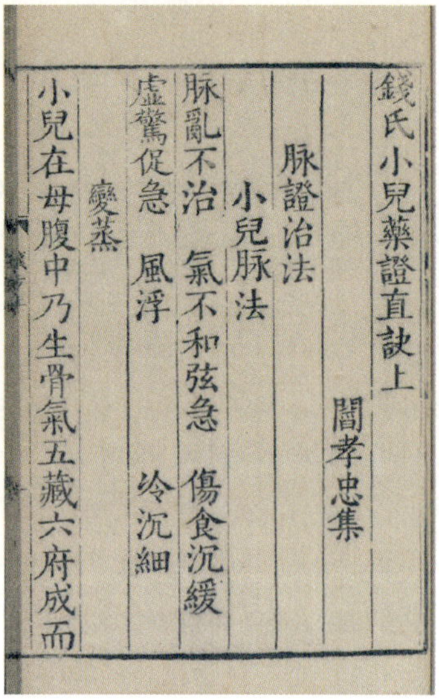
錢氏小兒藥證直訣上
閻孝忠集
脉證治法
小兒脉法
脉亂不治　氣不和弦急　傷食沉緩
虛驚促急　風浮　冷沉細
變蒸
小兒在母腹中乃生骨氣五藏六府成而

《小儿药证直诀》
*Xiaoer Yaozheng Zhijue (Key to Medicines and paterns of Children’s Diseases)*

他的《新校正》备受后人推崇。北宋医家王贶是考城（今河南兰考）人，著有《全生指迷方》，《四库全书提要》评价说：“此书于每证之前，非惟详其病状，且一一论其病源……无不辨其疑似，剖析微茫，亦可为诊家之枢要。”北宋末期的著名医家，《鸡峰备急方》（又称《鸡峰普济方》）的作者张锐是河南郑州人。

南宋的伤寒大家，《伤寒补亡论》的作者郭雍是洛阳（今河南洛阳）人。南宋法医学家郑克是开封（今河南开封）人，他著的《折狱龟鉴》是与宋慈的《洗冤集录》齐名的一部法医著作。

金元四大家之一，攻邪派的代表金代张子和是睢州考城（今河南兰考县，一说民权县）人。他的传世之作《儒门事亲》，是祖国医学园地的一朵奇葩，为中医学增添了异彩。

元代名医滑寿祖籍是襄城（今河南襄城县），他著有《读素问钞》《难经本义》，对《黄帝内经》和《难经》的研究做出了巨大贡献；他著的《诊家枢要》和《十四经发挥》分别是诊断学专著和针灸专著，均在中医发展史上占有光辉的一页。

*Steaming Bone Diseases*). Meng Shen of the Tang dynasty, a native of Ruzhou (today's Ruzhou city of Henan province), wrote *Shiliao Bencao* which is China's earliest dietary therapy monograph.

Wang Huaiyin of the Northern Song dynasty, the author of *Taiping Shenghui Fang* was from Suiyang of Songzhou (today's Ruzhou city of Henan province). Yan Xiaozhong, a famous pediatrician in the Song dynasty, was born in Xuchang, (today's Xuchang city of Henan province) and wrote *Xiaoer Yaozheng Zhijue* (*Key to Medicines and Paterns of Children's Diseases*), which enabled the theory of Qian Yi, a great pediatrician and his teacher, to be handed down. During the reign of Emperor Renzong in the Northern Song dynasty, several masters working for collating ancient medical books were Henan natives. For example, Zhang Yuxi, who wrote *Jiayou Bencao*, was a native of Yancheng of Xuzhou (today's Yancheng District of Luohe city of Henan province). Sun Zhao and Sun Qi from Heyang (today's Mengzhou city of Henan province) completed *Chongguang Buzhu Huangdi Neijing Suwen* (*Revised and Supplemental Annotation to Plain Question of Huangdi's Internal Classic*). In particular, Lin Yi, an important figure who worked in Bureau for Correcting Medical Books, was from Kaifeng (today's Kaifeng city of Henan province). His achievements in collating medical books were particularly outstanding. His *Xin Jiaozheng* (*The Newly-Revised Medical Books*) has been highly praised by later generations. Wang Yi, a physician in the Northern Song dynasty, was a native of Kaocheng (today's Lankao county of Henan province) and wrote *Quansheng Zhimi Fang* (*Life-Saving Formulas for Differentiating Confusion*). Regarding *Siku Quanshu Tiyao* (*Complete Library of the Four Branches of Literature*), people say, "In terms of each syndrome, the book not only describes its symptoms carefully, but also roots of diseases exactly··· Its delicate analysis can be very helpful for diagnosis and treatment." Zhang Rui, a famous doctor in late Northern Song dynasty, was born in Zhengzhou, Henan province. He wrote *Jifeng Beiji Fang* (*Jifeng Formulas for Emergency*) which is also called *Jifeng Puji Fang* (*Jifeng Formulas for Universal Relief*).

Guo Yong, an expert in cold damage diseases in the Southern Song dynasty, was the author of *Shanghan Buwang Lun* (*Supplement to What had been Lost from Treatise on Cold Damage*),was from Luoyang (today's Luoyang city of Henan province). Zheng Ke, a medicolegist in the Southern Song dynasty, was born in

明太祖朱元璋的五皇子朱橚，就藩在开封，为周定王，他著的《救荒本草》，以河南的灾荒为背景写成，开创了对野生可食植物的研究，对后世产生了深远影响。他主持编写的《普济方》收方 6 万余首，是中国古代最大的医方类书。论述云南药物的《滇南本草》，是颇受后人称道的地方本草典籍。其作者是明代的兰茂，原籍为河南洛阳。他常年在云南各地采集药物和治病，为群众所爱戴。著名的医史专家，明代的李濂是祥符（今河南开封）人，他的《医史》十卷，是我国首次以“医史”命名的医学史专著，书中为张仲景、王叔和、王冰等人补写了传记。

清代名医，《嵩崖尊生全书》的作者景日昣，是登封（今河南登封）人。清代温病学家的北方代表人物，《寒温条辨》的作者杨栗山是中州夏邑（今河南夏邑）人。清代著名的植物学家吴其濬，是河南固始县人，他撰写的《植物名实图考》和《植物名实图考长编》，不仅是植物学的一部名著，也是继《本草纲目》后最重要的本草类著作，对世界医学曾产生过重要影响。

据不完全统计，史传和地方志中有籍可考的河南古代医家多达 1000 余人。《周易・系辞》曰：“子曰：书不尽言，言不尽意。’”这些著名的医家，犹如璀璨的群星，照亮了中医学发展的历史道路。他们的医疗实践及其留下的宝贵著作，积淀了数千年的中医精华，养育了难以计数的杏林英才，构建了宏伟的中原古代中医药文化大厦，极大地彰显了中医药文化。

为了保护和传承这笔宝贵的文化财富，让广大读者顺利阅读这些古籍，并进一步深入研究中原医学，河南科学技术出版社组织了河南一大批中医专家和从事中医文献研究的专家，由许敬生教授担任主编，编写了《中原历代中医药名家文库・古代卷》。现已校注出版了 30 余部，随后陆续整理出版。

Kaifeng (today's Kaifeng city of Henan province). His book *Zheyu Guijian* (*A Collection of Model Judicial Cases*) is a forensic work with the same fame as Song Ci's *Xiyuan Jilu* (*Records for Washing Away of Wrong Cases*).

Zhang Zihe of the Jin dynasty, one of the four great masters of Jin and Yuan dynasties, the representative of the school of eliminating pathogenic factors, came from Kaocheng of Suizhou (today's Lankao county or Minquan county of Henan province). His handed-down work *Rumen Shiqin* (*Confucians' Duties to Parents*) is a wonderful flower in TCM garden, which adds splendor to TCM.

Hua Shou was a famous doctor of the Yuan dynasty, whose ancestral home was Xiangcheng (today's Xiangcheng County of Henan province). He compiled *Du Suwen Chao* (*Notes for Reading Plain Questions*), and *Nanjing Benyi* (*The Original Meaning of the Classic of Difficulties*), which made great contributions to the study of *Huangdi Neijing, and Nanjing* (*Classic of Difficulties*). He compiled *Zhenjia Shuyao* (*Essentials for Diagnosticians*) and *Shisijing Fahui* (*Elucidation on Fourteen Channels*), which are monographs on diagnostics and acupuncture and moxibustion respectively. Both are significant in the history of TCM development.

Zhu Su, the fifth son of Zhu Yuanzhang, the Emperor Taizu of the Ming dynasty, was the king of Zhou Ding in Kaifeng. His book, *Jiuhuang Bencao* (*Materia Medica for Famine Relief*), was written based on the famine in Henan province. He initiated the study of wild edible plants and exerted a far-reaching influence on later generations. *Puji Fang* (*Formulary of Universal Relief*) also under his general editorship, which collected more than 60,000 formulas, became the largest medical book in ancient China. *Diannan Bencao* (*Materia Medica of South Yunnan*) is a classic on local materia medica which is praised by later generations. Its author is Lan Mao of the Ming dynasty. His ancestral home was today's Luoyang in Henan Province. He had collected medicinals and treated diseases all over Yunnan, and was widely loved by people. Li Lian, a famous expert in medical history, was born in Xiangfu (today's Kaifeng city of Henan province) in the Ming dynasty. His ten volumes of *Yishi* (*Biography of Medical Figures*) are the first monographs on medical history named after "medical history" in China. The book supplements the biographies of Zhang Zhongjing, Wang Shuhe and Wang Bing.

Jing Rizhen, a famous doctor of the Qing dynasty, the author of *Songya Zunsheng Quanshu* (*Songya's complete Treatise on Respecting Life*) was from

## 二、新时期的河南名医

中华人民共和国成立以后，政府对中医药事业格外重视，采取了一系列保护发展的政策和措施。河南是中国人口第一大省，又是医圣张仲景的故乡，中医药基础深厚，有一大批全国知名的老中医。

1964 年经河南省卫生厅批准备案的老中医有 99 名，如：河南中医学院的郑颉云、李雅言、刘彦桐、袁子震、张永瑞，河南医学院的陈少坪，河南省人民医院的杨慈云，豫北医专的裴孝先，开封医专医院的张文甫，洛阳正骨研究所的高云峰，郑州中医院的胡世锐等。

1991 年，国家中医药管理局公布了第一批全国老中医药专家学术经验继承工作指导老师名单，河南省有 16 人。他们是：河南中医药大学吕承全、石冠卿、李振华、赵清理、邵经明、娄多峰，河南中医药研究院张海岑、毕福高、翟明义，河南医科大学冯化驯，洛阳正骨医院郭维淮，深圳平乐骨伤科医院郭春园，洛阳市第二中医院乔保钧，南阳地区人民医院李鸣皋，开封市第二中医院武明钦，邓州中医院唐祖宣。

之后，分别于 1996 年、2003 年、2008 年、2012 年、2017 年，国家中医药管理局又相继公布了第二批至第六批全国老中医药专家学术经验继承工作指导老师名单。到目前为止，河南省的国家级名老中医已有 150 余人。

从 2009 年 6 月起至今，国家先后评定了三届“国医大师”，并由人力资源和社会保障部、卫生部和国家中医药管理局联合下文公布。每次都在北京举行隆重的颁奖仪式。河南有三位名医荣登“国医大师”之列，分别是河南中医药大学李振华教授、张磊教授和邓州中医院唐祖宣主任医师。

全国首届国医大师李振华教授（1924 — 2017 年），河南洛宁县人，出身中医世家，从医 70 余年，从教 50 余载，曾任河南中医学院院长。是

Dengfeng (today's Dengfeng city of Henan province). Yang Lishan, the author of *Hanwen Tiaobian* (*Detailed Analysis of Cold and Epidemic Febrile Diseases*), and a representative of treaments on febrile diseases in northern China in the Qing dynasty was from Xiayi (today's Xiayi county of Henan province). Wu Qijun, a famous botanist in the Qing dynasty, was a native of Gushi county of Henan province. He compiled *Zhiwu Mingshi Tukao* (*Illustrated Reference of Botanical Nomenclature*) and *Zhiwu Mingshi Tukao Changbian* (*Detailed Analysis of Illustrated Reference of Botanical Nomenclature*), which are not only masterpieces of botany, but also the most important herbal books after *Bencao Gangmu.* They have exerted an important influence on world's medicine.

According to statistics, there are more than 1, 000 ancient doctors in Henan's history biography and local chronicles. *Zhouyi: Xici* (*The Book of Changes*) has also some records of them. These famous doctors, like bright stars, have illuminated the historical road of the TCM development. Their medical practice and valuable works have accumulated the essence of TCM for thousands of years, nurtured countless talents, constructed a magnificent ancient TCM culture building in the Central Plains and greatly demonstrated the culture of TCM.

In order to protect and pass down this precious cultural wealth, and to help the readers to easily find these ancient books for the purpose of advancing their study of TCM, Henan Science and Technology Publishing House has organized a large number of TCM experts and experts to engage in TCM literature research in Henan province. Professor Xu Jing-sheng as an editor-in-chief, has compiled *TCM Masters of the Past Dynasties in the Central Plains*. More than 30 publications have been published and the others with be published subsequently.

## Ⅱ. Henan Famous Doctors in the New Era

After the founding of People's Republic of China, the government has emphasized the cause of TCM and adopted a series of policies and measures to protect its development. Henan is the most populated province in China, and also the hometown of medical sage, Zhang Zhongjing. It has a deep foundation of TCM. There are a large number of nationally well-known TCM doctors.

In 1964, 99 elderly TCM practitioners were approved by Henan Provincial

李振华先生
Master Li Zhenhua

当代中国著名中医学家、中医教育家，被誉为治脾胃病国手。电影《精诚大医》即以他为原型拍摄而成。

李先生继承古代诸家脾胃学思想，力倡金元四大家之一李东垣的“内伤脾胃，百病由生”之论，形成了治病重视脾胃的学术思想。他主编了《中国传统脾胃病学》，多次承担国家及河南省重点科技攻关项目。他创立的香砂温中汤和沙参养胃汤，有效率达 98.7%，治愈率达 32%。政府建有“国医大师李振华学术思想传承工作室”，由其学术继承人李郑生教授、郭淑云教授等主持学术团队工作。

国医大师、河南中医药大学第三附属医院张磊教授，生于 1928 年，河南固始县人。幼读私塾，诵读经史，深受儒学熏陶，崇尚致中和平，从医 70 余载，博采百家，医术精湛。擅治内科杂症，在临证中，明辨求本，洞悉症结，知常达变。创立了独具特色的临证八法：疏利法、涤浊法、轻清法、灵动法、运通法、燮理法、达郁法、固元法。体现了他“动、和、平”的学术思想，即：和态下的运动发展观、和态失常的疾病发生观、病

Health Department, such as Zheng Jieyun, Li Yayan, Liu Yantong, Yuan Zizhen and Zhang Yongrui of Henan College of TCM; Chen Shaoping of Henan Medical College; Yang Ciyun of Henan People's Hospital; Pei Xiaoxian of North Henan Medical College; Zhang Wenfu of Kaifeng Medical College; Gao Yunfeng of Luoyang Orthopedic Institute; Hu Shirui of Zhengzhou Hospital of TCM, etc.

In 1991, the State Administration of TCM (SACM) published a list of the first batch of instructors on inheritance of academic experience among experts of TCM in China. There were 16 instructors in Henan province. They were as follows:

Lü Chengquan, Shi Guanqing, Li Zhenhua, Zhao Qingli, Shao Jingming, Lou Duofeng of Henan University of TCM; Zhang Haicen, Bi Fugao, and Zhai Mingyi of Henan Institute of TCM; Feng Huaxun of Henan Medical University; Guo Weihuai of Luoyang Orthopedic Hospital; Guo Chunyuan of Shenzhen Pingle Orthopedic Hospital; Qiao Baojun of Luoyang Second Hospital of TCM; Li Minggao of Nanyang People's Hospital; Wu Mingqin of Kaifeng Second Hospital of TCM; and Tang Zuxuan of Dengzhou Hospital of TCM.

Then, in 1996, 2003, 2008, 2012 and 2017 respectively, SACM published lists of the second to sixth batches of instructors on inheritance of the academic experience of the experts of TCM. So far, there are more than 150 famous TCM doctors in Henan Povince.

Since June 2009, China has assessed three batches of "Masters of TCM," which were jointly announced by the Ministry of Human Resources and Social Security, the Ministry of Health and SACM. A grand ceremony was held in Beijing every time. Three famous doctors in Henan were listed as "Masters of TCM". They were: Professor Li Zhenhua and Professor Zhang Lei of Henan University of TCM, and Chief physician Tang Zuxuan of Dengzhou Hospital of TCM.

Professor Li Zhenhua (1924–2017), one of the first batch of "Masters of TCM" in China, was born in a TCM aristocratic family in Luoning county, Henan province. He had been a doctor for more than 70 years and had taught for more than 50 years. He was once the president of Henan College of TCM. He was a famous TCM doctor, educator in modern China, and master in treating the spleen-stomach diseases. The movie *A Great Master of Chinese Medicine* was filmed featuring him as a prototype.

Professor Li inherited the thought of spleen and stomach in ancient times

张磊先生
Master Zhang Lei

症变化的动态观、动态的和平辨治观、动态的求本治本观。

张先生以 89 岁高龄坚持工作在医疗第一线，素以“方精、药少、量小、效奇”载誉中原，以“10 元处方治大病”造就医界传奇。他德高望重，博学多闻，在河南中医界有口皆碑。

国医大师唐祖宣主任医师，生于 1942 年 3 月，河南省邓州市人，身居仲景故里，长期担任邓州市中医院院长。从医 50 余年，学术经验丰富，对仲景学说尤为推崇，在诊治周围血管病上经验独到，研究成果曾获河南省科技进步一等奖。自 1981 年以来，历任县、市、省人大代表，第七届、九届、十届、十一届全国人大代表。他身在基层，时刻关注民生、民情，为国分忧，曾提出有关中医药事业方面的议案、建议 200 余件，充分发挥了人民代表的作用。

2017 年 6 月 29 日，国家人力资源社会保障部、国家卫生计生委和国家中医药管理局在京西宾馆联合举办国医大师、全国名中医表彰大会。河南中医药大学第一附属医院中医儿科专家丁樱教授、著名周围血管病专家崔公让教授，河南省中医院中医内科专家毛德西教授，被授予“全国名中医”

and advocates the theory of Li Dongyuan, one of the four great scholars in the Jin and Yuan dynasties, "That internal injury of the spleen and stomach results in all kinds of diseases." He compiled *Chinese Traditional Spleen and Stomach Diseases* and undertook many key scientific and technological projects in Henan province and China. He founded Xiangsha Decoction for Warming Middle Energizer, and Shashen Decoction for Nourishing Stomach. The effective rate was 98.7% and the cure rate was 32%. The government has set up a "National TCM Master Li Zhenhua Academic Ideology Inheritance Studio," and its academic successors, Professor Li Zhengsheng and Professor Guo Shuyun, are presiding over the academic team work.

Zhang Lei, "Master of TCM", a professor of Third Affiliated Hospital of Henan University of CM, was born in Gushi county of Henan province in 1928. He studied at a private school in his childhood and was familiar with classical works. He was deeply influenced by Confucianism and advocated the idea of harmony and balance. He has been a doctor for more than 70 years, learned from hundreds of schools and has grasped excellent medical skills. He is good at treating medical miscellaneous diseases. In his clinical practice, he discerns the origin and understands the treatment of the disease. He has created eight unique methods in clinical practice: dispersing, removing turbidity, clearing heat with light medicinals, moving, dredging, regulating, removing stagnation and consolidating primordial qi. These embody his academic thought of "movement, harmony and balance," namely, the view of movement development in harmony, the view of disease occurrence in harmony disorder, the dynamic view of disease change, peaceful differentiation and treatment, and seeking the root and curing.

Master Zhang Lei persists in working on the front line of medical practice even at the age of 89 at the time of writing. He is famous in the Central Plains for "simple prescription, few medicinals, small doses, and miraculous effect," and has created a medical legend of "10-yuan prescription for serious diseases." He is knowledgeable and highly respected, and widely known in the field of TCM in Henan.

Tang Zuxuan, a chief physician and master of TCM, was born in March 1942 in Dengzhou, Henan province. He is a resident of Zhongjing's hometown and has long served as the president of Dengzhou Hospital of TCM. He has been working as a doctor for more than 50 years and has rich academic experience. He especially

唐祖宣先生
Master Tang Zuxuan

称号。在大会上受到表彰。

这些“国医大师”和名医们，都在自己的岗位上为中医事业做出了杰出的贡献。

多年来，河南医家已出版了大量的中医学术和临证经验著作，遍及基础和临床各科。

advocates Zhongjing's theory and has unique experience in diagnosis and treatment of peripheral vascular diseases. His research achievements have once won the first prize of scientific and technological progress in Henan province. Since 1981, he has served as member of the county, city and provincial people's congresses, as well as a member of the Seventh, Ninth, Tenth and Eleventh National People's Congresses. At the grass-roots level, he always pays attention to people's livelihood and conditions, and shares his worries for the country. He has put forward more than 200 proposals on the cause of TCM, giving full play to the role of people's representative.

On June 29, 2017, the Ministry of Human Resources and Social Security, the State Health and Family Planning Commission, and SACM jointly organized a commendation conference for TCM masters, senior and famous TCM doctors in Jingxi Hotel. Professor Ding Ying, an expert in pediatrics of TCM; Professor Cui Gongrang, a famous expert in peripheral vascular diseases in the First Affiliated Hospital of Henan University of CM; and Professor Mao Dexi, an expert in internal medicine of Henan Hospital of TCM were awarded the title of "National Famous TCM doctors." They were commended at the conference.

These "Masters of TCM" and famous doctors have made outstanding contributions to the cause of TCM.

Over the years, Henan medical experts have published a large number of works on TCM academic and clinical experience, covering the foundations and clinical disciplines.

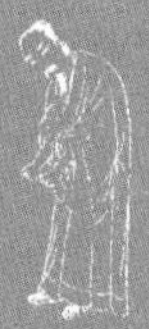

第四章

# 丰富的河南中药资源

Chapter Ⅳ

# Rich Chinese Materia Medica in Henan

关于中药，在民间有很多神奇的传说。不妨举个例子：相传很久以前，中原有两个古国发生了战争。强国把弱国打败了，占领了弱国的许多土地。后弱国军队只剩下千余人马，逃进了一座险要的山里。由于山势陡峭，易守难攻，强国军队几次进攻都未取胜，于是，便将这座山团团包围，坐等敌军投降。

几个月过去了，山上被包围的军队一直没有动静。山下军队的指挥官判断，敌军的粮草大约已吃完了。于是他让士兵高喊劝降，但被包围的军队并不回答，只是射出几支冷箭。

过了半年时间，山上仍然不见动静。山下的指挥官算定敌军已饿死多半，没什么抵抗力了。于是便放松警惕，整天饮酒作乐，等待收兵回营。一天晚上，山下军队正在酣睡，突然，从山中冲出一支兵马，径直杀向山下大营。结果山上军队大获全胜，后来又把失去的国土全部夺了回来。

山上军队被困半年，内无粮草，外无救兵，不但没有饿死，反而兵强马壮。这是为什么呢？原来山中到处长着一种草类植物，夏天开白色或淡绿色的花，地下的根茎呈圆柱状，可食用，原名薯蓣（又称“土薯”）。士兵们在山中以它充饥，而马就吃树叶和薯蓣的藤叶。半年时间，军队在山中得到休整，喂壮了疲劳待毙的马匹。于是趁敌军不备，黑夜杀下山去，大获全胜。

为了便于记住这种救命食物，人们给它起了一个名字，叫“山遇”，意思是刚好在山里正缺粮的时候遇到了它。后来又慢慢发现，它不仅能像粮食一样充饥，而且还有健脾胃、补肺肾的药用功效，吃了它可以治疗脾虚泄泻等症，于是就将“山遇”改名为山药。因怀地（今焦作一带）产者入药最佳，中药就有了“怀山药”之名。

中药是中医学宝库中的璀璨明珠，其疗效独特且副作用较少，受到广大患者的推崇。河南省蕴藏着丰富的中药材资源，有着悠久的历史和深厚的文化内涵。河南中药资源品种繁多，产量大，分布广，名列全国前茅，河南是得天独厚的中药大省。

There are many fantastic legends about Chinese materia medica among the people. The following is a classical example. It has been said that long long time ago, there was a war between two ancient countries in the Central Plains. The powerful nation began to defeat the weak one and occupy its land. Only about one thousand soldiers were left in the army of the weak country. They strategically fled into a mountain, where they would be inaccessible. Because the mountain was steep, it would be easy to defend and difficult to be attacked. The stronger army was not successful with several attacks, so they surrounded the mountain and waited for the enemy to surrender.

A few months passed, and there was no news of the enclosed troops in the mountain. The commander of the powerful army judged that the enemy's food and forage had been finished. Then he let the soldiers shout loudly to persuade the enemy to surrender, but the besieged troops did not answer, only shot out a few arrows.

After half a year, there was still no news of the enclosed troops in the mountain. The commander at the bottom of the mountain judged that most of the enemy had starved to death, and there was no resistance. So they relaxed their vigilance, drank wine, and enjoyed themselves all day, waiting to withdraw troops. One night, the soldiers at the foot of the mountain were sleeping soundly. Suddenly, a group of soldiers on horse rushed out of the mountain and directly attacked the camp down the mountain. The army in the mountain won a great victory, and later they took back all their lost territories.

The army in the mountain was trapped for half a year, without any provisions. Not only did they not starve to death, but they became stronger and stronger. What on earth happened? The fact was that there was a kind of grass abundantly growing in the mountain. In summer, they have white or light green flowers. The underground roots are columnar and edible. Its original name is Shu Yu (also known as "Tu Shu"). The soldiers ate it to satisfy hunger in the mountains, while horses ate tree leaves and Shu Yu leaves. During the half a year, the army was able to rest and reorganize in the mountains. The tired horses were well fed. Therefore, they were able to attack the enemy when the enemy trooped and won.

In order to remember this kind of life-saving plant, people gave it a name, "Mountain Encounter", which means that people tend to encounter them when there is a shortage of food in the mountain. Later, people slowly found that these

# 一、历史悠久的中药材市场和中药老字号

早在北宋时期，宋太宗赵光义于公元976年执政，亲自下诏在京师东京（今开封市）置香药交易院。此举促进了中外名贵药材的交流，并产生了许多以香药为主的中成药，如苏合香丸等。熙宁九年（1076年）东京设立的“熟药所”，为全国最早的官办药局。

元代安阳已有人工种植的药畦、药圃，并出现官办的药材种植场——汤阴艾园。

河南历史上曾有多处较大规模的中药材市场，明末清初，禹州、百泉（今辉县市辖）、归德（今商丘市睢阳区）、马山口（今南阳内乡县辖）四大药材集散地已经形成。全国药商结帮而至，药材贸易十分兴旺。

宣统三年（1911年）在德国柏林举办的“万国卫生博览会”上，河南有“九制大熟地”、柿霜等10种中成药和牛膝、山药等11种中药材被选参展。

1. 禹州药市及药商会馆

禹州市位于中原腹地，交通便利，乃历史上形成的全国四大中药材集散地（河北安国、河南禹州、安徽亳州、江西樟树）之一，素有“药过禹州倍生香”之说。早在明洪武元年（1368年），明太祖朱元璋曾诏令全国各地药商在此集结，初步形成了药材行市。至清乾隆二十七年（1762年），多个药帮商行云集禹州，开张近2000家药店，拥有药工5000余人，形成了禹州中药材市场的鼎盛时期。

在长期的药材交易和竞争中，为保护自身利益不受侵害，药商之间自发形成同乡性质的行帮。自康熙年间起，药商们在禹州相继建成“山西会馆”“十三帮馆”“怀帮会馆”“江西会馆”四处。其中尤以怀帮会馆规模最大，建筑水平最高。

改革开放以后，古老的“药都”焕发了新的生机，在政府的大力支持下，

plants can not only satisfy hunger like grain, but also have the medicinal effects of invigorating spleen and stomach, invigorating lung and kidney, treating spleen deficiency, diarrhea, and thirst, and so on. They then renamed it "Shanyao (common yam rhizome)". Because Huai prefecture (today's Jiaozuo area) produces the best Shanyao for medicine, Huai Shanyao has begun to appear among Chinese materia medica.

Chinese materia medica is a bright pearl in the treasure house of TCM. Its unique efficacy and fewer side effects are highly respected by the majority of patients. Henan province is rich in Chinese materia medica resources, and has a long history and profound cultural connotation. Henan is one of the largest provinces with Chinese materia medica in China because of its variety, large output and wide distribution.

## Ⅰ. Chinese Materia Medica Market with a Long History and Reputable Herbal Shops

As early as in the Northern Song dynasty, Zhao Guangyi, Emperor Taizong of the Song dynasty, held power in 976 A.D., and personally ordered to establish Perfume-Medicine Exchange in Dongjing (today's Kaifeng city of Henan). This promoted the exchange of rare materia medica between China and foreign countries, and produced many Chinese patent medicines taking perfume as the principal thing, such as Storax Pill, etc. In the ninth year of Xining (1076 A.D.), "The Prepared Pharmacy Institution" established in Dongjing was the earliest official pharmacy bureau in China at that time.

In the Yuan dynasty, there were already planted medicine beds and medicine gardens in Anyang city, and Tangyin Ai Yuan became an official medicine plantation.

History shows that there were once many large-scale Chinese materia medica markets in Henan. In the late Ming and early Qing dynasties, Yuzhou, Baiquan (under the jurisdiction of today's Huixian county), Guide (under the jurisdiction of today's Suiyang District of Shangqiu city), and Mashankou (under the jurisdiction of today's Neixiang county) had formed the four major distribution centers of medicinal materials. The pharmacists from all over the country would come in large numbers and trade in medicinal materials.

怀帮会馆旧址

The Former Site of “Huai Guild Hall”

形成了一条“内供外销”一体化的全新中药材基地。目前，禹州中药材市场已发展成为全国标准化、规范化的国家级中药材专业市场之一。

2. 百泉药会及药商会馆

百泉位于河南省辉县市中心西北五华里的苏门山南麓，因湖底遍布泉眼，故名百泉。素有“天然药库”之称，民间有“春暖花开到百泉，不到百泉药不全” 的赞誉。百泉药材交易会及卫源庙庙会即在此举办。卫源庙创修于隋，以祀河神灵源公。每年四月初八，百姓纷纷致祭，至今已延续千余年不断。

由于药材交易的发达，先后建立了药王庙及各地商人会馆。清康熙五十七年（1718 年），由药商李世荣联合华阴县药商同会、河内县（今沁阳县）药商同会集资，于百泉兴建药王庙。后经多次重修，有拜殿、正殿及东西配房 30 余间，另有戏楼 1 座。正殿祭祀药王三真人：华佗、韦慈藏、孙思邈。

辉县是晋豫商旅必经的重镇之一。此地山西商人众多，故晋商于乾

At Great Exhibition of Health of all Nations held in Berlin, Germany, in the third year's reign of Emperor Xuantong (1911 A.D.), 10 kinds of Chinese herbal patent formulas, such as "Ninefold Processed Rehmannia" and Shishuang (persimmon frost), and 11 single Chinese materia medica, such as Niuxi (wo-toothed achyranthes root) and Shanyao (common yam rhizome) were selected to participate in the exhibition.

1. Yuzhou Herbal Market and Pharmacist Guild Hall

Yuzhou city is located in the hinterland of the Central Plains with convenient transportation. It was once one of the four major distribution centers of Chinese medicinal materials (Anguo of Hebei province, Yuzhou of Henan province, Bozhou of Anhui province, and Zhangshu of Jiangxi province) in the history of China. At that time, among the common people there was a saying, "after medicine passes Yuzhou, it will always become better." As early as the first year of reign of Hongwu in the Ming dynasty (1368 A.D.), Emperor Zhu Yuanzhang ordered pharmacists from all over the country to assemble and established a market for medicinal materials. In the twenty-seventh year of the reign of Emperor Qianlong of the Qing dynasty (1762 A.D.), many pharmaceutical companies gathered in Yuzhou, opening nearly 2,000 herbal stores with more than 5,000 pharmaceutical workers, which formed the peak period of Yuzhou Chinese materia medica market.

In the long-term trade and competition of medicinal materials, in order to protect their own interests from infringement, pharmacists spontaneously formed associations of fellow townsmen. Since the reign of Emperor Kangxi of the Qing dynasty, pharmacists have successively built "Shanxi Guild Hall", "Thirteen Guild Halls," "Huai Guild Hall," and "Jiangxi Guild Hall" in Yuzhou. Among them, "Huai Guild Hall" has the largest scale and the highest building level.

Since the reformation and opening of China, the ancient "capital of Chinese materia medica" has taken on new vitality. With a strong support from the government, a brand-new base of Chinese medicinal materials has been formed, which integrates "domestic supply and export". At present, Yuzhou Chinese materia medica market has developed into one of the national-level standardized market of Chinese materia medica.

2. Baiquan Herbs Fair and Herbal Guild Hall

Baiquan is located in the south foot of Sumen Mountain, five miles northwest

卫源庙主殿
Mainhall of WeiYuan Temple

隆二十五年（1760 年）在此地捐款创建了山西会馆，后陆续增建，始成规模，又名同义会馆。山西会馆总建筑面积为 2706 平方米，位于辉县市区南关大街，又称“关帝庙”。建筑有大门、戏楼、拜殿、正殿，两侧建筑有两陪房、钟楼、鼓楼、东西厢房和两配殿。

改革开放以后，百泉药会更加展示了其勃勃生机。

3. 社旗药业和山陕会馆

河南省南阳市社旗县商业历史悠久，源远流长，兴于明末，盛于清朝乾隆、嘉庆年间，衰于民国时期。相传“医圣”张仲景常来赊旗店（现为赊店镇）行医，民间留下不少传说。“药王”孙思邈也曾到赊旗店采药行医。明清时，得山陕商人助力，赊旗店医药业遂大放异彩。社旗县药行、会馆林立。清末民初赊旗店药业发展到 30 余家，绝大多数是山陕商人所开。

山陕会馆座落在社旗县城中心，清代山西、陕西旅居赊旗店的富商大贾，在此联谊集会。因养有监管僧道，亦称山陕庙。道光年间（1821 ~ 1850 年）称鼎元社，民国十二年（1923 年）改称山陕会馆。会馆始建于清乾隆

of Huixian city, Henan province. It is named Baiquan because the bottom of the lake is covered with hundreds of springs (baiquan in Chinese). Baiquan is known as the "A Treasure House of Natural Medical Plants," and there is a saying among people: "In spring please come to Baiquan Herbs Fair, and you can find all you need here." Baiquan medicine trade fair and Wei Yuan Temple Fair are always held in Baiquan. Wei Yuan Temple was first built in the Sui dynasty for the sake of offering sacrifices to the god of river. On April 8th on the lunar calendar, people come to worship here to this day. This custom has been practiced for over one thousand years.

Due to the development of medicinal materials trade, The Pharmacist King Temple and businessmen guild halls in many places have been established successively. In the fifty-seventh year of Emperor Kangxi Reign of the Qing dynasty (1718 A.D.), the Pharmacist Li Shirong joined the Pharmacist Association of Huayin county and the Pharmacist Association of Henei county (today's Qinyang county) to raise funds to build the Pharmacist King Temple in Baiquan. It was rebuilt many times afterwards. Now, there is a worship hall, main hall with more than 30 wing-rooms, and opera tower. The main hall is for worshiping three real pharmacist kings: Hua Tuo, Wei Cizang, and Sun Simiao.

Huixian county is one of the most important towns for trade caravan between Shanxi and Henan. Many Shanxi businessmen traded there, so Shanxi businessmen donated money to establish Shanxi Guild Hall in the twenty-fifth year of Emperor Qianlong (1760 A.D.). Then it was expanded one after another, gradually forming a large-scale building which was also known as Tongyi Guild Hall. The total building area of Shanxi Guild Hall is 2,706 square meters, located in Nanguan Street, Huixian county. It was also called "Guandi Temple." The building of the guild hall includes gates, opera towers, worshipping halls, and main halls. On both sides, there are two accompanying rooms, bell tower, drum tower, East and West compartments, and two matching halls.

After the reformation and opening of China, Baiquan Medicine Association has shown its vitality to a higher degree.

3. Pharmaceutical Industry and Shan-Shaan Guild Hall

The business of Sheqi county in Nanyang city, Henan province, has a long history. It began in the late Ming dynasty, flourished in the reign of Qianlong and Jiaqing in the Qing dynasty, but declined in the Republic of China era. Zhang

山陕会馆

Shanxi-Shaanxi Guild Hall

二十一年（1756年），经嘉庆、道光、咸丰、同治至光绪十八年（1892年）落成，共历6帝136年。社旗山陕会馆无处不体现出厚重的商业氛围，药王殿的药王塑像、雕饰、匾额、楹联，更是与药材商业文化息息相关。

4. 四大怀药及怀邦会馆

焦作，古称覃怀、怀庆府，北依太行，南临黄河，山河相拱，有“三百里怀川”的称誉。山水奇秀的“覃怀”，造就了闻名海内的道地药材“四大怀药”——怀山药、怀牛膝、怀地黄、怀菊花。

牛膝，原产地就在焦作。在牛膝前冠以“怀”字的最早文献，是北宋苏颂的《本草图经》。地黄、山药、菊花，在怀地焦作也早有种植，而将怀庆府产的地黄、山药、菊花列为上品的道地药材，大概在明代中期以后。明代李时珍的《本草纲目》也有记载。明清之际，四大怀药在河南已有广泛种植。在焦作境内沁阳神农山一带，至今还保留有“山药沟”“地黄坡”“牛膝川”“菊花坡”等地名。

明代以后，怀药贸易日趋昌盛，药商队伍不断扩大，出现了怀帮，

Zhongjing, "the medical sage", would often come to Sheqi (now known as the town of Shedian) to practice medicine, leaving many legends behind. Sun Simiao, "the king of Chinese materia medica", once went to Sheqi to collect and practice medicine. In the Ming and Qing dynasties, with the help of Shaanxi merchants, Sheqi's pharmaceutical industry flourished. Pharmacies and guildhalls stood in great numbers. At the end of the Qing dynasty and the beginning of the Republic of China era, there were more than 30 pharmaceutical companies in Sheqi, and most of them were run by the merchants of Shanxi province and Shaanxi province.

Shanxi-Shaanxi Guild Hall lies in the center of Sheqi county. In the Qing dynasty, the rich merchants of Shanxi and Shaanxi who lived in Sheqi Town often gathered here for social gatherings. Because monks supervised the Guild Hall, it was also known as Shanxi-Shaanxi Temple. In the reign of Emperor Daoguang (1821 A.D.-1850 A.D.), it was called Ding Yuan Society. In the 12th year of the Republic of China era (1923 A.D.), it was renamed Shanxi-Shaanxi Guild Hall. The Guild-Hall was first established in 1756 A.D., the 21st year of Emperor Qianlong, then went through the reigns of Emperor Jiaqing, Daoguang, Xianfeng, and Tongzhi. During the 18th year of Emperor Guangxu (1892 A.D.), it was completed. Altogether, it went through 6 emperors and lasted for 136 years. Shanxi-Shaanxi Guild-Hall in Sheqi county reflects a strong commercial atmosphere in every aspect. The statues, sculptures, plaques, and couplets of the Pharmaceutical King's Hall are closely related to the commercial culture of medicinal materials.

4. The Four Huaiqing Herbs and Huai Guild Hall

Jiaozuo city, known as Qinhuai or Huaiqing Prefecture in ancient times, is adjacent to Taihang Mountain in the north and the Yellow River in the south. It has the reputation of "Huaichuan Plains Three Hundred Li from East to West." Its beautiful scenery of mountains and rivers has created the famous genuine medicinal herbs known as "The Four Huaiqing Herbs"– Huai Shanyao (common yam rhizome), Huai Niuxi (two-toothed achyranthes root), Huai Dihuang (Rehmanniae), and Huai Juhua (chrysanthemum flower).

Niuxi (two-toothed achyranthes root) is native to Jiaozuo. The earliest document of "Huai" put before Niuxi was Bencao Tujing (Illustrated Classic of Materia medica) of Su Song in the Northern Song dynasty. Dihuang, Shanyao, and Juhua were planted very early in Jiaozuo. Dihuang, Shanyao, and Juhua produced by Huaiqing

举办了怀药大会。为了便于怀药贸易，各地药商富贾主动集资，先后在武汉、禹州、北京、天津、西安、周口等地建立了便于怀庆商人联谊的场所——“怀庆会馆”。如明清著名的药材市场禹州，曾有“十三帮会馆”，其中“怀邦会馆”规模最大，如鹤立鸡群。民间曾有“十三帮一大片，不如怀帮一个殿”的美誉。由此可知怀药昔日的辉煌。“四大怀药”也随之名满全国。

清代中期，怀庆府的中药材贸易走向鼎盛时期，一跃成为全国“五大”（武汉、安国、樟树、禹州、怀庆）中药材集散地之一。

1911 年，河南“怀药”曾走出国门，参加了在美国旧金山举行的“万国商品博览会”，获得了较高的国际声誉。

如今四大怀药及其各种制品，更是日新月异，早已走进千家万户而享誉全球。

5. 禹州中药“四大九蒸货”

中药炮制是根据医疗需要以及药材的自身特点，以中医理论为指导，对原生药材采取的一项制药技术，是临床用药安全的有效保证。禹州作为药材集散地，集中了各地多种炮制技术和经验，逐渐形成了自己的特色，打造了一批极富盛名的炮制中药品。其中最有代表性的就是“四大九蒸货”，即九蒸九晒熟地、九蒸九晒黄精、九蒸九晒何首乌、九蒸九晒槐角。在禹州药市鼎盛的清代，赵隆太中药堂药铺遵从古法炮制出的“四大九蒸货”最为著名。如“九蒸大熟地”，是采用纯净的一级生地作原料，经过十几道工序的洗、渍、馏、蒸、揉、晒等反复处埋，成为色泽鲜艳、药香纯正、疗效显著、放置数年不会变质的珍品，热销全国。清朝宣统三年(1911 年)，赵隆太中药堂生产的“赵隆太熟地黄”在德国柏林“万国博览会”上荣获金奖，被列为清宫贡品。

国家中医药管理局命名的“老药工”、禹州朱清山先生是一位 85 岁高龄的老人，14 岁进药铺当学徒，练就了一手过硬的中药炮制技艺，他历经多次试验，恢复了九蒸九晒的技艺。这些产品已由河南省青山药业有限公司恢复生产。

Prefecture were listed as the top-grade genuine medicines probably after the mid-Ming dynasty. Li Shi-zhen in the Ming dynasty also recorded this point in *Bencao Gangmu* (*Compendium of Materia medica*). During the Ming and Qing dynasties, the Four Huai Medicinals were widely planted in Henan. In the area of Shennong Mountain of Qinyang in Jiaozuo, the names of "Shanyao Gou (Yam Ditch)", "Dihuang Po (Rehmannia Slope)", "Niuxi Chuan (Achyranthes Plain)" and "Juhua Po (Chrysanthemum Slope)" are still preserved.

After the Ming dynasty, the trade of Huai medicinals became more and more prosperous, and the sizes of pharmacists continued to grow. Many Huai Guild Halls appeared and the Huai medicinal congress was held. In order to promote the development of Huaiqing pharmaceutical trade, the local pharmacists and rich businessmen took the initiative to raise funds, and successively established "Huaiqing Guild Hall" in Wuhan, Yuzhou, Beijing, Tianjin, Xi'an, Zhoukou, and other places, where it was convenient for Huaiqing businessmen. For example, Yuzhou, a famous market of medicinal materials in the Ming and Qing dynasties, once had "Thirteen Guild Halls," among which the "Huai Guild Hall" was the largest, just like a crane standing among chickens. Among the common people, there was a saying, "All the financial resources of Thirteen Guild Halls are still less than a small part of Huaiqing Guild Hall." From this saying, we can see the glorious past of Huai medicinal. Then "The Four Huai Medicinals" also became famous throughout China.

In the mid-Qing dynasty, Huaiqing Prefecture's trade in Chinese materia medica reached its peak and became one of the five major distribution centers of Chinese materia medicas in China (Wuhan, Anguo, Zhangshu, Yuzhou, and Huaiqing).

In 1911, the "Four Huai Medicinals" in Henan province went abroad and participated in "Great Exhibition of Goods of all Nations" held in San Francisco, USA, and gained a high international reputation.

Nowadays, the "Four Huai Medicinals" and related products are changing with each passing day, and they have already entered thousands of households and enjoyed worldwide fame.

5. Yuzhou's "the Four herbs Processed with Nine Cycles of Steaming and Drying"

Processing of Chinese materia medica is a pharmaceutical technology, which

## 二、河南地道、大宗药材和中药种植基地

据崔建强、李惠民等编写的《河南中药资源集锦》（中国健康出版社，2007 年版）一书记载，经过多年普查，全省中药资源共有 2773 种，其中植物药材 2299 种，动物药材 365 种，矿物药材 84 种，其他类药材 25 种。

河南有地道、大宗药材 94 个品种。如怀山药、怀牛膝、怀地黄、怀菊花、金银花、山茱萸、冬凌草、连翘、柴胡、红花、白芷、半夏、银杏、麦冬、丹参、茯苓、桔梗、栀子、白芍等。

据李正昌等著《河南大中药产业发展研究》一书（河南大学出版社，2015 年版）记载，河南省规范化中药材种植示范基地有 45 个，其中有 18 种中药材的规范化种植技术研究分别通过了国家和省组织的验收，有 4 个药材种植基地已经通过了国家 GAP 认证，15 种药材获得国家地理标志性产品保护，中药材生产初步形成了良性机制。目前河南全省中药材种植面积达到 400 多万亩，中药农业产值 100 多亿元。

朱青山先生
Mr. Zhu Qing-shan

is guided by TCM theory and based on the medical needs and the characteristics of medicinal materials. It is an effective way to make the herbs safe. As a gathering and distributing center of medicinal materials, Yuzhou has gradually formed its own characteristics and created a number of well-known processed Chinese materia medicas by integrating various processing techniques and experiences from different places. The "four Herbs processed with Nine Cycles of Steaming and Drying" are the most well-known, which include Shudi (Radix Rehmanniae Praeparata), Huangjing (Rhizoma Polygonati), Heshouwu (Radix Polygoni Multiflori), and Huaijiao (Fructus Sophorae). In the Qing dynasty when Yuzhou pharmaceutical market was prosperous, the "four famous nine-steamed goods" produced by Zhao Long-tai Pharmaceutical Hall in compliance with the ancient law were the most famous. For example, the nine-steamed Shudi (Rehmannia Processed with Nine Cycles of Steaming) was made of pure first-grade raw Shengdi (rehmannia root) , which had been washed, stained, distilled, steamed, kneaded, and sundried repeatedly in more than a dozen processes. It finally becomes a precious product with bright color, pure medicinal fragrance, and remarkable curative effect. There would be no deterioration after several years' storage, and it was sold throughout the country at that time. In the third year of the reign of Emperor Xuantong in the Qing dynasty, in 1911 A.D., "the Zhao Long-tai Shudihuang" produced by Zhao Long-tai Pharmaceutical Hall won the gold medal at the World Expo in Berlin, Germany, and was listed as a tribute only offer to the Qing dynasty Royal families.

Mr. Zhu Qingshan of Yuzhou, the "veteran pharmacist" named by the SACM, is 85 years old. At age 14, he became an apprentice in a pharmacy and trained in a superb Chinese materia medica processing technique. After many experiments, he has resumed nine-steaming and nine-drying techniques. These products have been restored and produced by Qingshan Pharmaceutical Co., Ltd. of Henan province.

## Ⅱ. Henan's Authentic, Staple Herbs, and Their Cultivation Bases

According to Cui Jianqiang and Li Huimin's *A Collection of Henan Chinese Materia Medica Resources* (published by China Health Publishing House in June 2007), after many years of census, there are 2,773 kinds of Chinese materia medica

## 三、河南中药产业体系逐步形成

2001 年科技部批准建立国家中药现代化科技产业（河南）基地，这是国家选定的首批中药现代化建设基地之一。借助这一东风，河南中药产业实现了历史性的快速发展，现代中药产业体系初步形成。

药材种植不同于一般的农作物栽培，既要保持药材的应有药用品质，又要适应中药加工工艺的特殊要求，因而规范中药材种植技术，提高中药材栽培的科技水平，显得十分重要。

河南省是中药资源大省，栽培中药材产量及销售额在全国名列前茅，在药材市场具有举足轻重的地位。在中药现代化产业基地建设过程中，河南省根据市场需求和企业生产需要，统一规划，合理布局，强力推进中药材生产质量管理规范，按照 GAP 标准发展中药材种植，中药材种植基地管理水平显著提升。

例如：西峡县山茱萸种植基地是全省最早获得 GAP 认证和无公害基

九蒸地黄

Rehmannia Processed with Nine Cycles of Steaming

resources in the whole province, including 2,299 kinds of plant medicines, 365 kinds of animal medicines, 84 kinds of mineral medicines, and 25 kinds of other medicines.

There are 94 kinds of authentic, staple medicinal and herbal medicines, such as Huaishanyao (common yam rhizome), Huainiuxi (two-toothed), Huaidihuang (rehmannia root), Huaijuhua (chrysanthemum), Jinyinhua (honeysuckle flower), Shanzhuyu (cornus), Donglingcao (blush red rabdosia), Lianqiao (weeping forsythia capsule), Chaihu (bupleurum), Honghua (carthamus tinctourius), Baizhi (angelica dahurica), Banxia (pinellia rhizome), Yinxing (ginkgo), Maidong (dwarf lilyturf tuber), Danshen (salvia miltiorrhiza root), Fuling (porin), Jiegeng (platycodon root), Zhizi (gardenia), Baishao (paeonia lactiflora root), etc.

According to *Research on the Development of Comprehensive Traditional Chinese Materia Medica Industry in Henan Province* by Li Zhengchang and others (published in Henan University Press in 2015), there are 45 demonstration bases for standardized cultivation of Chinese materia medica in Henan province. Eighteen of them have passed the acceptance of the state and provincial organizations respectively. Four have already been approved as the national GAP, and 15 kinds of medicinal materials have been protected by national geographical landmark products. The production of Chinese medicinal materials has formed a benign mechanism. At present, the planting area of Chinese medicinal herbs in Henan province has reached about over 2600 $km^2$, and the output value of Chinese materia medica is about 1,000 million yuan.

## Ⅲ. Gradually Formed Herbal Medicine Industry System in Henan

In 2001, the Ministry of Science and Technology approved the establishment of a national scientific and technological base for the modernization of TCM in Henan, which is one of the first batches of bases selected by the state for the modernization of TCM. With the help of this advantage, Henan's Chinese materia medica industry has achieved historically rapid development, and the modern Chinese materia medica industry system has initially formed.

Chinese materia medica cultivation is different from general crop cultivation. It should not only maintain the medicinal quality of medicinal materials, but also meet

九暴地黄
Rehmannia Processed with Nine Cycles of Drying

地认证的药材基地，全县山茱萸种植总面积达22万亩，年产量1800吨，占全国山茱萸年总产量的二分之一，其规模、产量、产值均居全国第一。南召县辛夷种植基地是全国辛夷的主产区，占全国产量的40%，种植规模和产量均居全国首位。卢氏县连翘种植基地的连翘每年产量占全国总产量的四分之一，国内行销20多个省市和港、澳特区，外贸出口到日本、马来西亚、新加坡、泰国等地。汝阳县杜仲种植基地的杜仲面积已达17.8万亩，总产量达到3000多万吨，成为一项富县富民的支柱产业。嵩县柴胡种植基地的柴胡种植面积达3万余亩，年产量15万公斤，因该县柴胡质量好、产量高，被人们誉为“中国柴胡之王”。

河南在中药材基地建设中，药农与科研机构、制药企业相结合，较好地解决了这一系列问题。

河南中医药大学与河南省中医药研究院等科研单位合作，在药农配合下，对河南省8种大宗中药材的69个农家品种进行了普查和品种整理，在此基础上，将现代高科技手段和常规育种相结合，提纯复壮优良品种，选育适宜无公害药材新品种，较好地解决了一些中药材

the special requirements of Chinese materia medica processing technology. Therefore, it is very important to standardize the cultivation techniques of Chinese materia medica and improve the level of science and technology in the cultivation of Chinese materia medica.

Henan province is a province with large resources of Chinese materia medica. The output and sales of cultivated Chinese materia medica rank first in China and play an important role in the market of medicinal materials. In the process of building a modern industrial base of Chinese materia medica, Henan province, according to market demand and enterprise production needs, has unified planning, made a rational layout, vigorously promoted the quality management standards of Chinese materia medica production, and developed Chinese materia medica planting in accordance with GAP standards. The management level of Chinese materia medica planting base has been significantly improved.

Shanzhuyu (Fructus Corni) planting base in Xixia county is the earliest medicinal base in Henan province and has been certified by GAP and had non-pollution base certification. The total planting area of Shanzhuyu in the county is 150 $km^2$, with an annual output of 1,800 tons, which accounts for one-half of the total annual output of Shanzhuyu in China. Its scale, output and output value rank first in China. The planting base of Xinyi (blond magnolia flower) in Nanzhao county is the main production area of Xinyi in China, accounting for 40% of the national output. The planting scale and output rank first in the country. The annual output of Lianqiao (weeping forsythia capsule) planting base in Lushi county accounts for one quarter of the total output of whole China. Domestically they're sold to more than 20 provinces and municipalities, Hong Kong and Macao Special Administrative Regions. Foreign exporting nations includes Japan, Malaysia, Singapore, Thailand, and other places. The annual output of Duzhong (eucommia bark) planting base in Lushi county accounts for one quarter of the total output of whole China. Chaihu (bupleurum) planting base in Songxian county covers an area of more than 20 $km^2$ with an annual output of 150,000 kg. It is known as the "King of Chaihu" because of its good quality and high yield.

In the construction of Henan herbal medicine base, the combination of herbal farmers, scientific research institutions and pharmaceutical enterprises have solved series of problems.

野生变家种的难题。

河南中药生产，各地因地制宜，依托龙头企业，基本实现生产运营模式多样化。如以宛西制药有限公司为龙头企业所建的山茱萸肉基地，采取“公司 + 基地 + 农户”的模式，与农户签订了 30 年不变的合同，使 20 万粮农变药农。从而河南中药制药业也明显改观，产值大幅提升，涌现了一批产值超亿元的中药企业。天方、辅仁、宛西 3 家中药企业已进入全国医药百强行列。

在现代中药产业服务体系建设中，政府注重加强中药材市场建设，提高中药材专业市场标准化、规范化水平。目前，以禹州和百泉中药材市场为基地，一个联结焦作、南阳、商丘、洛阳、安阳、济源等河南中药材主产地的中药材信息服务网络已经建立。

Henan University of CM, in cooperation with Henan Institute of TCM and other scientific research institutes, has carried out a general survey and variety sorting of 69 farm varieties of 8 kinds of large-scale Chinese materia medica in Henan province. On this basis, they have combined modern high-tech means with conventional breeding, purified and rejuvenated excellent varieties, and selected and bred new varieties suitable for nuisance free medicinal materials, and have solved some difficult problems of changing Chinese medicinal herbs from wild into house-planted.

Henan Chinese materia medica production has basically realized the diversification of production and operation mode relying on leading enterprises. For example, Shanzhuyurou Base built by Wanxi Pharmaceutical Co., Ltd. as the leading enterprise adopts the model of "company + base + farmer", has signed a 30-year-old contract with farmers, making 200,000 farmers change from grain farmers to herbal farmers. Henan Chinese materia medica pharmaceutical industry has also significantly improved. The output value has been greatly increased, and a number of Chinese materia medica enterprises with output value exceeding 100 million yuan have emerged. Tianfang, Furen, and Wanxi Chinese materia medica enterprises have entered the ranks of the national top 100 pharmaceutical companies.

In the construction of modern Chinese materia medica industry service system, the government pays attention to strengthening the construction of Chinese materia medica market and improving the standardization level of Chinese materia medica professional market. At present, based on Yuzhou city and Baiquan city Chinese materia medica market, a Chinese materia medica information service network linking Jiaozuo, Nanyang, Shangqiu, Luoyang, Anyang, Jiyuan, and other main producing areas of Henan Chinese materia medica has been established.

第五章

# 独具特色的诊疗技术

Chapter V

# Characteristic Diagnostic and Therapeutic Technologies

经过多年的发展，河南中医已经实现了跨越式发展，涌现了一大批著名的独具特色的诊疗技术和中医医院及机构。

## 一、河南对专病的研究及治疗

1. 洛阳平乐郭氏正骨

平乐郭氏正骨，也称平乐正骨，发源于洛阳城外的孟津县平乐村，平乐村是郭氏的世居之地。平乐正骨不但继承了中医学的传统理论，而且不断创新发展，形成了一套比较系统的治疗法则。主张骨科证治应整体辨证，手法整复，夹板固定，内外用药，筋骨并重，按摩活筋，动静互补。

关于平乐正骨的学术来源虽有不同说法，但平乐村郭氏第十七代郭祥泰（清代乾隆嘉庆年间人）被誉为平乐郭氏正骨的创始人。由于其医术高，医德好，疗效高，从他起才正式有了“平乐正骨”的名号。郭祥泰之后，郭氏一族更是国手辈出，郭氏平乐正骨日益发展壮大。

高云峰先生铜像

A Bronze Statue of Mr.Gao Yunfeng

After years of development, TCM in Henan province has realized leap-forward development. There have emerged a large number of famous characteristic diagnostic and therapeutic technologies, TCM hospitals and institutions.

# Ⅰ. Research and Treatment on Special Diseases in Henan Province

1. Pingle Guo's Bone-setting in Luoyang city

Pingle Guo's Bone-setting, also known as Pingle Bone-setting, originated at Pingle village, Mengjin county, Luoyang city. Pingle village is the hometown of Dr. Guo's family. Pingle Bone-setting has not only inherited TCM theory, but also continuously made innovation and development, and finally formed its systematic therapeutic methods. It advocates that orthopedic treatment should follow the principles of "holism and pattern differentiation, manual reduction, splint fixation, internal and external medication administration, equal concern about bones and sinews, activating tendons by Tuina, and coordination of exercise and rest."

Though there are different opinions about the academic source of Pingle Bone-setting, Dr. Guo Xiangtai (during the years of the reign of Emperors Qianlong and and Jiaqing in Qing dynasty), the 17th generation of the Guo's family at Pingle village, is respected as the founder of Pingle Guo's Bone-setting. Owing to his great clinical skills, noble medical ethics, and good therapeutic effect, the formal name of "Pingle Bone-setting" began to be well-known. Since then, a large number of famous doctors of Guo's family have been cultivated, and Pingle Guo's Bone-setting was rapidly developing and expanding.

After the People's Republic of China was founded, Pingle Guo's Bone-setting was well appreciated and protected by the government. Ms. Gao Yunfeng is the wife of Guo Jingxing, the fifth-generation of Guo's family. After her husband's death at the young age, Ms. Gao shouldered the banner of Guo's Bone-setting, and started medical practice. As her fame grew, a folk saying was spread, "Out of ten bone diseases, Yunfeng can cure eight."

What is more commendable is that, in 1952, Ms. Gao Yunfeng broke the family regulation and made their secret prescription public. In 1956, with the support of the Luoyang government, she held the "the First Bone-setting Training Course

新中国成立以后，郭氏平乐正骨得到国家的重视与保护，第五代传人高云峰本为郭景星之妻，郭景星早逝之后，高云峰承担起郭氏正骨一门的大旗，悬壶济世，声名远播。民谚有“天下骨病一石，云峰能医八斗”之说。

更值得称道的是，1952年，高云峰冲破秘方不外传的族规，将郭氏一门骨科秘方公诸社会，并于1956年在洛阳市政府的支持下举办了“河南第一届正骨学习班”，公开向社会传授平乐郭氏正骨医术。在此基础上，1958年9月，高云峰又创建了我国第一所中医骨伤科大学——河南省平乐正骨学院，并亲自担任院长，开创了我国中医骨伤学高等教育之先河，为传承发展中医骨伤事业做出了卓越的贡献。从而将植根于中原沃土的平乐郭氏正骨术，引上了科学发展的道路。

时至今日，郭氏正骨，这一中医骨伤流派，已成长为一棵参天大树，走出了中医药界第一位“白求恩奖章”获得者郭维淮、被誉为“精诚大医”的郭春园等多位骨科大师。以郭氏正骨手法为核心技术而成立的河南省洛阳正骨医院，如今也已发展为全球规模最大的骨伤专科医院，成为了中华医药界之翘楚。

2. 对艾滋病的研究和防治

河南中医学院第一附属医院艾滋病临床研究中心是国家中医药管理局中医重点专科（病）、传染病协作艾滋病组长单位，拥有国家中医药管理局艾滋病重点研究室、中医传染病学（艾滋病）重点学科和艾滋病检测三级科学研究实验室，是科技部国际交流合作基地。拥有一支专职和兼职相结合的研究队伍。

中心成立了名老中医工作室，建立了艾滋病临床科研信息共享系统，在国内创立了临床研究人员到艾滋病高发区（河南上蔡县）以临床治疗为基础进行临床研究的新模式，担负着全省艾滋病患者的中医药诊治任务。

研制了益艾康胶囊、参芪除热胶囊、柴藿达原合剂、解表清理颗粒等多种医院制剂，已在临床推广运用。利用数字化中医四诊仪，全面采集

in Henan province," publicly teaching and introducing Pingle Guo's Bone-setting therapy to the society. Based on the training course, in September 1958, Ms. Gao Yunfeng founded the first TCM orthopedics-traumatology school in China—Pingle Bone-setting College in Henan province. As the president of the college, she pioneered the higher education of TCM orthopedics-traumatology, and made outstanding contributions to the inheritance and development of TCM orthopedics-traumatology. Since then, rooted in the fertile soil of the Central Plains, Pingle Guo's Bone-setting had stepped into the path of scientific development.

In the present time, Guo's Bone-setting, as a school of TCM orthopedics-traumatology, has grown into a towering tree. For example, Guo Weihuai is the first TCM doctor winner of "Dr. Bethune Medal"; Guo Chunyuan is known as "Well-skilled and respectable TCM doctor." Luoyang Bone-setting Hospital of Henan province, founded with the core technology of Guo's Bone-setting, has now developed into the world's largest orthopedics-traumatology hospital, and has become an outstanding leader in the field of TCM.

2. Research, Prevention and Treatment on AIDS

The AIDS Clinical Research Center of the First Affiliated Hospital, Henan University of Chinese Medicine (HUCM), is the leader institute of AIDS program of the special and infectious diseases working group under National. Administration of Traditional Chinese Medicine (NATCM). The center has the AIDS Key Laboratory of NATCM, the Key Discipline of Epidemiology (AIDS), and Level 3 scientific research laboratory of AIDS testing, international exchange and cooperation base of the Ministry of Science and Technology. A research team of full-time and part-time staff works in the center.

The center has established famous veteran TCM doctors' studio, and information sharing system of AIDS clinical scientific research. A new model of clinical research on the basis of clinical treatment has been founded by clinical research staff sent to the high AIDS incidence area (Shangcai county, Henan). The center is in charge of TCM diagnosis and treatment for AIDS patients in Henan province.

A number of patent herbal medicinals prepared in the hospital such as *Yiaikang* Capsule, *Shenqi* Heat-relieving Capsule, *Chaihuo Dayuan* Mixture and Exterior-Relieving and Interior-Cleaning Granules have been developed and applied in the clinical practice. Digital "TCM diagnostic instrument" is used to comprehensively

病人的四诊中医信息，积极开展中医辨证治疗、艾灸配合中药敷脐等中医特色诊疗技术。结果已显示中医药治疗可以明显改善艾滋病患者的临床症状，显著提高生活质量，减少病人机会性感染发生频率。

3. 对脉管炎的研究和治疗

全国名老中医、河南中医药大学第一附属医院崔公让教授以中医、中药为主治疗血栓闭塞性脉管炎、动脉硬化闭硬塞症、动脉栓塞、静脉栓塞及变态性小血管炎性疾病等周围血管病取得了显著成就。提出“病在脉者调之于血，病在血者调之于络”的治疗法则。通过临床实践研制出通脉丸、补气和血通脉丸等多种用之有效的中成药。

1963 年，崔公让教授在河南中医学院第一附属医院创建了河南省首家周围血管病专科，后发展成为河南中医药大学周围血管病研究所、河南

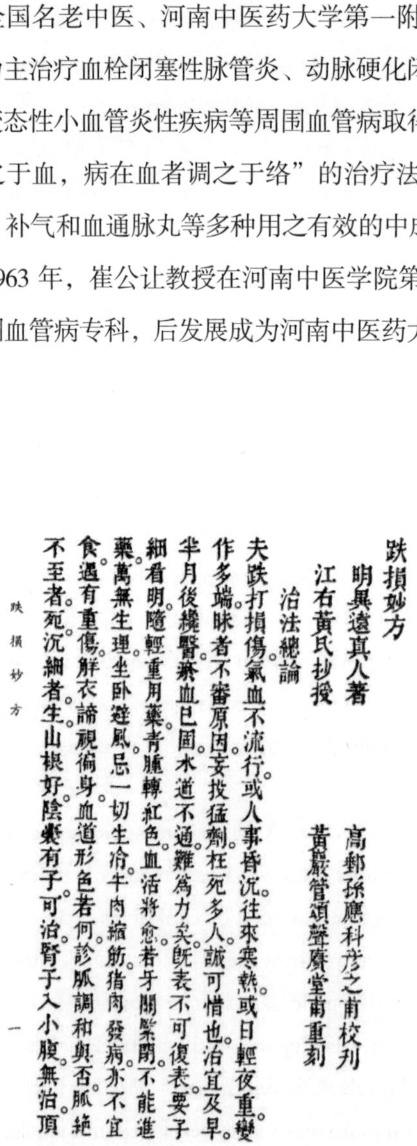
跌損妙方

明異遠真人著　高郵孫應科彥之甫校刊
江右黃氏抄授　黃巖管頌聲賡堂甫重刻

治法總論

夫跌打損傷。氣血不流行。或人事昏沉。往來寒熱。或日輕夜重。變作多端。昧者不審原因。妄投猛劑。枉死多人。誠可惜也。治宜及早。半月後。纔醫。瘀血已固。水道不通。難爲力矣。既表不可復表。要子細看明。隨輕重用藥。青腫轉紅色。血活將愈。若牙關緊閉。不能進藥。萬無生理。坐臥避風。忌一切生冷。牛肉。縮筋。猪肉。發病。亦不宜食。遇有重傷。解衣。諦視徧身。血道形色若何。診脈調和與否。脈絶不至者。死。沉細者。生。山根好。陰囊有子。可治。腎子入小腹。無治。頂

跌損妙方　一

跌损妙方
The Effective Prescriptions For Trauma

collect patients' information by four diagnostic methods. Herbal treatment and other TCM characteristic therapies such as moxibustion and umbilicus application are jointly used in the clinical practice. The results have shown that TCM treatment can significantly improve the clinical symptoms and life quality of AIDS patients, and reduce the frequency of opportunistic infections.

3. Research and Treatment on Vasculitis

Professor Cui Gongrang, a National Famous Veteran TCM Doctor from the First Affiliated Hospital of HUCM, has made significant achievements on TCM medicinals in treating peripheral vascular diseases, such as thromboangiitis obliterans, arteriosclerosis obliterans, arterial embolism, venous embolism and allergic small vessel vasculitis. He brought forward the therapeutic rule of "regulating blood when the disease is in the vessel; treating the collateral when the disease is in the blood." By means of the clinical practice, he has developed a series of effective Chinese patent medicines, such as *Tongmai* Pill, *Buqi Hexue Tongmai* Pill and so on.

At the First Affiliated Hospital of HUCM in 1963, Professor Cui Gongrang founded the first department of peripheral vascular in Henan province. Later, it developed into the Institute of Peripheral Vascular Diseases of HUCM, the Center of Diagnosis and Treatment on Peripheral Vascular Diseases, and the Key Specialized Department of NATCM.

Dr. Tang Zuxuan, a Great TCM Master and chief physician of Dengzhou TCM Hospital in Henan province, has unique therapy in treating peripheral vascular diseases. His research projects on the treatment of thromboangiitis obliterans have won the Henan Provincial Science and Technology Great Achievement Award. In 1998, he successfully developed the "*Mailuo Shutong* Granule", which was awarded the new medication certificate issued by the Ministry of Health. It was the first new herbal medication approved for venous thrombosis, and has been applied clinically both domestically and abroad.

Dr. Ma Tongchang, director of Anyang Vasculitis Hospital, founded the first specialized hospital for vasculitis in China in 1984, and achieved remarkable effects with TCM therapy in the treatment of vasculitis. Through repeated exploration, he successfully developed a series of *Rongshuan* (Thrombolytic) Pills (1# to 5#). He took full advantage of TCM external treatment, and carried on the holistic treatment by combining internal treatment with external treatment, TCM with Western medicine,

省中医周围血管病诊疗中心、国家中医药管理局重点专科。

国医大师、河南邓州中医院院长唐祖宣主任医师，对周围血管病有独特疗法。他的治疗血栓闭塞性脉管炎多项课题研究，获河南省重大科技成果奖。1998 年，他研制成功的“脉络疏通颗粒”获卫生部颁发的新药证书，成为我国第一个获批治疗静脉血栓的中药新药，至今畅销国内外。

安阳脉管炎医院院长马同常先生，于 1984 年创办了国内第一家脉管炎专科医院，用中医疗法治疗脉管炎取得了显著成就。在反复探索中，他成功地研制出以虫类药为主的 1 ～ 5 号系列溶栓丸，颇受患者欢迎。充分发挥中医外治疗法的优势，开展内治与外治相结合，中医与西医相结合，临床治疗与康复相结合的整体治疗。

毛氏济世堂位于河南省新蔡县，至今已历五代。其“脱骨疽症治疗法”主要治疗疑难杂症“老烂腿”（脉管炎），被认为是豫东南地区治疗脱骨疽病首选疗法。在治疗血栓闭塞型脉管炎方面已研制出多种纯中药制剂，并获得国家医学发明专利。

4. 少林伤科和禅医

在少林寺历史上产生了许多擅长伤科的僧医。唐代有昙宗、志操、惠书等开创了少林伤科。宋金时期，东林志隆禅师任少林寺住持，少林寺成立少林药局，不仅为僧众，亦为周边百姓提供医疗服务。元代著名学者元好问曾亲撰《少林药局记》予以记载。

明嘉靖年间，少林僧人异远真人经过多年的搜集整理，写成《跌损妙方》一书，少林伤科的真传秘方始为世人所知，异远真人成为少林伤科之集大成者。其后众多伤科学家皆宗其说，从而形成少林伤科学派。清代高僧湛举、湛化进一步补充、完善，整理为《少林跌打损伤秘方》。近年来在释永信方丈的领导下，少林寺组织僧医和中医药方面的专家进行了一系列的整理和挖掘，出版了《少林武功医宗秘笈》，受到学界重视。

历代高僧武医相兼，其处方遣药多遵循中医理论，成为中华骨伤科一重要组成部分。如少林活络膏古称“少林断续膏”，其秘方为宋代少林

clinical treatment with rehabilitation.

Mao's Jishitang Clinic is located in Xincai county, Henan province. It has been practicing TCM for five generations. Its "Anti-gangrene Therapy" is mainly for treating vasculitis, and is considered to be the first choice for the disease in the southeastern Henan province. In the treatment of thromboangiitis vasculitis, a variety of TCM herbal preparations have been developed with the national invention patents.

4. Shaolin Traumatology and Zen-medicine

There were many medical monks who were good at traumatology in the history of Shaolin Temple. In the Tang dynasty, Tanzong, Zhicao, Huishu and others had ever opened Shaolin traumatological clinics. During the Song and Jin dynasties, Zan-Buddhist Master Donglin Zhilong was appointed as the Abbot of Shaolin Temple. At that time, Shaolin Pharmacy was established, and provided medical services not only to the monks but also to local residents. The famous scholar Yuan Haowen of the Yuan dynasty once wrote a book named *Shaolin Yaoju Ji* (*Record of Shaolin Pharmacy*).

During the reign of Emperor Jiajing of the Ming dynasty, Yiyuan Zhenren, a monk in Shaolin Temple completed *Diesun Miaofang* (*The Effective Prescriptions for Trauma*) after many years of collection and reorganization. The Shaolin secret prescriptions for traumatology have been known to the public. Therefore, Yiyuan Zhenren is regarded by the late generations as the great master of Shaolin traumatology, and the doctrine of Shaolin traumatology was formed. By means of further supplementation and optimization by senior monks Zhanju and Zhanhua in the Qing dynasty, the book *Shaolin Dieda Sunshang Mifang* (*Shaolin's Effective Prescriptions for Trauma*) had been systematized and completed. In recent years, under the leadership of Abbot Shi Yongxin, Shaolin Temple organized medical monks and TCM experts to make a series of collation and exploration, and published *Shaolin Wugong Yizong Miji* (*The Secret of Shaolin Martial Art and Classical Medicine*), which was valued by the academic fields.

Throughout the history, many respectable eminent monks were good at martial arts and medicine. When making formulas and prescribing herbs, they mostly followed TCM theory. Therefore, Shaolin Traumatology has become an important component of TCM orthopedics-traumatology. For example, Shaolin *Huoluo* Plaster (Collateral-quickening Plaster) was once called Shaolin "*Duanxu* Plaster

寺福居大和尚所传，每获良效，方园数百里远近闻名，人称“少林神膏”。

少林医学深受佛学的影响。自汉代经中原传入中国的佛学，至魏晋以后广为流行，迅速渗透到社会各个领域，为中国所固有的文化融合与吸收，成为中国传统文化的组成部分。佛学与中国老庄哲学、魏晋玄学相结合，形成了禅宗。禅宗独特的思维方式与中医学的直觉体验不谋而合。

因此，思想上禅和医可以互相溶通，形成一种禅医文化，对中医的养生学产生了一定的影响。佛教的参禅让人们摒弃杂念，安静专一，修炼身心，这实际上也是一种佛家气功。历代医家从中汲取了很多积极有益的东西，从而进一步丰富了中医气功养生的内容。

在少林寺的发展过程中，少林僧人长期参禅打坐，习武导引，并且充分利用嵩山当地的药材治疗僧众和附近居民的各种疾病，因而形成了独特的少林禅医文化。少林禅医不同于我国传统中医流派之处，在于具有“禅”的特质。

少林禅医是在佛教医学和中医药学的基础上形成的医学流派，禅医突出以禅定为基础法门，运用气化、导引、点摩等为治疗手段，以提高生命力，激发潜能，而自成医学体系。

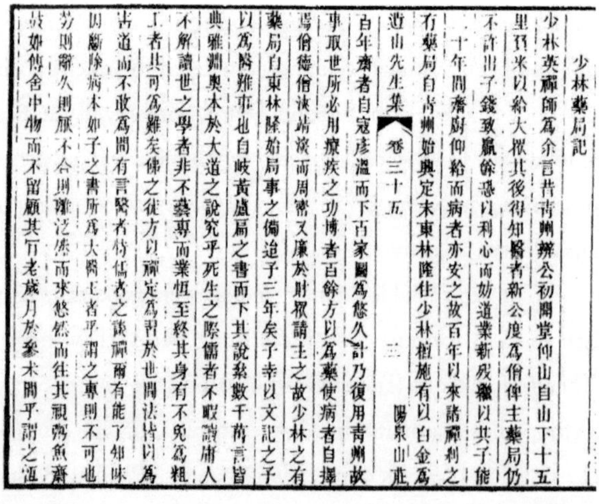
少林藥局記
少林英禪師爲余言昔青州辨公初開堂仰山自山下十五
里負米以給大衆其後得知醫者新公度爲僧俾主藥局仍
不許出子錢致贏餘恐以利心而妨道業新殁繼以其子能
十年間齋厨仰給而病者亦安之故百年以來諸禪刹之
有藥局自青州始興定末東林隆住少林樹施有以白金爲
遺山先生集 卷三十五 三 陽泉山莊
百年齋者自寇彥温而下百家圖爲悠久計乃復用青州故
事取世所必用療疾之功博者百餘方以爲藥使病者自擇
焉僧德僧泳靖深而周密又廉於財衆請主之故少林之有
藥局自東林隆始局事之備迨予三年矣予幸以文記之予
以爲醫難事也自岐黃盧扁之書而下其說殺數千萬言皆
典雅淵奧本於大道之說究乎死生之際儒者不暇讀庸人
不解讀世之學者非不藝專而業恒至終其身有不免爲粗
工者其可爲難矣佛之徒方以禪定爲習於世間法皆以爲
害道而不敢爲間有言醫者特儒者之談禪爾有能了知味
因斷除病本如子之書所爲大醫王者乎謂之專則不可也
勞則辭久則厭不合則離泛然而來悠然而往其視齋魚齋
鼓如傳舍中物而不留顧其肯老歲月於參术間乎謂之逼

少林药局记
Record of Shaolin Pharmacy

(Fracture-setting Plaster)." Its secret prescription was handed down by Fuju, a Great Monk of Shaolin Temple in the Song dynasty. With the good fame and effects, the plaster was called "Shaolin Magic Plaster."

Shaolin medicine is deeply influenced by Buddhism. Buddhism was introduced to China through the Centre Plains during the Han dynasty. After the Wei and Jin dynasties, Buddhism was widely spread and quickly penetrated into all fields of society. It was integrated and absorbed by Chinese culture, and became one part of Chinese traditional culture. Buddhism combined with Chinese philosophical ideas of Laozi and Zhuangzi and metaphysics in the Wei and Jin dynasties, and then developed into Zen Buddhism. Zen's unique way of thinking coincides with the intuitive experience of TCM.

Therefore, Zen and medicine can be mutually integrated, forming a Zen-medicine culture, which has a certain impact on the health preservation of TCM. Buddhist meditation allows people to abandon distracting thoughts, keep quiet and concentrative, and cultivate body and mind. This is actually Qigong of Buddhism. Doctors of late generations absorbed a lot of positive and beneficial thoughts, and further enriched the content of Qigong and health preservation of TCM.

During the development of Shaolin Temple, Shaolin monks insisted on practicing meditation, martial arts and breathing exercises. They took advantages of the local herbal medicinals in Songshan Mountain to treat various diseases of the monks and local residents, and formed a unique Shaolin Zen-medicine culture. Shaolin Zen-medicine is different from other TCM traditional schools in the aspect of its characteristic of "Zen".

Shaolin Zen-medicine is a medical school formed on the foundation of Buddhist medicine and TCM. Zen-medicine emphasizes Zen as the foundational principle. By using such therapeutic methods as qi transformation, breathing exercises, and finger-pressing and Tuina, Zen-medicine can improve vitality and activate the potential, and further develop into a special medical system.

5. Li's Innovative Research on Prevention and Treatment of Respiratory Diseases with TCM

Dr. Li Jiansheng, a famous Scholar in the Central Plains, academic leader of chronic obstructive pulmonary disease (COPD) in National TCM Clinical Research Base, a professor of HUCM, has long been dedicating himself to the

5. 李氏对中医药防治呼吸疾病的创新研究

著名中原学者、国家中医临床研究基地慢性阻塞性肺疾病学术带头人、河南中医药大学李建生教授，长期致力于中医药防治呼吸疾病的理论传承与创新研究及医疗工作，主持建立了《中医肺病文献数据库》，创新性提出了“正虚积损”“衰老积损、热毒损肺”“正虚络痹、积损难复”为慢阻肺、老年人肺炎和间质性肺疾病的病机新理论，建立了13项辨证标准，并通过学会发布推广，提出了10项中医、中西医结合诊疗方案，丰富了诊疗体系。

通过建设全国中医临床呼吸疾病数据库、呼吸疾病生物样本库及其规范化流程和60家推广示范基地，搭建了中医防治呼吸疾病研究合作与转化推广平台，促进了学科发展。由于成绩突出，李教授被评为国家万人计划——百千万工程领军人才，荣获吴阶平医药创新奖、河南省科技杰出贡献奖、国家科技进步二等奖等荣誉。

6. 娄氏对风湿病的研究和治疗

首批全国名老中医专家、河南中医药大学娄多峰教授，从事风湿病及骨伤科教学、临床和科研工作70余年，他是河南中医学院骨伤系和河

邵经明先生
Professor ShaoJingming

research and clinical practice of theoretical inheritance and innovation with TCM for prevention and treatment of respiratory diseases. He presided and established *Database of Literature on TCM for Pulmonary Diseases.* He innovatively proposed the new theory of pathogenesis of COPD, senile pneumonia and interstitial lung diseases, namely "retention and impairment due to deficient vital qi", "retention and impairment due to aging", "impairment of the lung by toxic heat", "obstruction of collaterals due to deficient vital qi", and "difficulty in recovery due to retention and impairment." His 13 standards of pattern differentiation have been issued and popularized through academic society. He proposed 10 diagnostic and therapeutic protocols of TCM and TCM-WM (Western Medicine) Integrated Medicine, which enriched the diagnosis and treatment system.

Through the establishment of the National TCM Clinical Database of Respiratory Diseases, Biological sample bank and its standardized procedure of respiratory diseases, and 60 promotion demonstration bases, the platform of cooperation, transformation and promotion with TCM in prevention and treatment for respiratory diseases was established. Owing to his outstanding achievements, Professor Li was awarded the Leading Talent of National "Ten Thousand Talents Plan" and "Hundred-Thousand Talents Project," Wu Jieping Medical Innovation Award, Henan Provincial Science-technology Outstanding Contribution Award, as well as Second Prize of National Science-technology Progress Award (twice).

6. Lou's Research and Treatment on Rheumatism

Professor Lou Duofeng, a National Famous Veteran TCM Doctor, professor of HUCM, has engaged in teaching, clinical practicing and scientific research on rheumatology and orthopedics for more than 70 years. He founded the Department of Orthopedics and Traumatology in Henan College of Traditional Chinese Medicine (the former name of HUCM), and Henan Rheumatology Hospital. He is the chief editor of *Rheumatism and Arthritis*, one of the series journals under China Association of Chinese Medicine (CACM).

His systematic theory of "deficiency, pathogenic factors, and blood stasis" for Bi-obstruction syndrome has been incorporated into the textbook for national medical higher education. His medications "*Biku Naiting*" and "*Bilong Qing'an*" for intractable Bi-obstruction syndrome (rheumatoid arthritis) won the National (Ministry) Major Science-technology Achievement Award as early as 1986.

南风湿病医院创始人。任中华中医药学会主办杂志《风湿病与关节炎》主编。

他创立的“虚、邪、瘀”治痹系统理论编入了全国高等医药院校普通教材；研制的“痹苦乃停”和“痹隆清安”两种药物治疗顽痹（类风湿性关节炎），早在 1986 年曾荣获国家（部级）重大科技成果奖。

1995 年，娄多峰教授在郑州黄河岸边创建了河南风湿病医院。在娄教授及其学术继承人娄玉钤院长带领下，医院针对不同证型，辨证治疗各类风湿病。研制出热痹清片、舒督丸、骨痹舒、瘀痹平等多种中药制剂。形成医院的专病专科特色优势，患者遍布国内外。

7. 邵氏“三穴五针法”治疗哮喘

首批全国名老中医、著名针灸专家、河南中医药大学邵经明教授（1911.3—2012.10），享年 102 岁，是当代河南省针灸事业发展的奠基人之一，从医 80 余载。针灸取穴少而精，重视特定穴的应用，善用背俞穴治疗脏腑病；针刺手法师古而不泥古，将针刺与气功融为一体。

他创立一种收效迅速的治疗哮喘方法，该法以肺俞、大椎、风门作为治疗哮喘的主穴，人们称之为“三穴五针一火罐”。2007 年国家中医药管理局已向全国推广，形成了国内外较有影响的“河南邵氏针灸流派”。现由其学术继承人邵素菊、邵素霞等传承发扬。

8. 宋氏对大肠肛门疾病的研究和治疗

全国名老中医、郑州市大肠肛门病医院院长宋光瑞教授，从事大肠肛门疾病诊疗 60 年，采用内服、直肠给药的方法，中西医结合进行治疗，特色显著。

他根据大肠的生理病理特点，用药以疏导为主，慎用涩敛，重视直肠给药的治疗方法。又据“同病异治”的原则制定个体化方案，分为保留灌肠法、直肠点滴给药法、直肠喷粉法和栓剂塞肛法等。研制的专科制剂如“云竹润肠丸”“益气润肠丸”“通便液”等，在临证中收效显著。

1985 年他主编出版的《中国大肠肛门病学》，为我国首部出版的关

In 1995, Professor Lou Duofeng founded Henan Rheumatology Hospital on the bank of the Yellow River in Zhengzhou. Under the leadership of Professor Lou and his academic inheritor Director Lou Yuqian, the hospital treats various rheumatism according to different types of syndromes, and developed TCM herbal preparations such as *Rebiqing* Tablet, *Shudu* Pill, *Gubishu* Pill and *Yubiping* Pill. The hospital has formed its advantage in treating special diseases, and treated patients from China and abroad.

7. Shao's "Three-point Five-needle"Therapy for Asthma

Professor Shao Jingming (1911—2012), a National Famous Veteran TCM Doctor, well-known acupuncture expert, professor of HUCM with more than 80 years' clinical experience, is one of the founders of the contemporary acupuncture in Henan province. He selected a few points with accurate location, and was good at the clinical application of specific points, especially back-*shu* points for *Zangfu* diseases. He learned and followed the ancient acupuncture, but never rigidly adhered to it, and integrated acupuncture with Qigong.

He created a "Three-point Five-needle One-cupping" Therapy for asthma, which mainly selects Feishu (BL13), Dazhui (GV14), and Fengmen (BL12) for acupuncture treatment. In 2007, NATCM started promoting the therapy national-wide, and "The Doctrine of Henan Shao's Acupuncture" was gradually formed with domestic and international good fame. At present, it is inherited and innovated by Professor Shao Suju and Dr. Shao Suxia as its academic inheritors.

8. Song's Research and Treatment for Anorectal Diseases

Dr. Song Guangrui, a National Famous Veteran TCM Doctor, the director of Zhengzhou Anorectal Diseases Hospital, has been engaged in the diagnosis and treatment of anorectal diseases for 60 years. His treatment is characterized by combination of oral decoction with rectal administration, and combination of TCM and Western medicine.

On the basis of physiological and pathological characteristics of the large intestine, he treated the diseases by using herbs mainly for dredging function, cautionally for astringency, and advisably for rectal administration. According to the principle of "different treatments for the same disease," the individualized programs are formulated, including retention enema method, rectal drip administration method, rectal powder spraying method, and anal suppository method, etc. The

于大肠肛门病的诊疗专著。1986 年 9 月，他在郑州市创建了郑州市大肠肛门病医院。2007 年被国家中医药管理局定为“全国重点肛肠专科医院”。

9. 韦氏对疼痛病的研究和治疗

全国名老中医、河南省中医药学会民间传统诊疗技术与验方整理研究分会主任委员、安阳市疼痛专业学会主任韦绪性教授，出身中医世家，长于疼痛及疑难病诊疗，长期致力于中医疼痛学的研究。先后主编出版了《中医痛证诊疗大全》《中西医临床疼痛学》《辨治疼痛病精要》等著作，系统地论述了中医疼痛学理论。

10. 买氏中医外治法

周口买氏中医外治法始创于清朝，最早有文献记载为第三代传人买锡冕，得先祖真传。几百年来，买氏家族已经 8 代人世袭相传。

第八代传承人买建修，研创出汝怡通、买怡帖（乳体散结膏，国家级十一五科技支撑项目）等药剂，主治骨科、妇科风湿病，享誉省内外。

## 二、河南的中医药非物质文化遗产项目

作为中医大省的河南有众多的中医药老字号，有一部分已被评为省级以上中医药非物质文化遗产项目。

到目前为止，河南省共评选了四批省级非物质文化遗产代表性项目，其中中医药非物质文化遗产项目 53 项。项目类别从最初第一批的民间手工技艺（四大怀药种植与炮制、禹州中药加工炮制技艺）、生产商贸习俗（百泉药会、禹州药会）、民间信仰（医圣张仲景祭祀）、民间知识（洛阳正骨、针灸铜人）等名称类别散乱分布，到第二、三、四批集中以“传统医药”类别，统领中医药非物质文化遗产项目，名下有中医学的各学科项目。

如妇科（象庄秦氏妇科、李楼李八先生妇科）、烧伤科（黄家烧伤药膜、烧伤自然疗法与自然烧伤膏、潘氏烧伤传统疗法）、眼口腔咽喉科（张氏喉科、秦李庄周氏口腔咽喉科、纯德堂口疮散、杜氏口疮治疗技法、杨

specialized herbal preparations such as "*Yunzhu Runchang* Pills", "*Yiqi Runchang* Pills" and "*Tongbian* Liquid" have achieved remarkable results in the clinical practice.

In 1985, he authored and published the book *Chinese Anorectal Diseases*, which was the first published monograph on the diagnosis and treatment of anorectal diseases in China. In September 1986, he founded Zhengzhou Anorectal Disease Hospital, which was designated as the "State Key Anorectal Specialty Hospital" by NATCM in 2007.

9. Wei's Research and Treatment for Pain Diseases

Dr. Wei Xuxing, a National Famous Veteran TCM Doctor, the chairman of the Folk Diagnostic and Therapeutic Technology and Prescription Research branch of Henan TCM Association, the director of the Anyang Pain Management Specialty Committee, was born in a TCM family. He is good at treating pain and difficult diseases, and has long devoted himself to the research of pain management by TCM. He authored and published *Compendium of TCM Diagnosis and Treatment of Pain Syndrome, Clinical Study on Pain by TCM and Western Medicine, and Differentiation and Treatment of Pain Syndrome* and systematically illustrated the TCM theory on pain syndrome.

10. Mai's TCM External Therapy

Mai's TCM external therapy in Zhoukou city was founded in the Qing dynasty. Mai Ximian, the third generation of his family, was the earliest recorded successor who inherited from his ancestors. For hundreds of years, the therapy has been handed down in Mai's family for eight generations.

Mai Jianxiu, the eighth-generation inheritor, created *Ruyi Tong, Maiyi* Plaster (*Ruti Sanjie* Plaster, National 11th Five-year Science-technology Support Project) and other medications, which are mainly indicated for orthopedic, gynecological and rheumatic diseases.

## Ⅱ. Intangible Cultural Heritage Projects of TCM in Henan Province

As a big province of TCM, Henan has many honored TCM brands. Some of them have been rated as TCM Intangible Cultural Heritage Projects at or above the provincial level.

氏珍珠散治疗口疮技艺）、中医正骨疗法（快庄李氏中医正骨、刘氏正骨、陈氏正骨、杨家正骨疗法）、中医外科（张八卦中医外科、世医堂中医外科、买氏中医外治疗法）、针灸（贵氏针灸、石氏中医针灸、张氏耳病针灸疗法）、中医传统制剂方法（五更太平丸制备工艺、黑虎丸、李氏膏药、姚家膏药、黄氏膏药、黄塔膏药）等。

入选“国家级非物质文化遗产代表性项目名录”6 项，即中药炮制技术（四大怀药种植与炮制）、中医正骨疗法（平乐郭氏正骨法）、药市习俗（百泉药会、禹州药会）、中医诊疗法（买氏中医外治法、毛氏济世堂脱骨疽症疗法）。

## 三、河南著名的中医院

河南省 100 多个县市，每个县都有中医院，充分发挥中医的特长，为人民的健康服务。著名的三甲中医院有：河南中医药大学第一附属医院、河南省中医院（又称河南中医药大学第二附属医院）、河南中医药大学第三附属医院、河南省中医药研究院、郑州市中医院、开封市中医院、安阳市中医院、濮阳市中医院、洛阳第一中医院、焦作市中医院、三门峡市中医院、南阳市中医院、商丘市中医院、许昌市中医院、周口市中医院、郑州市大肠肛门病医院等。这些医院，都各具特色。

河南中医药大学第一附属医院，始建于 1953 年，是一所集医疗、教学、科研、预防、保健、康复为一体的全国百佳医院。是全国中药制剂与剂型改革基地、国家中医临床研究基地、国家中医药国际合作交流基地，并设有博士后科研工作站。于 2008 年 12 月被确定为国家中医临床研究基地建设单位，艾滋病、慢性阻塞性肺疾病为基地重点研究病种。

医院设有 55 个临床科室、47 个病区和 13 个医技科室，开放床位 2600 张。其中儿科、心血管科、肝病科、肺病科、脑病科、周围血管科、康复科、肛肠科、妇产科、骨伤科、耳鼻喉科、护理学科、感染性疾病科、

So far, four batches of provincial-level representative projects of Intangible Cultural Heritage have been voted in Henan province, including 53 TCM intangible cultural heritage projects. The project categories of the first batch were not well-organized, and TCM were included in many categories. In the category of Folk Handicrafts, there are the planting & processing of the four major *Huai* herbs, and the preparing and processing technology of herbs in Yuzhou county. In the category of producing and trading customs, there are herbal trade fairs in Baiquan and Yuzhou. In the category of folk belief, there is the worshipping ceremony for Medical Sage Zhang Zhongjing. In the category of folk knowledge, there are Pingle Guo's Bone-setting therapy in Luoyang city, and acupuncture bronze status. However, the second, third and fourth batches were sorted under the category of "Traditional medicine." In the category, TCM intangible cultural heritage projects are classified by medical specialty.

For example, Gynecology includes Qin's Gynecology in Xiangzhuang, and Li Ba's Gynecology in Lilou village. Burns includes Huang's burns medical membrane, natural therapy and ointment for burns, and Pan's traditional therapy for burns. Ophthalmology and otolaryngology include Zhang's laryngology, Zhou's stomatology and laryngology at Qinlizhuang village, aphtha powder of Chundetang clinic, Du's therapy for aphtha, and Yang's therapy with Pearl Powder for aphtha. TCM bone-setting includes Li's TCM bone-setting at Kuaizhuang village, Liu's bone-setting, Chen's bone-setting, and Yang's bone-setting. TCM external medicine includes Zhang Bagua's TCM external medicine, TCM external medicine of Shiyitang clinic, and Mai's external therapy. Acupuncture includes Gui's acupuncture, Shi's TCM acupuncture, and Zhang's acupuncture for ear diseases. TCM traditional preparation methods include preparing technique of *Wugeng Taiping* Pills, Black Tiger Pills, Li's Plaster, Yao's Plaster, Huang's Plaster, and *Huangta* Plaster.

Among them, six items were selected as the "National Intangible Cultural Heritage Representative Project List." i.e. preparing and processing technology of herbs (planting & processing of the four major *Huai* herbs), TCM Bone-setting therapy (Pingle Guo's Bone-setting therapy), Herbal producing and trading customs (Herbs trade fair at Baiquan village, Herbs trade fair at Yuzhou county), and TCM diagnostic and therapeutic method (Mao's Anti-gangrene therapy of Jishitang Clinic, Mai's TCM external therapy).

## Ⅲ. Well-known TCM Hospitals in Henan Province

There are more than 100 counties and cities in Henan province. Every county

临床中药学等，为国家临床重点专科或国家中医药管理局重点学科。

如该院儿科为河南省中医名科，是国内首家中医儿科医院，拥有全国中医儿科最大的临床、教学基地及国家中医药管理局三级科研实验室。在治疗过敏性紫癜（紫癜性肾炎）、功能性便秘、多发性抽动症等病症小儿方面，疗效显著。脾胃肝胆病科在治疗肝硬化、非酒精性脂肪性肝病、慢性萎缩性胃炎等常见病方面，积累了丰富经验，达到国内先进水平。

has been facilitated with one TCM hospital to provide TCM service to local residents. The famous Level-Three Grade-A hospitals are the First Affiliated Hospital of HUCM, Henan Provincial TCM Hospital (also known as the Second Affiliated Hospital of HUCM), the Third Affiliated Hospital of HUCM, the Affiliated Hospital of Henan TCM Research Institute, Zhengzhou TCM Hospital, Kaifeng TCM Hospital, Anyang TCM Hospital, Puyang TCM Hospital, The First TCM Hospital of Luoyang, Jiaozuo TCM Hospital, Sanmenxia TCM Hospital, Nanyang TCM Hospital, Shangqiu TCM Hospital, Xuchang TCM Hospital, Zhoukou TCM Hospital, and Zhengzhou Anorectal Diseases Hospital. All these hospitals have their own unique characteristics.

The First Affiliated Hospital of HUCM, founded in 1953, is one of the 100 Best Hospitals in China, and is integrated with medical treatment, teaching, scientific research, prevention, health preservation and rehabilitation. It is a National Base of TCM Herbal Preparation and Dosage Form Reform, National Base of TCM Clinical Research, National Base of TCM International Cooperation and Exchange, as well as the postdoctoral research station. Construction Unit of National base of TCM Clinical Research approved in December 2008 focuses on AIDS and COPD researches.

The hospital has 55 clinical departments, 47 wards with 2,600 open beds, and 13 medical technology departments. The departments of pediatrics, angiocardiopathy, hepatopathy, pneumopathy, encephalopathy, peripheral angiopathy, rehabilitation, coloproctology, obstetrics and gynecology, orthopedics and traumatology, otolaryngology, nursing, infectious diseases, and clinical TCM pharmacology are national clinical key specialties or key disciplines of NATCM.

For example, the pediatrics department of the hospital is the well-known department in Henan. It is also the first TCM Children's Hospital in China with the largest clinical and teaching base and the Level III scientific research laboratory of the NATCM. In the treatment of allergic purpura in children (purpuric nephritis), functional constipation, Tourette's syndrome and other children diseases, the therapeutic effects are significant. Besides, the department of gastroenteric and hepatobiliary diseases has reached the domestic advanced level in the treatment of common diseases such as cirrhosis, nonalcoholic fatty liver diseases and chronic atrophic gastritis.

第六章

# 河南中医药文化旅游资源

Chapter Ⅵ

# TCM Cultural Tourism Resources in Henan Province

# 一、中医药文化寻根游

1. 新郑、新密岐黄文化遗迹

新郑、新密一带为古有熊国，是河洛文化的核心区域，有着极其丰富的历史文化资源。

黄帝故里在新郑，每年农历三月三，河南省政府都要在这里举行隆重的拜祖大典。在以具茨山为轴心的文化圈，保留了大量的黄帝文化积淀。如轩辕丘位于新郑和新密交界处。在具茨山及诸山的命名中，多与黄帝臣属有关。如具茨山主峰风后顶，即因大臣风后而得名；大鸿山（在风后顶南）即因大鸿而得名。21世纪初，考古学者在具茨山发现的3000多处岩画，更是为研究中原地区包括黄帝文化在内的远古文化，提供了重要的实物资料。

岐黄文化就是中医药文化，截至目前，新密境内发现与岐黄文化有关的遗址、遗迹约40余处。新密市有大量关于轩辕黄帝活动的遗迹和传说，

新密黄帝宫
Huangdi's Palace in Xinmi City

## Ⅰ. Chinese Herbal Culture Root-seeking Tour

1. Qihuang Culture Relics in Xinzheng City and Xinmi City

Xinzheng city and Xinmi city belonged to Youxiong country in ancient times, which are central areas of Heluo culture and have extremely rich historical and cultural resources.

The hometown of Huang Di is in Xinzheng city. In the third lunar month of each year, the Henan provincial government holds a grand ancestor-worshipping ceremony there. In the cultural circle centered around the Juci Mountain, there is a large amount of cultural accumulation of Huang Di. For example, Xuanyuan hill is located at the junction of Xinzheng city and Xinmi city. In the name of the Juci Mountain and other mountains, it is mostly related to Huangdi and his officials. For example, Fenghou peak, the main peak of the Juci Mountain, was named after the minister Feng Hou; Dahong Mountain (in the south of Fenghou Peak) was named after Dahong. At the beginning of the 21st century, more than 3,000 rock paintings discovered by archaeologists in the Juci mountain provided important material information for the study of ancient cultures in the Central Plains including Huangdi culture.

Qihuang culture is the culture of TCM. Up to now, more than 40 historical and cultural sites related to Qihuang culture have been found in Xinmi city, which has a large number of sites and legends about Xuanyuan Huangdi's activities, such as Xuanyuan Hill and Huangdi's Palace; there are also relics of activities of the ancient physician Qi Bo and Da Hong (also called Wei Yuqu), such as the Qibo Spring, the Qibo Mountain, the Qibo Temple, and the Qibo Cave, which are famous in the era of Huangdi.

Although *Huangdi Neijing* was attributed to Huang Di, and has something to do with Huang Di. It should be said that Huang Di, Qi Bo, Wei Yuqu and other courtiers discussed the medical doctrine together. It was taught orally, and generation after generation of sages constantly supplemented and perfected it. During the Warring States and the Qin and Han dynasties, the book *Huangdi Neijing* was finally published and considered as a TCM classic. It can be inferred that it was Huang Di who led Qi Bo from the Qishan area in Shaanxi province to the place

如轩辕丘和黄帝宫等，更有黄帝时期著名的上古医家岐伯、大鸿（鬼臾区）等活动的遗迹，如岐伯泉、岐伯山、岐伯庙、岐伯洞等。

《黄帝内经》虽是托名黄帝而作，但这个托名绝不是空穴来风，而是同黄帝确有关系。应该说是黄帝与岐伯、鬼臾区等臣子在一起讨论医道，经过口耳相传，一代又一代先贤们不断地补充完善，到了战国和秦汉之际，终于使《黄帝内经》成书，成就了中医的经典之作。可以推想，是黄帝西行把岐伯从陕西岐山一带引载到自己的部落有熊氏所在地，拜为医学之师。而新密正是黄帝和岐伯等名臣讨论医学之道的主要活动场所之一，因而成为《黄帝内经》思想形成诞生的主要地区之一。（详见本书第一章。）

2. 焦作沁阳神农山、神农坛和道教上清派第一代宗师魏夫人祠

神农山，位于河南省焦作沁阳市城区西北 23 千米的太行山麓。乾隆年间编纂的《怀庆府志》，有“垅实自于炎农”的记载。这里不仅是神农氏尝百草、辨五谷、设坛祭祀的圣地，也是道教创始人老子炼丹升仙之所在，同时，韩愈、李商隐等历代文人都曾在此留下传世佳作。在沁阳神农山老君洼一带，至今还保留有“山药沟”“地黄坡”“牛膝川”“菊花坡”

神农坛
Shennong Altar

where his Youxiong tribe was located and worshipped him as a medical teacher. Xinmi city was one of the main places where Huang Di and famous officials like Qi Bo discussed the medical doctrine, and became one of the main areas where the thought of *Huangdi Neijing* was produced. (See Chapter I of this book for details.)

2. Shennong Mountain, Shennong Altar and Weifuren Ci (Madam Wei's Temple, Commemorating the First Generation of Taoist Master in Shangqing School) in Qinyang City of Jiaozuo City

Shennong mountain is located at the foot of Taihang mountain, 23 km northwest of Qinyang city of Jiaozuo city in Henan province. *Huaiqingfu Zhi* (*The Annals of Huaiqing Prefecture*), compiled during the reign of Qianlong emperor, has a record of "long (ridge) actually originated from the era of Yan emperor and Shennong". This is not only the holy land where Shennong tasted hundreds of herbs, distinguished grains and set up altars and sacrifices, but also the place where Laozi, the founder of Taoism, practiced alchemy and became immortal. At the same time, Han Yu, Li Shangyin and other ancient scholars have all left outstanding works here. In the area around Laojunwa in Shennong mountain of Qinyang city, ancient names such as "Shanyao Gou (Yam Ditch)", "Dihuang Po (Rehmannia Slope)", "Niuxi Chuan (Achyranthes Plain)" and "Juhua Po (Chrysanthemum Slope)" are still preserved. This mountain, which combines nature with humanity, attracts people to follow Shennong's footsteps and feel the beauty of TCM culture.

Shennong Altar ( Shennong's Sacrifice Altar to the Heaven) is located at the top of the Shennong mountain, 30 meters wide from east to west and 22 meters deep from north to south, and is oval in shape. The main content of Shennong's sacrifice to heaven is closely related to agriculture and people's life to thank God for giving him wisdom to teach his people to plant grain and make hemp as clothing. Then, agriculture began to arise. He was also able to recognize the nature of the herb, relieve the sufferings of the people, and reduce the pain and death from then on. A number of archaeological and architectural experts came to Shennong mountain for field visit. They believed that the construction history of Shennong temple was earlier than that of Beijing Temple of Heaven, which could be called "the first altar in China", the birthplace of Chinese civilization created by Yan emperor Shennong.

The Weifuren Temple ( Erxian Temple) is located in the Erxian Temple Scenic Area in Shennong mountain of Qinyang city, and was built in memory of Wei

二仙祠
Erxian Ci (Two Immortals' Shrine)

等古地名。这座自然与人文兼具的山峰,吸引着人们赶来,追寻神农氏之踪,感受中医药文化之美。

神农坛(神农祭天坛)在神农山极顶紫金顶,东西宽30米,南北深22米,呈椭圆形。神农祭天的主要内容与农业和人民生活密切相关。谢祭上天赐予他智慧,使他教民树艺五谷,制麻为衣,从此农业兴起。又使他辨认出百草性味,疗民疾苦,从此减少病痛和死亡。多位考古专家、建筑专家来到神农山实地考察,他们认为,神农坛的建造历史要早于北京天坛,可以称为"中华第一坛",是炎帝神农创造华夏文明的发祥地。

魏夫人祠(二仙祠)位于沁阳神农山二仙庙景区,是为纪念道教上清派第一代宗师魏华存而建。魏华存是晋代女道士,字贤安,博览百家,通儒学五经,尤耽老、庄之学。为了使上清派的炼修功夫深入人心,她把原来在晋武帝太康九年(288年)时接收到的《黄庭内景经》草本,加以修订整理后,并予注述,撰为定本,传抄问世。

魏夫人定本的《黄庭经》,是早期道教重要的经典之一。成为后世

Huacun, the first Taoist master of the Shangqing school (see photo). Wei Huacun, a female Taoist priest of the Jin dynasty, with the style name Xian'an, read works of numerous schools extensively with a thorough understanding of the Five Classics of Confucianism, especially the study of the *Laozi* and *Zhuangzi*. In order to make Shangqing school's meditation skills deeply rooted in the hearts of the people, she revised and collated the *Huangting Neijing Jing* (*Inner Meditation Classic of the Huangting School*) which was originally published in the 9th year of the Tai Kang reign of the Wu Emperor of Jin (288 A.D.) and made a note of it. It was written as a book and copied by people.

Lady Wei's *Huangting Jing* (*Huangting's Classic*) is one of the important classics of the early Taoism. It has become the most famous classic of Taoist practice in later generations. Based on the understanding of the human body in TCM, the book uses Taoist thinking and language to briefly describe the organs and functions of the human body, summarizes the physiological functions of various systems of the human body, and puts forward three *dantian* (including the upper, middle, lower *dantian*): the upper *dantian* is the place where the Governor vessel is in charge of the temple, also known as the "Niwan Palace"; the middle *dantian* is at Danzhong acupoint (CV 17) in the chest, where the pectoral qi gathers; the lower *dantian* is the Guanyuan acupoint (CV 4) of Conception Vessel, three inches below the navel, where essence is stored) and other Taoist cultivation theory. It can be said that it is an important work that integrates medicine and Taoism, and has become a monograph on Taoist health practice that has influenced China for more than 1,000 years. This will not only reveal the evolution of the Taoist "Nei Dan (Inner *Dantian*)" thought, but also expose the evolution of TCM theory.

Wei Huacun spent most of her life in Qinyang. With the cultivation place Yangluo Mountain as the center, she hung the pot (being a doctor) in the Huaichuan Plain in the area of the ancient Huaiqing prefecture, and preached there. She has done many good things for the local people and won the love of the people. After her death, people built a "Weifuren Ci (Lady Wei's Shrine)" for her in Mujian mountain, the branch of Yangluo mountain in Qinyang city. For more than 1,700 years, on "March the 3rd" of the lunar calendar, people in the area of Fuyang held a temple fair there to commemorate her.

道教修炼“内丹”最有名的经典。该书以传统医学对人体的认识为基础，运用道教思维及语言，简明扼要地描述了人身脏腑器官及其功能，概括了人体各系统的生理功能，提出了“三丹田”（有上中下三丹田：上丹田为督脉印堂之处，又称“泥丸宫”；中丹田为胸中膻中穴处，为宗气之所聚；下丹田为任脉关元穴，脐下三寸之处，为藏精之所）等道教修养理论。可以说是一部融汇医学、道学思想的重要著作，成为影响中国1000多年的道教养生修炼专著。借此不仅可以窥见中国道教“内丹”思想的演变，也可以考见中国医学思想的流变。

魏华存一生的大部分时间是在沁阳度过的。她以修炼地阳洛山为中心，在古怀庆府一带的怀川平原悬壶济世，布道度人，为当地的老百姓办了许多好事，深得百姓的爱戴。她仙逝后，人们在她当年修炼地——沁阳阳洛山支脉沐涧山为其建起“魏夫人祠”进行祭祀。1700多年来，每逢农历“三月三”，沁阳一带的老百姓就在此举行庙会，隆重纪念她。

## 二、以开封为中心的饮食文化游

开封的饮食文化源远流长，在古代曾长期处在显著的领先地位。

火祖燧人氏首创钻木取火，在开封东边几十公里处的商丘点燃了华夏文明之火，将中华民族带进了文明时代。由于火的发明，改变了先民的食性，熟食便是食养、食疗的开端，从此，我们的祖先“火食之道始成”，我国才真正进入了烹饪时代。商朝的开国元勋、著名的贤相伊尹，被中国烹饪界尊为“烹饪之圣”“中华厨祖”，也是中药汤剂的首创者。在开封、尉氏、虞城等地均有伊尹祠、伊尹墓和大量相关传说。《吕氏春秋·本味篇》记述了伊尹的生平和他同商汤论述饮食之道的情景，提出了著名的“五味调和”理论及“火候”说，这是中国饮食文化的经典理论。

追溯中国饮食文化的滥觞，河南居十分重要的位置。中华第一宴是夏启在今河南禹州的“钧台”举办的，史称“钧台之享”。豫菜源于夏商，

## Ⅱ. Food Culture Tour Centered in Kaifeng

Kaifeng's food culture has a long history and has been in a leading position for a long time in ancient times.

The fire ancestor Suirenshi pioneered drilling wood for fire, lighting the fire of Chinese civilization in Shangqiu city, dozens of kilometers east of Kaifeng, bringing the Chinese nation into a civilized era. Due to the invention of fire, the food habits of the ancestors were changed, and cooked food was the beginning of feeding and dietotherapy. From then on, our ancestors "began to eat after cooking by fire" and our country really entered the cooking era. Yi Yin, the founder of the Shang dynasty and a famous sage, was revered by the Chinese culinary circles as "the sage of cooking" and "the ancestor of Chinese chefs." He was also the pioneer of Chinese medical decoction. In Kaifeng city, Weishi city, Yucheng city and other places, there are Yiyin Temple, Yiyin Tomb and a large number of related legends. *"Lüshi Chunqiu "* describes the life of Yi Yin and his discussion with Shang Tang on the way of eating. The famous "five flavors" theory and "fire" theory are put forward, which is the classic theory of Chinese food culture.

Tracing back to the origin of the Chinese food culture, Henan occupies a very important position. The first Chinese banquet was held by Xia Qi in today's "Jun Tai" in Yuzhou of Henan province. It was called "Juntai's share" in history. Henan cuisine originated from the Xia dynasty and flourished in Bianjing of the Northern Song dynasty. It is the oldest kind of cuisine in China. Later, after the Southern Song dynasty going south, it had a great influence on the formation of several important cuisines in the south. Henan cuisine once thrived and still showed its charm until the first half of the last century.

Youyixin restaurant in Kaifeng, a famous Chinese restaurant recorded in the encyclopedia of China, was built in the Qing dynasty. The century-old shop in the 32nd year of Guangxu reign (1906 A.D.), formerly known as "Youyi Cun (Another Village)", inherited the traditional cuisine style of the Song dynasty and was praised as the first authentic Henan cuisine with a collection of master chefs with superb cooking skills.

One of China's four chefs' hometowns (Changyuan county in Henan province, Shunde district of Foshan city in Guangdong province, Lantian county in Shaanxi

兴盛于北宋汴京，是中国最古老的一种菜系。后来随南宋南下，对南方几个重要菜系的形成影响巨大。历史上，豫菜曾风光无限，直到上世纪前半叶，仍显示出其魅力。

被中国大百科全书收录的中国名餐馆开封“又一新”饭店是一家始建于清光绪三十二年（1906 年）的百年老店，前身名“又一村”，它继承宋菜传统风格，以名家高手荟萃，烹调技艺精湛，被誉为正宗豫菜第一家。

中国四大厨师之乡（分别是河南长垣县、广东佛山市顺德区、陕西蓝田县、安徽绩溪县）之一，也是第一个“厨师之乡”——河南长垣县，是开封北面的近邻。国内外许多名厨来自长垣县。2012 年 3 月 11 日，中国烹饪协会又向长垣县颁发了“中华美食名城”牌匾，并举行了隆重的授牌仪式。目前，长垣现有中国烹饪大师 38 人，从事烹饪工作的专业厨师达 3 万余人，遍及世界 46 个国家和地区。（见 2012 年 3 月 13 日《大河报》。）顺理成章，将“厨师之乡”和开封饮食共建一条饮食文化旅游线。

目前，已建有开封中医院中医治未病健康养生中心基地，开封大宋中医药文化博物馆（现为全国中医药文化教育基地），开封大梁门饮食文化博物馆，开封、尉氏、虞城等地伊尹故里遗迹等中医药文化基地。

在此基础上，以开封为核心，打造一条饱含着中原中医药文化特色的开封市中医药健康旅游线：

汴京饮食文化（含开封大梁门饮食文化博物馆）——中国第一个“厨师之乡”长垣县——中医治未病的健康养生中心基地——大宋中医药文化博物馆——开封、尉氏、虞城等地“中华厨祖”、中药汤剂的首创者伊尹故里遗迹。

## 三、中原特色的中医药文化遗迹

河南有众多的中医药文化遗迹已成为旅游资源。

province, and Jixi county in Anhui province) is also the first "chef's village"- Changyuan county in Henan, which is the neighbor to the north of Kaifeng. Many famous chefs at home and abroad come from Changyuan county. On March 11, 2012, the China Cuisine Association issued the"Chinese Cuisine City"plaque to Changyuan county and held a grand ceremony. At present, Changyuan has 38 Chinese cooking masters and more than 30,000 professional cooks, covering 46 countries and regions in the world. (See *Dahe Daily*, March 13, 2012) It is logical to build a tourism line of food culture between "the chef's hometown" and Kaifeng dietary culture.

At present, there are already some TCM cultural bases, such as Kaifeng TCM Hospital, Kaifeng Dasong TCM Cultural Museum (now the national TCM cultural education base), Kaifeng Daliangmen Food Culture Museum and Yi Yin's hometown relics in Kaifeng city, Weishi city, Yucheng city and other places.

On this basis, with Kaifeng as the core, TCM Health Travel Line in Kaifeng city has been established, with the TCM characteristics of the Central Plains:

Bianjing Food Culture (including Kaifeng Daliangmen Food Culture Museum)- Changyuan county, China's first "chef's hometown"- Health Care Center Base of TCM for Disease Prevention- Dasong Museum of TCM- Ruins of Kaifeng city, Weishi city and Yucheng city's "Chinese Kitchen Ancestors" and the TCM Decoction Creator Yi Yin's Hometown.

## Ⅲ. TCM Cultural Heritage and Characteristics of the Central Plains

There are many TCM cultural heritages in Henan province which have become tourist resources.

1. The Medical Sage Shrine and Zhang Zhongjing Culture Festival in Nanyang city

The "Medical Sage Shrine" in the hometown of Zhang Zhongjing in Nanyang city is said to be the location of Zhang Zhongjing's tomb. The construction date of the medical sage shrine is unknown. The existing building was built by the scholar-physician Shen Jin and others in the 25th year of Jiajing reign of the Ming dynasty (1536 A.D.). Zhu Yuwen, the seignior of the Ming dynasty (governing the Nanyang

1. 南阳医圣祠及张仲景文化节

南阳仲景故里的“医圣祠”，相传为仲景庐墓所在。医圣祠始建年月不详，现存建筑为明朝嘉靖二十五年（1536年）儒医沈津等人倡修，明代藩王朱宇温（就藩南阳府）亲撰《医圣张仲景祠墓志》一文，刊石立于墓前，残石现存祠内。其后，曾多次整饬修葺。中华人民共和国成立后，1956年重加修缮，1988年1月13日被国务院公布为第三批全国重点文物保护单位。时至今日，“医圣祠”一直为人们所崇敬而四时享祭。

医圣祠内建有仲景经方碑林，碑文由全国名老中医和书法大师题写，系统诠释《伤寒杂病论》经方精髓，是目前唯一以碑林形式记述仲景经方的人文壮举。

中国南阳张仲景医药科技文化节暨南阳张仲景医药文化节，由国家科技部、国家中医药管理局和河南省人民政府主办，从2002年至2017年已成功举办了12届，是一个展示中医药产业发展成果、弘扬中医药优秀传统文化、推进中医药科技创新的交流平台。

医圣祠

Zhang Zhongjing's Temple

Prefecture), wrote the article "Yisheng Zhang Zhongjing Ci Muzhi (Epitaph of the Medical Sage Shrine of Zhang Zhongjing)", with a stone standing in front of the tomb, the remnant stone of which still existing in the shrine. Since then, it has been repaired many times. After the founding of the People's Republic of China, it was rebuilt in 1956. On January 13, 1988, it was announced by the State Council as the third batch of national key cultural heritage protection units. Up to now, the "Medical Sage Shrine" has always been honored by people.

There is a stele forest of Zhongjing's classic formula in the medical sage shrine, inscribed by famous TCM doctors and calligraphers, which systematically interprets the essence of *Shanghan Zabing Lun* and is currently the only human feature to describe Zhongjing's formulas in the form of the stele forest.

The Medical Science and Technology Culture Festival of Zhang Zhongjing in Nanyang of China and the Medical Culture Festival of Zhang Zhongjing in Nanyang city were hosted by the Ministry of Science and Technology, the State Administration of TCM and the Henan Provincial Government of the People. They have been successfully held for 12 sessions from 2002 to 2017. It is a communication platform that demonstrates the development achievements of the TCM industry, promotes the excellent traditional culture and the scientific and technological innovation of TCM.

2. Prescription Cave of Longmen Grottoes in Luoyang City

Longmen Grottoes (a world cultural heritage) in Luoyang are located in the south of the ancient capital of Luoyang and were first excavated during the emperor Xiaowen's reign in the Northern Wei dynasty. Among the numerous Buddhist statues in Longmen grottoes, the famous Longmen grottoes' prescription cave is the 3000-word prescription engraved on the cliff inside the cave.

The prescription cave is located on the western mountain cliff of Longmen Grottoes in Luoyang. There are 140 prescriptions in the cave in the north and south cliffs, 65 of which consist of complete characters and more than 40 cases of treatment. There are 117 prescriptions for herbal treatment and 23 prescriptions for moxibustion treatment, including nearly 40 kinds of diseases such as malaria, vomiting and nausea, abscess effusion of the back, lacquer sore, plague, jaundice, five stranguries, cholera, red and white dysentery, fish bones stuck in the throat and vomiting, etc., involving the internal medicine, surgery, gynecology, pediatrics,

2. 洛阳龙门石窟药方洞

洛阳龙门石窟（世界文化遗产）地处古都洛阳以南，始开凿于北魏孝文帝年间。在龙门众多的石龛石窟佛教造像中，引人瞩目的是镌刻在洞内石壁上长达3000字的药方，这就是有名的龙门石窟药方洞。

药方洞位于洛阳龙门西山窟群崖壁上，洞内南北石壁现存药方140首，文字完整的有65首，治疗病名达40余例。药物治疗方117首，灸法治疗方23首，治疗疾病包括疟疾、呕吐反胃、发背、漆疮、瘟疫、黄疸、五淋、霍乱、赤白痢疾、鱼骨鲠喉、呕哕等近40种疾病，涉及内、外、妇、儿、肿瘤等多科。药方洞不仅展现了辉煌的中华文化艺术宝库的风采，也承载了漫漫中医药史中浓重的一笔。

洛阳龙门药方洞所刻药方在唐代已传入日本，为日本医家所尊崇，将其称为“龙门方”。

3. 汤阴扁鹊庙及艾园

艾草是常用的中药材，与中国人的生活息息相关。在古代，河南汤

药方洞
Prescription Cave

ontology and other specialities. The prescription cave not only shows the elegant demeanour of the splendid Chinese culture and art treasure house, but also keeps an important record in the long history of TCM.

The prescriptions carved in Luoyang Longmen Prescription Cave were introduced to Japan in the Tang dynasty and honored by Japanese doctors, calling it "Longmen Prescriptions".

3. Bianque Temple and the Mugwort Garden in Tangyin County

The mugwort is not only a common Chinese herbal medicine, but also closely related to the life of Chinese people. In ancient times, the mugwort was produced in the Mugwort garden of the Bianque temple in Fudao village of Henan province.

Fudao Village, located in the southeast of Tangyin county of Anyang city, is called Fudao township presently. It is said that Bianque was stabbed here after falling into an ambush, so the place was called "Fu Dao (a road with ambush)". After Bianque's assassination, the local villagers remembered Bianque's merits and built a memorial hall for him, offering sacrifices to him, which was the origin of the Bianque Temple in Tangyin county. According to *Tangyin Xianzhi* (*Records of Tangyin County*), there were hundreds of acres of mugwort next to the Bianque Temple, known as "the Mugwort Garden." In the Ming dynasty, the mugwort beside the Bianque Tomb was honored as "Xian'ai (magical mugwort)" and was listed as a tribute in the imperial court.

After thousands of years of war and turmoil, the mugwort garden beside Bianque's tomb is no longer what it used to be. In 1988, the Tangyin county government repaired the Bianque Tomb and rebuilt the Mugwort Garden at the original site to plant mugworts.

4. Chrysanthemum Altar in Nanyang City

Chrysanthemum is a famous flower in China, and it is also a commonly used medicinal. Chrysanthemum is a treasure. Henan has an indissoluble bond with chrysanthemum. In addition to the "Bianju (chrysanthemums in Kaifeng city)" and "Huaiju (chrysanthemums in the Huai district)" which are famous all over the world today, there is also a "Liju (chrysanthemums in Li county)." According to records in Su Song's *Bencao Tujing* (*Illustrated Classic of Materia Medica*), "Chrysanthemums are produced along rivers and pools or in fields of Yongzhou, which are everywhere today, with products of the Chrysanthemum Pond in Nanyang being the best." The

阴伏道村扁鹊庙艾园所产艾草非常有名。

伏道村，在今安阳市汤阴县东南，今为伏道乡。据传当年扁鹊遇伏被刺于此，故此地得名“伏道”。扁鹊遇刺后，当地村民感念扁鹊功德，为之建墓立祠，四时祭祀，绵延至今，这就是汤阴扁鹊庙的由来。据《汤阴县志》记载，扁鹊庙旁旧有艾数百亩，号称“艾园”。到了明代，扁鹊墓所产艾草又被尊称为“仙艾”，名列朝廷贡品。

历经千年的战乱动荡，扁鹊墓艾园已非昔日模样。1988年汤阴县政府对扁鹊墓进行了修复，并在原址复建艾园，种植艾草。

4. 南阳菊坛

菊花是中国的名花，也是常用的药物，菊花一身都是宝。河南与菊花有着不解之缘，除了今日扬名四海的“汴菊”“怀菊”，更有一种“郦菊”。宋·苏颂《本草图经》载：“菊花生雍州川泽及田野，今处处有之，以南阳菊潭者为佳。”苏颂所提到的菊潭，即在今河南省南阳市西峡县菊花山，此地既是菊潭所在，也是“郦菊”的产地。

扁鹊庙
Bianque Temple

chrysanthemum pool mentioned by Su Song is now in the chrysanthemum mountain in Xixia county of Nanyang city in Henan province, where the chrysanthemum pool is located and where "chrysanthemums of the Li county" are produced.

Ju Tan (chrysanthemum pool) is short for Juhua Tan (chrysanthemum flower pool), also known as the chrysanthemum spring. In history, the pond was once as clear as mirror. The water was very sweet and the chrysanthemums on the mountain were reflected on the surface. The scenery was beautiful. Because the chrysanthemums in the valley fell into the pond and nourished the water all year round, the pond water began to have a medicinal property. It was called Ju Tan (chrysanthemum pond) in history. The surrounding village was a famous longevity town in ancient times. Li county, set by King Zhaoxiang of the Qin dynasty, later belonged to Neixiang county of Nanyang county (the present Nanyang region), was divided into Neixiang county and Xixia county after the founding of the People's Republic of China. Because of the early records of chrysanthemum in ancient times, it has the honorable name of "the chrysanthemum's hometown". Li Ju (chrysanthemums in the Li county) was named after the Li county.

Although not many people know Li Ju and Ju Tan today, there has been a lot of praises in ancient books. Li Ju and Ju Tan were recorded in Ying Shao's *Fengsu Tongyi* (*General Discussions of Customs*) of the Later Han dynasty, Ge Hong's *Baopuzi* of the Jin dynasty, Li Daoyuan's *Shuijing Zhu* (*Commentary on the Water ways Classic*) of the Northern Wei dynasty, and Li Shizhen's *Bencao Gangmu* of the Ming dynasty.

Many scholars and literati have written wonderful poems to praise Ju Tan and Li Ju, such as: "White chrysanthemums of the Nanyang city have a lot of benefits, thus many longevous people live along the chrysanthemum pond." [*Wuyue Yuanfu Xian Baiju* (*A Garden Farmer Presenting White Chrysanthemums in May*), written by Suzhe of the Song dynasty]; "Nanyang chrysanthemum water feeds many longevous people, which is a kind of flower to prolong life." [*Yong Ganju* (*Chanting the Sweet chrysanthemum*), written by Zheng Banqiao of the Qing dynasty]

After the Ming and Qing dynasties, the pond in the chrysanthemum mountain was blocked, and chrysanthemums in the mountain decreased, being not so flourishing as before.

The Chrysanthemum Mountain and Chrysanthemum Lake have obvious

菊潭是菊花潭的简称，又名菊泉。历史上曾潭清可鉴，水极甘馨，山上菊花影映其中，风景秀丽。因谷上菊花堕其中，常年滋液，潭水具有药用功能，史称菊潭。周围村庄是古代著名的长寿之乡。郦县，秦昭襄王所置，后皆属南阳郡（今南阳地区）内乡县，1949 年后被划分为内乡县与西峡县。因古代早有种菊的记载，故有“菊花故乡”之誉。郦菊，因郦县而得名。

今人虽少有知郦菊与菊潭者，但历代典籍却不乏推崇之词。后汉应劭《风俗通义》、晋代葛洪《抱朴子》、北魏郦道元《水经注》、明代李时珍《本草纲目》等专著，均有郦菊与菊潭的相关记载。

众多文人墨客更是留下了称颂菊潭与郦菊的佳句，如：“南阳白菊有奇功，潭上居人多老翁”（宋·苏辙《五月园夫献白菊》），“南阳菊水多耆旧，此是延年一种花”（清·郑板桥《咏甘菊》）。

明清以后，菊花山碧潭淤塞，山菊敛迹，已无复当年盛景。

菊花山、菊潭地域优势非常明显，它逶迤于 800 里伏牛山中，而今

菊潭

Ju Tan (Chrysanthemum Pond)

regional advantages. They stretch around 800 miles in Funiu mountain and now have a convenient transportation environment. Neixiang county, 25 kilometers apart, has a famous plaque of "Jutan Guzhi (ancient chrysanthemum pond)," reflecting the ancient beauty of the pond. Known as the miracle of the world, the dinosaur egg fossils in Xixia city, the dinosaur ruins park in Danshui town, which is famous overseas, and the endless kiwifruit forest are not far from the chrysanthemum mountain and the chrysanthemum pond. We should recreate the beauty of the chrysanthemum pond, reconstruct the culture of the chrysanthemum pond, and turn these unique cultural resources into cultural and tourist resorts.

5. Bronze Statue of Acupuncture and Moxibustion in the Northern Song Dynasty

On January 18, 2017 in Geneva, Switzerland, President Xi Jinping presented a bronze statue of acupuncture and moxibustion to the World Health Organization (WHO). The bronze sculpture, covered with acupuncture points, immediately attracted the world's attention. Presenting acupuncture bronze as a national gift to the WHO also implies giving the wisdom of Chinese civilization to the world. The bronze statue of acupuncture and moxibustion is a symbol of TCM and has a deep historical origin. It first appeared in the Song dynasty nearly one thousand years ago.

The bronze statue of acupuncture and moxibustion in the Tiansheng reign of the Northern Song dynasty was designed by Wang Weiyi, built up by craftsmen organized by the government of Song in 1027 A.D.. The bronze statue of acupuncture and moxibustion in the Tiansheng reign was the earliest bronze man of acupuncture and moxibustion in China and even in the world. It created the world's precedent of using bronze man as a human body model for acupuncture and moxibustion teaching and has attracted great attention at home and abroad.

Wang Weiyi, or Weide (roughly 987 A.D. to 1067 A.D.), an acupuncture doctor in the Northern Song dynasty, served as the medical officer during the reign of Ren emperor and Ying emperor of the Song dynasty. In the fourth year of the Tiansheng reign (1026 A.D.), The emperor ordered Wang Weiyi to collect the old news, correct the mistakes, and revise the acupuncture works. He drew the front and side views of the human body according to the human figure, marked the precise position of the acupoints, searched for ancient and modern clinical experiences, pooled the theory of acupuncture and moxibustion, and compiled 3 volumes of the *Tongren Shuxue*

交通便利。相距 25 公里的内乡县衙，至今遗有著名的“菊潭古治”匾牌，传播着菊潭美景的古老信息。被誉为“世界奇迹”的西峡恐龙蛋化石群、名扬海外的丹水镇恐龙遗迹园、一望无际的猕猴桃林，都与菊花山、菊潭相距不远。再造菊潭美景，重构菊潭文化，让这些得天独厚的文化资源成为文化旅游胜地是当务之急。

5. 北宋针灸铜人塑像

2017 年 1 月 18 日于瑞士日内瓦，国家主席习近平向世界卫生组织赠送针灸铜人雕塑。这个浑身布满穴位的铜人雕塑，顿时吸引了世界目光。将针灸铜人作为国礼送给世界卫生组织，这也寓意着把中华文明智慧送给全球。针灸铜人是中医药的象征，历史渊源很深，最早出现在近千年的大宋年间。

北宋天圣针灸铜人是在北宋天圣年间，由王维一负责设计，宋政府组织全国能工巧匠进行铸造，于 1027 年铸成的两具针灸铜人。天圣针灸铜人是中国乃至世界上最早铸成的针灸铜人，它开创了世界上用铜人作为人体模型进行针灸教学的先河，在海内外引起极大关注。

王惟一，或名惟德（约 987—1067 年），北宋针灸医家，任宋仁宗、宋英宗两朝医官。天圣四年（1026 年），王惟一奉皇帝命令，纂集旧闻，订正谬误，考订针灸著作。他按人形绘制人体正面、侧面图，标明腧穴的精确位置，并搜采古今临床经验，汇集诸家针灸理论，编成《铜人腧穴针灸图经》3 卷，共载腧穴 354 个，采用经络和部位相结合的腧穴排列方法，既使人了解经络系统，又便于临症取穴。并铸造两具针灸铜人，一具放在朝廷医官院，用于学医者观摩练习之用；另一具放置在京城大相国寺的仁济殿，供百姓前来参观。体现了当时高超的人体美学和铸造工艺。

针灸铜人自铸成之后，其命运坎坷，历经沧桑。元代至元年间 (1264–1294 年)，由于元朝定都北京，将宋针灸铜人从河南开封移至北京。此时宋铜人已经历 200 来个寒暑，其形象已经昏暗，穴名或已不清，并有缺损者。至公元 1265 年，曾请尼伯尔匠人阿尼哥对针灸铜人进行修整。经过修复后，

*Zhenjiu Tujing*, with a total of 354 acupoints. The acupoint arrangement method with the combination of meridians and locations not only helps people understand the meridian system, but also is convenient for selecting acupoints. Two more bronze acupuncture and moxibustion figures were cast, one of which was placed in the medical officer's hospital in the imperial court to be used for the observation and practice of medical practitioners. The other was placed in the Renji Hall in the Daxiangguo temple in the capital city for people to visit. It reflects the superb human body aesthetics and casting technology at that time.

After being cast, the bronze statue had a bumpy fate and experienced vicissitudes. During the Zhiyuan reign of the Yuan dynasty (1264 A.D. – 1294 A.D.), the bronze man was moved from Kaifeng city of Henan province to Beijing due to the capital movement of the Yuan dynasty. At that time, the bronze statue in the Song dynasty had been more than 200 years old. Its color was becoming dim, and the names of some acupuncture points were not clear or visible. By 1265 A.D., the Nepalese craftsman Anigo was asked to repair the bronze statue. After the restoration, the image of the statue became new again.

After the restoration of the bronze statue in the Song dynasty, after nearly 200 years, in the eighth year of the Zhengtong reign in the Ming dynasty (1443 A.D.), Zhu Qizhen, Ying emperor of the Ming dynasty, found the holes and meridians of the bronze statue dim and indistinguishable. He then organized gold craftsmen to imitate the model and make a new one. The original bronze statue of the Northern Song dynasty has been lost.

After the production of the bronze statue in the Tiansheng reign of the Northern Song dynasty, there have been bronze statues made in all generations. During the Jiajing era of the Ming dynasty (1522 A.D. -1566 A.D.), the acupuncturist Gao Wu cast bronze statues with the shape of a man, a woman and a child respectively. In 1742 A.D., the Qing government ordered Wu Qian to compile the *Yizong Jinjian* (*Golden Mirror of the Medical Ancestors*). In order to award the chief editors, a number of small bronze statues were built and presented to them for collection. Now there is a statue in the medical history museum at Shanghai University of Traditional Chinese Medicine. During the reign of emperor Guangxu of the Qing dynasty, after the Eight-Power Allied Forces entered Beijing, the bronze statue of the Ming dynasty, stored in the imperial hospital, was taken away by the

针灸铜人

Bronze Statue of Acupuncture and Moxibustion

其形象焕然一新。

经此修复的宋针灸铜人，又经近 200 年至明代正统八年（1443 年），明英宗朱祁镇见铜人之孔穴经络已昏暗难辨，组织金工范铜仿作。而北宋铜人原件遂被遗弃，下落不明。

自北宋天圣铜人之后，历代均有铜人制作。明嘉靖年间（1522 ~ 1566 年），针灸学家高武铸造男、女、儿童形状的针灸铜人各一具。1742 年，清政府令吴谦等编撰《医宗金鉴》，为奖励主要编撰者，曾铸造若干具小型针灸铜人发给他们收藏。现上海中医药大学医史博物馆即藏有一具。清代光绪年间，八国联军进京以后，存放在太医院的明正统仿宋铜人被列强抢走。后清代太医院为弥补空缺，又根据明代南京太医院珍藏的明堂图，结合北京太医院的明正统铜人体例，制作了清代光绪年间的铜人。现藏于国家博物院。国家主席习近平向世界卫生组织赠送的针灸铜人雕塑，就是仿清代光绪年间的这座针灸铜人。

现在韩国首尔市德昌宫秘苑的仁政殿车行阁，还保存有我国元明间

intruders. In order to make up for the vacancy, the imperial hospital of the Qing dynasty made the bronze statue during the reign of Emperor Guangxu of the Qing dynasty according to the Mingtang chart stored in Nanjing Imperial Hospital, in combination with the style of the bronze statue in the Ming dynasty recorded in Beijing Imperial Hospital. It is now stored in the National Museum. The bronze statue presented by President Xi Jinping to the WHO is a replica of the bronze statue in the Qing dynasty.

At present, there are still bronze statues of acupuncture and moxibustion made in the Yuan and Ming dynasties in Chexing Cabinet of the Renzheng Hall at the Secret Garden in Dechang Palace of Seoul in South Korea. In France, there is a small bronze statue of acupuncture and moxibustion from the Qing dynasty. In Russia, there is a collection of acupuncture bronze figures made in the eighth year during the Zhengtong reign of the Ming dynasty in China.

In 1958, Professor Li Ding and others collaborated with Shanghai Teaching Model Factory to create different kinds of acupuncture models, including "plaster statue", "plastic statue" and "glass statue", which took a new step for visual teaching. In 1978, Nanjing College of Traditional Chinese Medicine cooperated with the Chinese Academy of Traditional Chinese Medicine to develop a copy of the bronze statue in the Song dynasty, which is now stored in the Chinese Academy of Traditional Chinese Medicine. In 1987, He Baoyi, an official in the health bureau of Kaifeng city in Henan province, cast a copy of the bronze statue made in the Song dynasty, which is now being stored in the Daxiangguo temple of Kaifeng city. In 2009, Professor He Puren, a master of TCM, made a special kind of bronze statue and obtained a national patent.

Inspired by the bronze statue made in the Song dynasty, many medical equipment companies produced acupuncture models with different functions for teaching and medical treatment. The bronze statue has become the image symbol of acupuncture and moxibustion.

6. Yaowang Cave in Wuyan Mountain of Hebi City

Sunzhenren cave in Wuyan mountain of Hebi city is an earlier relic of Sun Simiao, a medicinal king in Henan province, built around the Song and Jin dynasties.

Wuyan mountain is the remnant of the Taihang mountains, which is named Wuyan mountain because it has five valleys, five caves and five peaks. According to

针灸铜人。法国人粟理氏保存有我国清朝乾隆时期的一座针灸小铜人。俄罗斯收藏有我国明代正统八年制作的针灸铜人。

1958 年李鼎教授等与上海教学模型厂合作，创制了不同种类的针灸经穴模型，有“石膏人”“塑料人”“玻璃人”等，为形象化教学迈出了新的一步；1978 年，南京中医学院和中国中医研究院合作，研制仿宋针灸铜人一具，现存中国中医研究院；1987 年，河南省开封市卫生局何保仪等根据历史文献，铸造仿宋针灸铜人一具，现存开封相国寺。2009 年，国医大师贺普仁教授制作了贺氏仿真针灸铜人，并取得了国家专利。

在宋代针灸铜人的启发下，许多医疗器械公司生产了不同功能的针灸模型，供教学医疗之用。铜人已成为针灸的形象标识。

6. 鹤壁五岩山药王洞

鹤壁五岩山孙真人洞，是河南较早的一处药王孙思邈遗迹，约建在宋金时期。

五岩山为太行山余脉，因山有五谷、五洞、五峰，故名五岩山。据明代《彰德府志・山川》记载：“五岩山在汤阴县西四十里，山有五谷，东南一大窟，孙真人室也。”在这里流传着孙思邈“针刺救虎”等许多神奇的传说。

五岩山孙真人洞，全长约 400 余米，为一天然崖洞。洞口面向东北，入口处建有拜棚，据壁间残存碑刻所记，约始建于金大定二十三年（1183 年），后于明弘治元年（1488 年）、清道光十年（1830 年）重修。

现存的拜棚，是在清代旧址上于20世纪80年代复建的，门额上有清道光年间题刻“大唐名医”四字，洞侧有石刻门联“胆欲大而心欲小，智欲圆而行欲方”。

孙真人洞正中供奉有孙思邈木雕神像，神像石座是明代旧物。

洞内尚残存有两处题记，可证孙真人洞悠远的历史。神像上方，即洞顶壁与南壁交界处，有石刻题字“崇宁元年（1102 年）九月初五日，游孙真人洞，相州人赵永昌”，字体浑朴苍劲。

*Zhangdefu Zhi* (*Records of the Zhangde Prefecture*), "Wuyan mountain is forty miles west of Tangyin county with five valleys in the mountain and a large cave in the southeast, which is Sunzhenren's room." There are many magical legends of Sun Simiao, such as "Acupuncture Saves Tiger".

Sunzhenren cave in Wuyan mountain, about 400-meter long, is a natural cliff cave. The entrance of the cave faces northeast, and a worshipping shed is built at the entrance. According to the inscriptions left in the walls, it was built around the 23rd year of Dading reign in the Jin dynasty (1183 A.D.), and then rebuilt in the first year of Hongzhi reign in the Ming dynasty (1488 A.D.) and the 10th year of Daoguang reign in the Qing dynasty (1830 A.D.).

The extant worship shed was rebuilt in the 1980s on the site of the Qing dynasty, with the inscription "Datang Mingyi (A Famous Doctor of the Tang dynasty)" on the forehead of the gate and the inscription on the side of the cave "Be bold and careful; be flexible and upright".

In the center of Sunzhenren's cave is a wooden statue of Sun Simiao, the stone base of which is an antique made in the Ming dynasty.

There are still two inscriptions in the cave, which reflects the long history of the cave. Above the statue, at the junction of the ceiling wall and the south wall, there is the inscription "Zhao Yongchang from Xiang zhou (an administrative division in former times) visited Sunzhenren cave on the 5th of the lunar September in the first year of Chongning reign (1102 A.D.)", written with a bold vigorous handwriting.

The inscriptions on the south wall were severely damaged, but most of them were distinguishable. The title "A Reconstruction Record of Sun Zhenren's Statue in Sumenjixian Cave" was inscribed with a signature "Weina, on the 23rd Year of Dading reign". "Chongning" is the title of Zhao Ji, Hui emperor in the Northern Song dynasty, which shows that Yaowang cave was already a place where scholars and writers rushed to worship as early as the Northern Song dynasty. "Weina" was the name of the monk official in charge of Buddhist affairs in the 23rd year of Dading reign in the Jin dynasty (1183 A.D.). This also shows people's strong belief of Sun Zhenren at that time. Wuyan mountain is not only rich in medicinal materials, but also an important part of Henan's "King of Medicine Culture".

7. The Birthplace of Chinese Taijiquan—Chenjiagou in the Wen County

Taijiquan originated from Chenjiagou of Wen county in Henan province, which

五岩山
Wuyan Mountain

南壁题刻，字迹残损严重，但大都依稀可辨。标题“苏门集仙洞重修孙真人像记”，落款“维那——大定二十三年岁次癸卯丙寅”。“崇宁”是北宋徽宗赵佶年号，这说明早在北宋时期，药王洞已经是文人墨客争相访古朝拜之处。“维那”为金代主管佛教事务的僧官名，时值金大定二十三年（1183年）。由此也可见当时信徒对孙真人的信仰程度。五岩山不仅药材资源丰富，也是河南“药王文化”的重要组成部分。

7. 中国太极拳发源地——温县陈家沟

太极拳发源于河南省温县陈家沟，至今已有300多年的历史。明朝末年，陈家沟人陈王廷根据祖传拳术，结合导引、吐纳和中医经络学说，创编一新的拳种，按阴阳转换之意取名太极拳，世称陈式太极拳。数百年来，已由陈氏一家的独得之秘，衍变出杨式、武式、吴式、孙式、和式等。太极拳是集技击、强体、健身、益智和修性为一体的独特的运动方式，蕴藏着东方哲学的深刻内涵。它将阴阳、动静、正反、有无、形神等对立统

has a history of more than 300 years. In the last years of the Ming dynasty, Chen Wangting of Chenjiagou, combined the ancestral boxing technique, with Daoyin (an ancient breathing exercises, a branch of Qigong), Tuna (a kind of breathing exercises) and the meridian theory of TCM, and a new type of boxing was created. It is what is known as Taijiquan according to the meaning of yin and yang conversion, and sometimes called Chen-style Taijiquan. For hundreds of years, it has been transformed from the secret of the Chen style to the Yang style, Wu (武， with a falling and rising tone in Chinese) style, Wu (吴， with a rising tone in Chinese) style, Sun style, and He style. Taijiquan is a unique movement that combines martial arts, body building, fitness, intelligence enhancement and cultivation. It contains the profound connotations of the eastern philosophy. It combines the philosophy of unity of opposites such as yin and yang, movement and rest, positive and negative, presence and absence, and form and spirit. Spiritual resources such as martial arts, medicine and art are combined into a new form of martial arts, strengthening physical fitness in the form of exercises conforming to the laws of human movement, and reflecting the vitality of the Chinese nation. It has caught worldwide attention.

The boxing theory of Taijiquan originates from the classics of traditional Chinese philosophy, medical skills, and martial arts, such as *Yi Jing*, *Huangdi Neijing*, *Huangting Jing* (*Huangting's Classic*), and *Jixiao Xinshu* (*A Book on the Art of War*, written by Qi Jiguang in the Ming dynasty). It has absorbed reasonable contents of Taoism, Confucianism, Buddhism and other philosophies during its development. Therefore, Taijiquan is called the "quintessence of the nation".

At present, Wen county has built more than 20 Taijiquan scenic spots and developed more than 30 military schools. In 2006, Taijiquan was included in the first batch of national intangible cultural heritage. In 2007, Wen county was officially named "the birthplace of Chinese Taijiquan" and "the research base of Chinese Taijiquan culture" by the Chinese Association of Martial Arts and the Folk Artists Association. In 2010, Wen county was jointly awarded the honorary title of "One of China's Top Ten Cultural Leisure Tourism Counties" by the World Overseas Chinese Association, the Chinese Culture Promotion Association and the International Leisure Economy Promotion Association. In 2011, Wen county was awarded the title of "Hometown of Chinese Martial Arts".

一的哲理和武学、医学、艺术等精神资源融入武术之中，以符合人体运动规律的演练形式强体健身，体现了中华民族生生不息的活力，受到了全世界的关爱。

太极拳拳理来源于《易经》《黄帝内经》《黄庭经》《纪效新书》（明·戚继光著）等中国传统哲学、医术、武术等经典著作，并在其长期的发展过程中又吸收了道、儒、释等文化的合理内容，故太极拳被称为“国粹”。

目前，温县已建成太极拳景点20多个，发展武校30余所。2006年，太极拳被列入首批国家级非物质文化遗产名录；2007年，温县被中国武术家协会、民间文艺家协会正式命名为“中国太极拳发源地”和“中国太极拳文化研究基地”；2010年，温县被世界华侨华人社团、中华文化促进会、国际休闲经济促进会联合授予“中国十大文化休闲旅游县”荣誉称号；2011年，温县被评为“中国武术之乡”。

陈家沟太极拳祖祠

The Ancestral Temple of Taijiquan in Chenjiagou

8. Botanist Wu Qijun's Hometown

In the late Qing dynasty, internal and external troubles were like "ten thousand horses stand mute (describing an atmosphere of political oppression)", but at that time there appeared a book that had a profound impact on traditional herbal science and later botany- Wu Qijun's *Zhiwu Mingshi Tukao.*

Wu Qijun, a native of Gushi county in Henan province, ranked the first during the imperial examination in the 22nd year of Jiaqing reign (1817 A.D.) in the Qing dynasty. During his official career, he has served in the Hanlin Academy, as a Xuezheng official in Jiangxi and Hubei provinces, as an assistant minister of the Ministry of Military Affairs, and as a governor of of Hunan, Hubei, Yunnan, Guizhou, Fujian and Shanxi provinces.

*Zhiwu Mingshi Tukao* consists of 38 volumes, recording 1,714 species of plants, with more than 1,700 attached drawings, divided into 12 categories, including grain, vegetable, mountain grass, grass, stone grass (including mosses), aquatic plants (including algae), creeping weed, aromatic grass, poisonous grass, flowers (including fungi), fruits, and wood. This is a monograph which specially records plants and reflects their medicinal value and biological characteristics. Some of the plants collected in this book are recorded for the first time in history, such as "Hezhangxiao" in Jiangxi province. Some are supplements to previously found plants, such as the "yam egg" in Shanxi. The book also corrects mistakes in the description of ancient herbal medicines. It has raised the traditional herbalism of our country to a new level and also had a profound impact on the world's botany.

After the publication of the *Zhiwu Mingshi Tukao* in the 28th year of Daoguang reign (1848 A.D.), it was widely praised at home and abroad.

The former residence of Wu Qijun (also known as Gongbao mansion) was built during the reign of Emperor Qianlong of the Qing dynasty. There were three gatehouses along the street, two wooden pillars in front of the gate, and a wooden square bucket on it. It was called "Fayue Door" and was the symbol of the official family. Inside the gate, there is a courtyard, which is divided into three residences: the east courtyard gate, the west courtyard gate and the main entrance. Currently, there are three reading buildings in the west of the west courtyard, named "Lüyun Veranda".

The former residence of Wu Qijun was originally larger than it is now. Now,

8. 植物学家吴其濬故里

清代后期，内忧外患，“万马齐喑”，而在这时却出现了一部对传统本草学乃至后世植物学产生了深远影响的著作——吴其濬的《植物名实图考》。

吴其濬，今河南固始县人，清嘉庆二十二年（1817年）丁丑科状元。一生宦游天下，先后历任翰林院修纂，江西、湖北学政，兵部侍郎，湖南、湖北、云南、贵州、福建、山西总督、巡抚等职。

《植物名实图考》，全书38卷，记载植物1714种，附图1700多幅，分谷、蔬、山草、隰草、石草（含苔藓类）、水草（含藻类）、蔓草、芳草、毒草、群芳（含菌类）、果、木等12大类。这是一部专门记载植物，又集中反映其药用价值及生物学特性的专著。该书所收植物中，有的是首次登录记载，如江西的“合掌消”；有的是对新近植物的补充辑录，如山西一带的“山药蛋”等。该书对历代本草的著录错误也时有纠正。把我国传统本草学提升到了一个全新的水平，也对世界植物学产生了深刻影响。

吴其濬故居

Former residence of Wu Qijun

there are only 16 rooms remaining on the upper and lower floors of the storehouse and the reading building left. The whole building has typical architectural characteristics of the Qing dynasty and has high research and protection value. In September 2000, the former residence was announced by the People's Government of Henan province as a provincial-level key cultural heritage protection unit.

9. The Hot Spring Pool and the Orange Well in Shangcheng County

The hot spring pool, the first spring in Dabie mountain, is known as the "Magic Spring Pool". As a natural hot spring, it is located at the foot of Lei mountain in Shangcheng county, with its back on the luxuriant forest and its body alongside the rippling waters of the Nianyu mountain lake. It not only can be used to bathe, but also has high medicinal value. Li Zhi, a famous thinker and poet in the Ming dynasty, once visited there, leaving a poem "Wash your heart in streams, and clean your feet in the hot spring pool". Wang Diao, the literati of the Qing dynasty, also had a poem: "It is known that the spring breeze at the bottom of the pool is warm, and the bathing place is full of people."

According to the records of *Shangcheng Xianzhi*, "The hot spring, 30 kilometers southwest, flows out of the stone shovel. The color is green, being hot like boiled water, used to cure skin diseases." Therefore, it is also known as the "Medicinal Spring."

The local villagers who lived in the springs established the "Tangkengdian City". In the 25th reign of emperor Qianlong of the Qing dynasty (1760 A.D.), emperor Qianlong once patrolled the hot spring pool and wrote "Tang Keng (Hot Spring Pool)" as a monument for it. During the Jiaqing reign of the Qing dynasty, the local government officially founded the "Hot Spring Academy" there.

It is said that when the army of Liu Bocheng and Deng Xiaoping went into the Dabie mountains for a thousand miles, the soldiers couldn't adapt to the local environment and suffered from skin diseases. Liu Bocheng and Deng Xiaoping heard that the hot springs were magical. They seized the Hot Spring Pool to help soldiers heal wounds. As a result, they were able to destroy the enemy' s crazy "encirclement and suppression".

"Orange Well" and "Fragrant Orange Well" are famous allusions in the field of TCM. According to *Shenxian Zhuan* (*Biography of the Immortals*), written by Ge Hong of the Jin dynasty, in Guiyang county (now Chenzhou city of Hunan

《植物名实图考》于道光二十八年（1848 年）刊印发行问世后，受到国内外的一致推崇。

吴其濬故居（又称“宫保第”）建于清乾隆年间。原沿街有门楼三间，门前有两根木柱，上面有一木方斗，称“阀阅门”，是世宦门第的标志。进大门后是天井院，分东院门、西院门和正门三个住宅，目前保留的就是西院内宅堂楼西的三间读书楼，名“绿云轩”。

吴其濬故居原规模很大，现仅存堂楼和读书楼上下两层共 16 间。整个建筑有典型的清代建筑特征，具有较高的研究保护价值。2000 年 9 月，故居被河南省人民政府公布为省级重点文物保护单位。

9. 商城汤泉池及橘井

汤泉池，大别山麓第一泉，有“神汤”之称。它地处商城县雷山脚下，背依林木郁翠的雷山，身傍碧波荡漾的鲇鱼山湖水，是一处天然温泉。不仅能洗浴，同时具有较高的药用价值。明代著名思想家、诗人李贽曾游览此处，留下了“洗心千涧水，濯足温泉宫”的诗句。清代文人王调也有诗曰：

苏仙石
Suxian Stone

province), before Su Xiangong became a fairy, he told his mother that there would be an epidemic next year, and the well water soaked with orange leaves can be used to treat the disease. The news was widely spread. Since then, "Orange Well" located in Chenzhou city of Hunan province has been well known. However, the Orange Well and Suxian Stone in Shangcheng county are not well-known.

In fact, there are two "Orange Wells" in China, one in Chenzhou city of Hunan province and another in Suxianshi township of Shangcheng county in the Dabie mountain. There is a mountain named Dasu mountain in the township. At the foot of the mountain, there are two stones standing opposite to each other, named "Suxian Stone". There are two deep footprints on the stones, and a thousand-year-old well 400 meters north, named "Orange Well". Su Xian announced to his mother that he could use the well water soaked with orange leaves to cure the disease. Similar stories are recorded in ancient books such as *Henan Tongzhi* (*General Records of Henan Province*), *Daqing Yitong Zhi* (*General Geographical Records*) *of Qing Dynasty* and *Guangzhou Zhi* (*Records of Guangzhou prefecture*).

There is a well-known legend of Suxian Stone: Su Dan, a native of Guiyang county in the Han dynasty, took his mother there to learn new skills. He built a house beside the river and lived there. One day, he stepped onto the stone, flew up to the heaven riding a fairy crane and became a fairy, leaving a pair of deep footprints on the stone. After he became a fairy, his mother used the well water soaked with orange leaves to cure diseases and saved countless people. The place to this day has been called "Suxian Stone" since the Han dynasty. There is also a well-known poem in this area: "Taizi peak lies in front of the Dasu mountain, with an ancient legend of Suxian. The immortal has gone by the yellow fairy crane, leaving footprints on the top of the mountain."

It can be seen that the "Orange Well" in the north of Shangcheng county has the same origin with the legend of the "Orange Well" in the south of Chenzhou city. It is all from the allusion that "Water in the orange well is fragrant". In Yufan village of Suxianshi township, there are also many ancient monuments such as "Dasu Mountain", "Suxian Stone", "Orange Well" and "Suxian Temple". Because the Suxianshi Township is located in the hinterland of Dabie Mountains, with mountains, rivers and beautiful forests, it has always been inconvenient for transportation. It has always been isolated like a fairyland, which was considered a

“共知池底春风暖，浴罢游人漫咏归。”

明嘉靖《商城县志》记载：“温泉，在西南三十公里，自石罅中流出，其色绿，其热如汤，人浴之可治疥癞。”故又有“药泉”之称。

当地乡民多依泉聚居，形成了万家辐辏的“汤坑店市”。清乾隆二十五年（1760 年），乾隆皇帝曾出巡汤泉池，御笔题书“汤坑”，并立碑志之。清嘉庆年间，地方官府曾在此创办“温泉书院”。

据传，当年刘邓大军千里跃进大别山后，战士水土不服，身生疥疮。刘、邓首长听说温泉神奇，专门派兵夺取了汤泉池，让广大战士洗浴疗伤，粉碎了敌人的疯狂“围剿”。

“橘井”“橘井泉香”是我国中医界著名的典故。东晋学者葛洪《神仙传》记：桂阳（今湖南郴州）人苏仙公成仙前，告其母明年有疫，可取橘叶井水以疗疫疾。好事者因传之。所以，一直以来，世人皆知“橘井”在湖南的郴州，却不知商城也有橘井和苏仙石。

其实，我国有两处“橘井”，一处在湖南郴州，一处在大别山区的商城县苏仙石乡。乡内有一山名大苏山。山下子安河边有双石对峙，名“苏仙石”，上有两个深深的足印。石北 400 米处有千年古井，名“橘井”。苏仙公告其母，可取橘叶井水以疗疫疾的故事，《河南通志》《大清一统志》《光州志》等古籍中均有类似记载。

当地有个妇孺皆知的传说：汉代桂阳人苏耽携母至此拜师学艺，于河边结庐而居，后踏石跨鹤飞升而去，石上留下一对深深的足迹。苏仙飞升后，其母用井水橘叶疗疫，救人无数。该石从汉代以后便因此而被命名为“苏仙石”，并沿用至今。当地还流传有一首耳熟能详的诗：“大苏山前太子尖，相传此地有苏仙；仙人已乘黄鹤去，留下足迹在山巅。”

可见商城之北“橘井”与郴州之南“橘井”的传说同根同源，皆出自《神仙传》“橘井泉香”典故。且在苏仙石乡境内的喻畈村也遗存有“大苏山”“苏仙石”“橘井”“苏仙寺”等众多古迹。因苏仙石乡位于大别山腹地，山河纵横，林海绵延，历来交通不便，似世外仙境，是古人隐居藏身修炼的

good place to hide and practice seclusion, so the northern "Orange Well" was not known to outsiders before.

10. Famous Museums of TCM in Henan Province

Henan Museum of TCM is located in Henan University of Chinese Medicine and became open to the public in June 2015, including the Medical History Museum, the Zhongjing Pavilion, the Chinese Medicine Museum, and the School History Museum. The museums are integrated but independent of each other. There are also independent venues such as the Human Science Museum, Medical Ethics Museum, Source of TCM, Light of Basic Medicine and Teleconsultation Center. There is also a corridor culture: Medicinals' Garden, formulas' Garden, Famous Doctors' Painting Exhibition Hall, Pharmaceutical Enterprise Culture Exhibition Hall, TCM Culture Exhibition Hall, the Exhibition Hall of the Central Plains' Culture, etc. It contains rich elements of traditional culture and filled with different styles from different periods of history. The related peripheral cultural landscapes include: South Gate Relief, Sculpture and Inscription in the Zhongjing Culture Square, Houmu Wuding (a tripod statue), Shennong Mountain Landscape and Li Shizhen Sculpture. Facing the Henan Museum of TCM, the Chinese Medicine Botanical Garden was built, covering an area of 138 mu (about 92,000 square meters). There are about 500 kinds of medicinal planted in the park.

Reliefs on the east and west sides of the south gate of the school were named "Heluo Xuri (The Rising Sun in the Heluo District)" and "Songshan Xiaoyue (The Moon Before Dawn in the Song Mountain)" respectively, meaning that mountains and rivers are together with TCM culture, and that the sun and moon shine with TCM culture. The content of the relief picture reflects the concept of yin-yang opposition, coordination and unity of thinking in TCM. Inside the gate, there is a statue of the medical sage Zhongjing. The back of the sculpture displays the life of Zhongjing. The back of the wall is covered with the inscription of the preface of the *Shanghan Zabing Lun*. The whole campus combines elements of China, Central Plains and TCM through venue construction, cultural landscape and the street names. It is a profound and colorful TCM culture of Henan province, and has become a beautiful poster for Henan TCM. It is widely welcomed by people from all walks of life.

Dasong Museum of TCM Culture is located on the sixth floor of the

佳地，故北“橘井”不为外人知晓。

10. 河南著名的中医药博物馆

河南中医药博物馆位于河南中医药大学内，于 2015 年 6 月开馆，包括医史馆、仲景馆、中药馆、校史馆等。各馆相互独立又浑然一体。另有人体科学馆、医德馆、中医源、基础医学之光、远程会诊中心等独立场馆。还有廊道文化：百药苑、百方苑、名医画传展厅、药企文化展厅、中医药文化展厅、中原文化展厅等。既包含传统文化的丰富元素，又充满了时代气息。配套的外围文化景观有：南大门浮雕、仲景文化广场雕塑及碑刻、后母戊鼎、神农山景观、李时珍雕塑等。在河南中医药博物馆对面建有中药植物园，占地面积 138 亩（约 9.2 万平方米）。园内分区种植各类药用植物 500 种左右。

学校南大门东西两侧浮雕，分别取名“河洛旭日”“嵩山晓月”，意为山河与中医药文化同在，日月与中医药文化同辉；浮雕画面内容，体现了中医学思维的阴阳对立又协调统一的理念。进入大门，映入眼帘的是医圣仲景塑像，后侧是展示仲景生平的浮雕影壁墙，墙背面是《伤寒杂病论·序》碑刻，融合了中国、中原、中医元素。整个校园从场馆建设、文化景观到道路命名等，都体现了中医药文化的内涵，向公众展示了河南博大精深、绚丽多彩的中医药文化，已成为河南中医药一张亮丽的名片，受到各界人士的普遍欢迎。

大宋中医药文化博物馆坐落在七朝古都开封的开封市中医院门诊大楼第六层，是一座综合性中医药博物馆。博物馆于2013年3月26日开馆，目前建筑面积约为1800$m^2$，陈列展出面积约980$m^2$。展览厅以中医药文化的发展为主线布展，共分为“朝尚医药　专设机构”“针灸大成　空前繁荣”“汇聚方药　济世惠民”“分科论病　承古创新”“文化繁荣　儒医辈出”“继承创新　续写辉煌”六大部分。在馆内特设宋代名医馆，针灸铜人文化墙，绘宋代制药、问诊等实景7处，有动植物中药标本数十件，陈列实物百余种。并挖掘了一些与宋代医药发展相关，且有

Outpatient Building of Kaifeng Chinese Medicine Hospital in Kaifeng city, the capital of seven dynasties, and is a comprehensive TCM museum. The museum opened on March 26, 2013. The current construction area is about 1,800 square meters, and the exhibition area is about 980 square meters. The exhibition hall takes the development of TCM culture as its main line, and is divided into six parts: "Worshipping the medical science and setting specialized institutions", "unprecedented prosperity of acupuncture and moxibustion", " bringing prescriptions and medicines together to benefit the people", "Treating diseases according to medical divisions and inheriting ancient knowledge to make innovations", "Culture prosperity producing scholar-physicians" and "inheriting and making innovations to rewrite a brilliant history". The museum exhibits the famous doctors in the Song dynasty, the culture wall of the bronze statue of acupuncture and moxibustion, and paintings of seven real scenes of the Song dynasty, such as the pharmaceutical production and interrogation examination, with dozens of specimens of the animals and plants and more than 100 kinds of objects. The museum also excavated some socially influential allusions and legends related to the development of medicine in the Song dynasty.

Dasong Museum of TCM reproduces the brilliant development history of TCM in the Song dynasty, and is named "National Base of TCM Culture Publicity and Education" by the State Administration of TCM.

As early as 2002, the People's Government of Dengzhou city allocated special funds and relied on Dengzhou Chinese Medicine Hospital to build the "Zhang Zhongjing Museum" with an exhibition area of 400 square meters. On October 12, 2011, the State Administration of TCM established the Zhangzhongjing Exhibition Hall in Dengzhou city as the construction unit of the national TCM culture publicity and education base. From the museum to the exhibition hall, the scale has been continuously expanded and the content has become more abundant. At present, the exhibition hall of this antique building has a total of 4 floors with a designed exhibition area of 18,000 square meters. The museum is divided into seven exhibition areas, exhibiting the medical sage Zhang Zhongjing, the TCM history, modern TCM, the development of Dengzhou's TCM, the famous old TCM doctors in Dengzhou city, health preservation, calligraphy and painting. The contents and various versions *of Shanghan Lun* (*Treatise on Febrile Diseases*) and *Jingui Yaolüe*

一定社会影响的典故传说。

大宋中医药文化博物馆再现大宋中医药灿烂辉煌的发展历史，被国家中医药管理局命名为“全国中医药文化宣传教育基地”。

早在2002年，邓州市人民政府就划拨专款，依托邓州市中医院，建成了展区面积400平方米的“张仲景博物馆”。2011年10月12日，国家中医药管理局下文，将邓州市张仲景展览馆确定为全国中医药文化宣传教育基地建设单位，从博物馆到展览馆，规模不断扩大，内涵愈加丰富。目前，这座仿古建筑的展览馆共4层，设计展出面积18000平方米。馆内分医圣张仲景、中医药发展史、蓬勃发展的现代中医、邓州市中医药发展、邓州市名老中医、养生保健、书画墨宝7个展区。展示了《伤寒论》和《金匮要略》的内容及各种版本，用南阳独山玉雕刻的张仲景生平组画，还展示了历经曲折的百年中医等多种内容，为张仲景的故里增添了异彩。

早在2005年，仲景宛西制药就以仲景品牌为中心，围绕“中医药文化体验、中医药科普教育、中医药养生健康”三大主题，立足南阳，先后投入数亿元，建成了中药现代化生产线、中药材标准化生产基地、中医药博物馆等基础设施。随之，仲景宛西制药中华医圣苑、仲景巨型雕像、医圣山文化广场、仲景百草园等设施亮相。每年农历正月十八，社会各界数万人齐聚中华医圣苑，拜祭仲景，自此成为仲景宛西制药一个标志性文化品牌。

仲景宛西制药推出了以中医药文化体验为主题的旅游项目，包含现代化生产线、图片展、仲景文化广场、紫铜浮雕墙、南阳张仲景中医药治未病体验中心、仲景大厨房公司、大药房国医馆、南阳张仲景医院中医药博物馆、南阳张仲景中药材公司中药材标本馆、仲景百草园、山茱萸生态基地等景点，集中医药文化体验、科普教育、养生于一体，成为宣传中医药文化的重要基地。

马同长天然药物收藏馆坐落在安阳职业技术学院医药卫生学院。在这个收藏馆里，摆放着两株将近1米长的千年野生灵芝王、重10千克的

(*Synopsis of the Golden Chamber*) are displayed. The paintings of Zhang Zhongjing, a sculpture made of Dushan jade in Nanyang province, also display a variety of contents such as the century-old TCM practitioners who have experienced twists and turns. It provides an extraordinary splendor to Zhang Zhongjing's hometown.

As early as 2005, Zhongjing Wanxi Pharmaceutical took Zhongjing brand as the center, based on the three major themes of "TCM cultural experience, TCM popular science education and TCM health preservation". They invested hundreds of millions of yuan to build the infrastructure in Nanyang such as the modern production line and standardized production base of Chinese herbs, TCM museum, etc. After that, other facilities of Zhongjing Wanxi Pharmaceuticals, such as China Medical Sage Garden, Zhongjing's Giant Statue, Medical Sage Mountain Cultural Square and Zhongjing Medicinal Garden were established. On the 18th of the first month of the lunar year, thousands of people from all walks of life gather in the Chinese Medical Sage Garden to worship Zhongjing. Since then, it has become a significant cultural brand of Zhongjing Wanxi Pharmaceuticals.

Zhongjing Wanxi Pharmaceutical has launched a tourism project with the theme of TCM culture experience, including modern production line, photo exhibition, Zhongjing Cultural Square, copper relief wall, Nanyang Zhang Zhongjing Chinese Medicine Preventative Treatment Center, Zhongjing Big Kitchen Company, Large Pharmacy of the National Medical Center, Chinese Medicine Museum of the Nanyang Zhang Zhongjing Hospital, Chinese Herbal Medicine Herbarium of the Nanyang Zhang Zhongjing Chinese Herbal Medicine Company, Zhongjing Herb Garden, and the Hawthorn Ecological Base. They focus on the medical culture experience, popular science education, and health preservation, which has become an important publicity base of the TCM culture.

Ma Tongchang's Collection of the Natural Medicinals is located in the School of Medicine and Health in Anyang Vocational and Technical College. In this collection, there are two nearly one-meter-long thousand-year-old wild Lingzhi (glossy ganoderma) kings, Rougui (cinnamon) weighing 10 kilograms, a huge honeycomb 60 centimeters tall, a one-meter-long turtle specimen, and a giant agarwood trunk standing against the ceiling, which is more than 3 meters high. There are also Tibetan mushrooms, mermaid bones, hundreds of colour photos of medicinal plants and animals used in TCM, and the medicine of other nationalities,

肉桂、高 60 厘米的特大蜂房、1 米多长的海龟标本、3 米多高已抵住天花板的巨型沉香树干，有西藏雪灵、美人鱼骨，有汉药、苗药、蒙药、壮药等数百幅药用动植物彩照，还有数千件动植物标本等等。这里收藏的一大批珍奇药材，吸引着参观者的眼球，让众人大开眼界，无不感到震撼。

马同长先生在深入研究脉管炎的同时，对中药材的研究也非常痴迷。为淘得药中珍品，他的足迹踏遍了祖国的奇山名川、雪域高原、茫茫草场。这些珍奇药材，就是多年来他历尽艰辛，一点一点收藏的。

such as Miao, Mongolian and Zhuang nationality, and several thousand specimens of animals and plants. A large number of rare medicinal materials collected here have attracted the attention of visitors and enriched their horizons.

While studying vasculitis in depth, Mr. Ma Tongchang is also fascinated with the study of Chinese herbal medicines. In order to find out the treasures of medicine, he has traveled all over the country, including famous mountains, rivers, snowy plateaus and vast pastures. These rare medicinal materials have been gradually collected by him through many years of hard work.

第七章

# 河南中医药文化国际传播与交流

Chapter Ⅶ

# International Communication and Exchange of TCM Culture in Henan

目前，中医药已传播到183个国家和地区。中国已同外国政府、地区主管机构和国际组织签署了86个中医药合作协议。世界卫生组织中103个会员国认可使用针灸，其中29个设立了传统医学的法律法规，18个将针灸纳入医疗保险体系。中医针灸列入联合国教科文组织《人类非物质文化遗产代表作名录》，《本草纲目》和《黄帝内经》列入《世界记忆名录》。国际标准化组织（ISO）成立中医药技术委员会（ISO/TC249），并陆续制定颁布46个中医药国际标准。以中医药为代表的传统医学首次纳入世界卫生组织国际疾病分类代码（ICD-11），中药逐步进入国际医药体系，已在俄罗斯、古巴、越南、新加坡和阿联酋等国以药品形式注册。中医药作为国际医学体系的重要组成部分，正为促进人类健康发挥积极作用。

河南中医药国际交往历史悠久，日趋频繁。近年来，河南中医药积极融入中医药世界发展的大格局中，在国际舞台上取得长足发展，开展国际合作与交流的国家越来越多，合作的领域不断扩大，中医药已成为河南与世界各国开展人文交流、促进东西方文明交流互鉴的重要内容，成为河南与相关国家和地区共同维护人民健康、增进人类福祉、建设人类命运共同体的重要载体。

## 一、河南中医药与世界各国的文化交流源远流长

河南中医药与世界各国的文化交流历史悠久。早在秦朝时，中国的医药文化已传到日本，相传方士徐福精于医药和炼丹，被日本人尊为“司药神”。西汉时张骞两次出使西域，拓宽了中原与西北、西南边疆的经济文化渠道，形成了驰名中外的“丝绸之路”。东汉班超继张骞之后治理西域，保持了丝绸之路的畅通。在同西域进行政治、文化交流活动的同时，也进行了医药的交流。他们将中原先进的医药知识介绍到西域，同时又把西域的医药知识带回中原。如西域的特产，石榴、葡萄、胡麻、核桃等，先后引进了中原。中医药传入越南后，越南的象牙、珍珠、玳瑁、犀角、

At present, TCM has been spread to 183 countries. China has signed 86 agreements on TCM with foreign governments, regional authorities, and international organizations. Among WHO member states, 103 have approved the use of acupuncture, 29 have established laws and regulations regarding TCM, and 18 have incorporated acupuncture into their medical insurance system. Acupuncture and moxibustion of TCM has been listed in *Representative List of the Intangible Cultural Heritage of Humanity* of United Nations Educational Scientific and Culture Organization (UNESCO). *Bencao Gangmu and Huangdi Neijing* have been enlisted into *Memory of the World Register*. The International Organization for Standardization (ISO) has established the Technical Committee of Traditional Chinese Medicine (ISO/TC249), and has formulated and promulgated more than 46 international standards of TCM. Chinese language represented by TCM has been first incorporated into the International Classification of Diseases Code (ICD-11) of the WHO. TCM has gradually entered the international medical system. It has been registered in Russia, Cuba, Vietnam, Singapore, and the United Arab Emirates in the form of medicinal. As an important part of the international medical system, TCM is playing an active role in promoting human health.

The international exchange of TCM in Henan has a long history and is becoming more frequent. In recent years, Henan's TCM has been actively integrated into the development of the world of TCM, and has made a great progress on the international stage. More and more countries have carried out international cooperation and exchange, and the fields of cooperation have been expanding. Henan's TCM has become the focus of carrying out cultural exchange with other nations and promoting exchange and mutual learning between with Western nations. It is important for Henan to jointly safeguard people's health, promote human welfare, and build a community of human destiny with other related countries and regions.

## Ⅰ. Henan TCM and Countries of the World: a Long History of Cultural Exchanges

As early as in the Qin dynasty, TCM culture had already spread to Japan. According to legend, Xu Fu, an alchemist, was skilled in medicine and alchemy, and

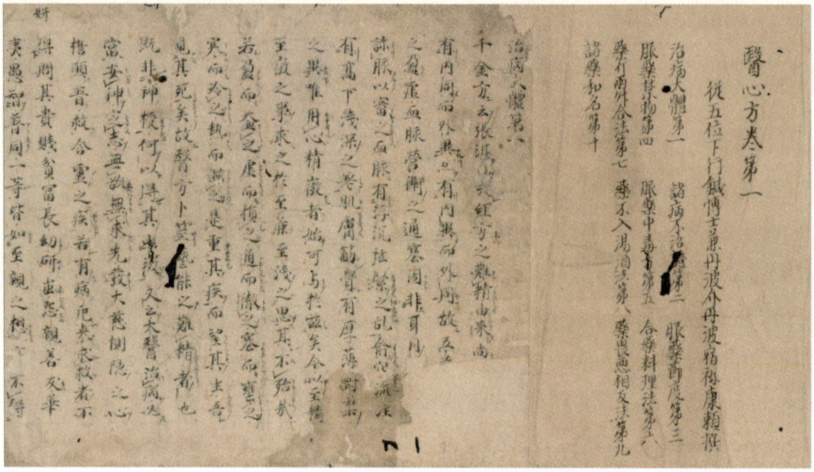
醫心方卷第一
從五位下行鍼博士兼丹波介丹波宿祢康頼撰

《医心方》
*Ishinpo*

龙眼、槟榔、菖蒲、薏米也进入中原。在我国第一部本草学专著《神农本草经》中，就记载有西域的药材。

汉代时，中国与印度的交往也早已开始，印度古代医药与佛教关系密切，汉明帝时印度僧人聂摩腾、竺法兰白马驮经书到河南洛阳白马寺，在皇家寺院翻译了佛经中的有关医药卫生知识，逐步融入中医，成为中医防病治病的组成部分。隋唐时期，出生于河南偃师县的僧人玄奘在印度取经，他的《大唐西域记》记载了印度医学随着佛教进入中原的线索，对中印两国的药物进行了比较。玄奘的活动足迹，足以说明中印、中尼、中巴之间的医药交流在唐代已趋于繁荣。

唐代中日医学交流已很广泛。洛阳龙门药方洞所刻药方在唐代已传入日本，为日本医家所尊崇。公元984年，日本古代医学家丹波康赖在其编著的《医心方》一书中，就收录了龙门石刻药方95例，并将其称之为“龙门方”。

张仲景著作早在日本平安时期（794 ~ 1192 年）之前，已传入日本，促进了日本汉方医学的进步。

北宋时期中医药教育得到充分发展，重视国际交流，宋真宗大中祥

was honored by the Japanese as the "The God of Herbal Administration."

During the Western Han dynasty, Zhang Qian made two trips to the Western Regions, broadened the economic and cultural channels among the Central Plains, Northwest, and Southwest frontiers, and formed the well-known "Silk Road." In the Eastern Han dynasty, Ban Chao managed the Western Regions after Zhang Qian and maintained the smooth passage of the "Silk Road." During the political and cultural exchange activities with the Western Regions, the exchange of medicine was also conducted. They introduced the advanced medical knowledge of the Central Plains to the Western Regions, and at the same time brought the medical knowledge of the Western Regions back to the Central Plains. For example, the special products from the Western Regions were brought back, such as Shiliu (pomegranate), Putao (grape), Huma (flax), and Hetao (walnut). After TCM was introduced to Vietnam, Vietnam's Xiangya (ivory), Zhenzhu (pearl), Daimao (hawksbill), Xijiao (rhinoceros horn), Longyan (longan), Binlang (areca), Changpu (acorus calamus), and Yimi (coix seed) also entered the Central Plains. In *Shennong Bencao Jing*, the first monograph of Chinese materia medica, the medicinal materials in the Western Regions are recorded.

In the Han dynasty, the contacts between China and India had already begun. Ancient Indian medicine and Buddhism were closely related. During the reign of the emperor Han Mingdi, the Indian monks, Nie Moteng and Zhu Falan, carried scriptures to Baima Temple in Luoyang, Henan province on white horses, where they translated the medical and health knowledge of Buddhist scriptures. They were gradually integrated into TCM and became an integral part of TCM in preventing and treating diseases. During the Sui and Tang dynasties, Xuan Zang (602-604), a monk born in Yanshi county, Henan province, went to India to seek Buddhist sutras. In *Datang Xiyu Ji* (*Records of the Western Regions of the Great Tang dynasty*), he records that the Indian medicine entered the Central Plains with Buddhism and compares the medicines of China and India. Xuan Zang's footprints showed that the medical exchanges between China, India, Nepal, and Pakistan had been prosperous in the Tang dynasty.

In the Tang dynasty, the medical exchanges between China and Japan were very extensive. The prescriptions carved on the Prescription Cave of Longmen in Luoyang, were introduced to Japan in the Tang dynasty and respected by Japanese doctors. In

符九年（1016年），曾向高丽使者赠送了中原名医王怀隐编纂的大型方书《太平圣惠方》1000卷。

明代时期，高丽著名医家许俊，参考数百部中医古籍，花了十多年功夫，用汉语编撰了《东医宝鉴》一书，并于1613年出版。对发展高丽医学起了很大作用，至今一直被韩国医学奉为经典。

诞生于中原的《黄帝内经》《神农本草经》《伤寒杂病论》三部经典著作，犹如金鼎之三足，承托起中医学宏伟之大厦。它们在历史发展的长河中，汇集众流，生生不息，对日本的医学发展也产生了巨大影响。

到了日本江户时期（1603～1867年），日本汉医届出现了研究《黄帝内经》《神农本草经》《伤寒杂病论》的高潮，涌现了一批高质量的研究著作，如丹波元简的《素问识》《伤寒论辑义》和《金匮玉函要略辑义》，森立之的《伤寒论考注》《金匮要略考注》《神农本草经》辑本等。使这几部经典成为日本汉方医界的主流学术思想。

中华人民共和国建立后，特别是改革开放以来，河南省对外交流与合作日益频繁，与美国、加拿大、英国、俄罗斯、德国、瑞士等50多个国家政府、大学、科研与医疗机构、企业等建立了广泛联系，政府搭台，高校、医院、企业多方参与，多渠道工作，开展了人才培养、科学研究、医疗服务、产品研发等多方面的国际合作与交流。

河南中医药教育国际合作与交流得到空前发展，合作领域不断拓展，国家中医药管理局中医药国际合作基地相继在豫落户，河南中医药的国际影响力不断扩大。河南有关高校及机构与美国纽约医学院、南阿拉巴马大学、澳大利亚西悉尼大学、新西兰中医学院、日本浜松医科大学、东京国立感染症研究中心、金泽大学药学部、韩国釜山大学、大邱韩医大学、韩国东义科学大学、美国哈佛大学医学院、加拿大安省中医学院、巴西若茵维莱大学、瑞典伦德大学、意大利那不勒斯第一卫生局、意大利那不勒斯东方大学、意大利素问中医培训中心、德国康斯坦茨市传统中医与自然疗法中心、苏丹非洲国际大学、香港大学等50多个海外教育、科研、

984 A.D., Tanba Yasuyori, an ancient Japanese medical expert, compiled *Yixin Fang* (*Ishinpo*), which is a collection of 95 prescriptions carved on the Prescription Cave of Longmen, and called them "Prescriptions Inscribed in the Longmen Cave."

Zhang Zhongjing's works had been introduced to Japan before the Ping'an Period (794 A.D.- 1192 A.D.), which promoted the progress of TCM in Japan.

In the Northern Song dynasty, TCM education was fully developed. The government attached great importance to international exchange. In the ninth year of Dazhong Xiangfu of Emperor Song Zhenzong(1016 A.D.), the Northern Song government presented 1,000 volumes of *Taiping Shenghui Fang* compiled by Wang Huaiyin, a famous doctor in the Central Plains, to the messenger of Koryo.

In the Ming dynasty, Xu Jun, a famous Koryo physician, consulted hundreds of ancient books of TCM, spent more than ten years compiling *Dongyi Baojian* (*Treasured Mirror of Oriental Medicine*) in Chinese language and had it published in 1613 A.D. This book played a great role in the development of Koryo medicine at that time and has been regarded as classic by Korean medicine to this day.

The three classics: *Huangdi Neijing, Shennong Bencao Jing, and Shanghan Zabing Lun* of the Central Plains, are like three feet of the golden tripod that support the magnificent edifice of TCM. In the long course of historical development, these classics have gathered the wisdom of the sage and had a great impact on the development of Japanese medicine.

By the time of the Edo Period in Japan (1603 A.D. – 1867 A.D.), the high tide of the study of *Huangdi Neijing, Shennong Bencao Jing*, and *Shanghan Zabing Lun*, a number of high-quality research works have emerged, such as Dan Bo-yuan-jian's *Suwen Shi* (*Corrections of Plain Questions*), *Shanghan Lun Jiyi* (*A Collection of Annonations on Treatise on Cold Damage Diseases*), *Jingui Yuhan Yaolue Jiyi* (*A Collection of Annotations on Synopsis of the Golden Chamber*), Sen Li-zhi's *Shanghan Lun Kaozhu* (*Collected Commentaries on Treatise on Cold Damage diseases*), *Jingui Yaolue Kaozhu* (*Collected Commentaries on Synopsis of the Golden Chamber*), and *Shennong Bencao Jing*. Later, these classics became the mainstream academic thoughts of the Japanese TCM medical circles.

After the founding of the People's Republic of China, especially since the reformation and opening of the country, Henan Province has increased foreign exchange and cooperation with more than 50 governments, universities, scientific

医疗机构，开展了联合办学、医疗和科技国际交流与合作。

河南省积极推进中医药高等教育国际化，大力支持留学生来豫学习，提供河南省政府奖学金，鼓励海外学子来河南学习中医。自1994年8月起，教育部批准河南中医高校为外国留学生和港澳台学生招生单位。目前在豫学习中医的外国留学生200余人，已毕业的各类学历教育留学生及港澳台地区学生1000余人。河南中医药大学在马来西亚设立分校，建立了“河南中医药大学MSU仲景学院”，成为中医药院校境外办学第一家。

## 二、中医药已成为河南省对外交流与合作的优势领域

在中医药全球发展的同时，河南中医药国际交流与合作纷繁活跃。厚重的中原中医药文化为河南中医药走出去奠定了良好根基，河南作为中医药大省，在全国具有举足轻重的地位。明显的历史优势、文化优势和资源优势，具备了建设中医药强省和快速发展的基础条件。已初步形成多形式、多渠道、多层次的交流与合作格局，进入较快的发展时期。

加强中医药对外交流合作，深化河南省与多国政府和世界卫生组织、

中医药合作基地（河南）
International TCM Cooperation Base

research and medical institutions, and enterprises in the United States, Canada, Britain, Russia, Germany, and Switzerland. Henan Province has been carrying out international cooperation and exchange in forms of personnel training, scientific research, medical services, product research and development with governments, universities, hospitals, and enterprises.

The international cooperation and exchange in education of TCM in Henan province has developed unprecedentedly, and the fields of cooperation are continuously expanding. The International Cooperation Bases of TCM of the SACM have settled in Henan province one after another, and the international influence of TCM in Henan province has been expanding. The relevant universities and institutions in Henan province have carried out joint international exchange and cooperation in running schools, medical care, science, and technology with more than 50 overseas educational, scientific, or medical institutions, including New York Medical College of Health Professions, University of South Alabama, University of Western Sydney in Australia, New Zealand College of Traditional Chinese Medicine, Hamamatsu Medical University of Japan, Tokyo National Infectious Disease Research Center, Pharmaceutical Department of Kanazawa University, Busan University of Korea, Daegu Haany University, Dong-Eui Institute of Technology, School of Medicine of Harvard University, Ontario College of TCM in Canada, University of Rheinville in Brazil, Lund University in Sweden, First Health Bureau of Naples in Italy, Italy Plain Questions TCM Training Center, Konstantz City TCM and Natural Therapy Centre in Germany, Sudan International University in Africa, and Hongkong University.

Henan province actively promotes the internationalization of higher education of TCM, vigorously supports foreign students to study in Henan, provides Henan government scholarship, and encourages overseas students to study TCM in Henan. Since August 1994, the Ministry of Education has approved Henan colleges and universities of TCM as units for recruiting students from Hong Kong, Macao, Taiwan, and internationally. At present, there are more than 200 foreign students studying TCM in Henan province, and more than 1000 students from foreign countries, Hong Kong, Macao and Taiwan have graduated from Henan. Henan University of CM has set up a branch in Malaysia and established MSU Zhong-jing College of Henan University of CM, which is the first overseas school of TCM

国际标准化组织等的交流与合作，积极参与国际规则、标准的研究与制订，营造有利于中医药海外发展的国际环境。本着政府支持、民间运作、服务当地、互利共赢的原则，支持河南中医药高校、药企走出去探索建设中医药海外中心。支持河南中医药机构全面参与全球中医药各领域合作与竞争，发挥中医药社会组织的作用。在国家援外医疗中进一步增加中医药服务内容。推进多层次的中医药国际教育交流合作，吸引更多的海外留学生来河南接受学历教育、非学历教育、短期培训和临床实习，把中医药打造成中外人文交流、民心相通的亮丽名片。

作为医圣张仲景的故乡，河南积极发挥河南中医药对外工作的优势，鼓励支持中医药走出去为世界人民健康服务；发挥河南国际航空港优势，鼓励河南中医药国际贸易，将中医药国际贸易纳入河南对外贸易发展总体战略，支持河南中医药机构参与“一带一路”建设，扩大中医药对外投资和贸易，为中医药服务贸易发展提供全方位公共资源保障。

## 三、河南中医药对外援助增进了国际友谊

中国在致力于自身发展的同时，坚持向发展中国家提供力所能及的援助，承担相应国际义务。目前，中国已向亚洲、非洲、拉丁美洲的 70 多个国家派遣了医疗队，在非洲国家启动建设中国中医中心，在科威特、阿尔及利亚、突尼斯、摩洛哥、马耳他、纳米比亚等国家还设有专门的中医医疗队（点）。截至目前，中国政府在海外支持建立了 10 个中医药中心。近年来，中国加强在发展中国家特别是非洲国家开展艾滋病、疟疾等疾病防治，先后派出中医技术人员 400 余名，分赴坦桑尼亚、科摩罗、印度尼西亚等 40 多个国家。援外医疗队采用中药、针灸、推拿以及中西医结合方法治疗了不少疑难重症，挽救了许多垂危病人的生命，得到受援国政府和人民的充分肯定。

河南省于 1973 年开始承担埃塞俄比亚、赞比亚和厄立特里亚 3 个国

of Henan province.

## Ⅱ. TCM as an Advantageous Field of Henan's International Exchange and Cooperation

In the global development of TCM, the international exchange and cooperation of TCM in Henan are numerous and active. The rich culture of TCM in the Central Plains has laid a good foundation for Henan to go out. Henan, as a big province of TCM, has a pivotal position in China. Its historical, cultural, and resourceful advantages make Henan a strong province of TCM and promotes the rapid development. Henan TCM has formed a multi-form, multi-channel, multi-level exchange and cooperation pattern, entered a relatively rapid development period.

Henan will continue to strengthen the exchange and cooperation of TCM with foreign countries, deepen the exchange and cooperation with other governments, the WHO, and the International Organization for Standardization, actively participate in the research and formulation of international rules and standards, and create an international environment conducive to the overseas development of TCM. In line with the principles of government support, non-governmental operation, local service and mutual benefit, colleges and universities of TCM and pharmaceutical enterprises in Henan should be supported to go out and explore the construction of overseas centers of TCM. We should support Henan TCM institutions to fully participate in global cooperation and competition in various fields of TCM and give full play to the role of TCM social organizations. The contents of TCM services should be further increased in the country's foreign aid. We should promote multi-level international educational exchange and cooperation in TCM, attract more overseas students to Henan for academic education, non-academic education, short-term training, and clinical practice, and make TCM a beautiful business card for cultural exchanges between China and foreign countries.

As the hometown of Zhang Zhongjing, the medical sage of TCM, Henan actively exerts the advantages of Henan's external work of TCM, encourages and supports TCM to go out and serve the world's people's health, gives full play to the advantages of Henan's international airport, encourages the international trade of TCM in Henan, and brings the international trade of TCM into the overall strategy

河南援外医疗表彰会
Awards Ceremony for Medical Aid Team to Africa of Henan Province

家的医疗援助任务，先后派出53批1069人次。基本上每个医疗队中都有中医药人员，约占医务人员总数的10%。历届医疗队在各地各单位的大力支持下，继承优良传统，坚持创新发展，出色地完成了各项援外任务，受到受援国政府和人民的高度评价。

河南省人民政府提出在“十三五”规划中创建1～2家国家康养旅游示范基地。促进旅游与中医药融合发展，推动中医药旅游产品创新、医疗资源开放共享，加强中医药健康旅游产品国际交流合作，创建2～3家全国中医药健康旅游示范区、5家省级中医药健康旅游示范区和10家全国中医药健康旅游示范企业（基地）、20家省级中医药健康旅游示范企业（基地）。积极引进国际高端医疗企业和研发机构，以健康检查、慢性病治疗康复、中医药养生保健等为重点，培育康复、健身、养生与休闲旅游融合发展新业态。完善以温泉为主题的度假、养生、娱乐、观光等复合型旅游产品体系，建设一批知名温泉养生度假目的地。展望未来，

of Henan's foreign trade development, supports Henan TCM institutions to take part in the construction of "one belt and one road," expands the external investment and trade of TCM, and provides all-round public resources protection for the development of TCM trade in services.

## Ⅲ. Henan's Foreign Aid in TCM and International Friendship

While devoting itself to its own development, China persists in extending assistance within its capacity to developing countries and undertakes corresponding international obligations. At present, China has dispatched medical teams to more than 70 countries in Asia, Africa, and Latin America. In Africa, China has initiated the construction of TCM centers. In Kuwait, Algeria, Tunisia, Morocco, Malta, Namibia, and other countries, there are also special medical teams of TCM. Up to now, the Chinese government has supported 10 TCM centers overseas. In recent years, China has been strengthening the prevention and treatment of AIDS and malaria in developing countries, especially in Africa. More than 400 Chinese medical technicians have been sent to more than 40 countries, including Tanzania, Comoros, and Indonesia. These foreign aid medical teams have adopted TCM, acupuncture, massage, and the combination of Chinese and Western medicine to treat a lot of difficult and severe cases, which have saved the lives of many patients and have been fully affirmed by the government and people of the recipient countries.

In 1973, Henan province began to undertake medical assistance tasks in Ethiopia, Zambia, and Eritrea and has sent 53 batches involving 1069 people to these countries. Basically, every medical team had TCM personnel, accounting for 10% of the total number of medical staff. With the strong support of various groups in various places, all the medical teams have inherited fine traditions and insisted on innovation and development. They have accomplished various foreign aid tasks successfully and have been highly praised by the governments and people of the recipient countries.

Henan provincial People's Government has proposed to establish 1-2 national health tourism demonstration bases, 2-3 national health tourism demonstration zones, 5 provincial health tourism demonstration zones, 10 national health tourism

河南中医药发展蓝图已经绘就，平台已经搭建，条件已经成熟，河南中医药事业必将迎来新一轮更快更好的发展，河南中医药文化国际交流与合作将在中原崛起中发挥更大作用。

demonstration enterprises (bases), and 20 provincial health tourism demonstration enterprises of TCM during the 13th Five-Year Plan period to promote the integration of tourism and TCM, drive the innovation of tourism products of TCM, open and share medical resources, and strengthen international exchange and cooperation of health tourism products of TCM. Henan has planned to actively introduce international high-end medical enterprises and research and development institutions, focusing on health examination, treatment and rehabilitation of chronic diseases, health care of TCM, to cultivate a new form of integration of rehabilitation, fitness, health care and leisure tourism, to perfect complex tourism product system regarding the hot springs as the theme of vacation, health care, entertainment, sightseeing and others forms. Looking forward to the future, the blueprint for the development of TCM in Henan province has been drawn, the platform has been built and the conditions have been ripe. Henan's cause of TCM will surely usher in a new round of faster and better development. Henan's culture of TCM will certainly play a greater role in international exchange and cooperation in the rise of the Central Plains.

# 附录一
Appendix Ⅰ

## 中国历史年代简表
## A Brief Chronology of Chinese History

| | | |
|---|---|---|
| 五帝时代<br>Period of the Five Legendary Rulers<br>c. 2600 B.C.—c. 2070 B.C. | | 黄帝 Huangdi (Yellow Emperor) |
| | | 颛顼 Zhuanxu |
| | | 帝喾 Diku (Emperor Ku) |
| | | （唐）尧 Yao |
| | | （虞）舜 Shun |
| 夏 Xia Dynasty | | c . 2070 B.C.— c . 1600 B.C. |
| 商 Shang Dynasty | | c . 1600 B.C.— c . 1046 B.C. |
| 西周 Western Zhou Dynasty | | c . 1046 B.C.— c . 771 B.C. |
| 东周<br>Eastern Zhou Dynasty 770 B.C.—256 B.C. | 春秋<br>Spring and Autumn Period | 770 B.C.—476B.C. |
| | 战国<br>Warring States Period | 475 B.C.—221 B.C. |
| 秦 Qin Dynasty | | 221 B.C.—206 B.C. |
| 汉<br>Han Dynasty206 B.C.—220 A.D. | 西汉<br>Western Han | 206 B.C.—25 A.D. |
| | 东汉 Eastern Han | 25—220 |
| 三国<br>Three Kingdoms 220—280 | 魏 Wei | 220—265 |
| | 蜀汉 Shu Han | 221—263 |
| | 吴 Wu | 222—280 |
| 晋<br>Jin Dynasty 265—420 | 西晋 Western Jin | 265—317 |
| | 东晋 Eastern Jin | 317—420 |

**续表 Continued Table**

| | | | |
|---|---|---|---|
| 南北朝 Southern and Northern Dynasties420—589 | 南朝 Southern Dynasties | 宋 Song | 420—479 |
| | | 齐 Qi | 479—502 |
| | | 梁 Liang | 502—557 |
| | | 陈 Chen | 557—589 |
| | 北朝 Northern Dynasties | 北魏 Northern Wei | 386—534 |
| | | 东魏 Eastern Wei | 534—550 |
| | | 北齐 Northern Qi | 550—577 |
| | | 西魏 Western Wei | 535—556 |
| | | 北周 Northern Zhou | 557—581 |
| 隋 Sui Dynasty | | 581—618 | |
| 唐 Tang Dynasty | | 618— 907 | |
| 五代十国 Five Dynasties and Ten States | 五代 Five Dynasties 907—960 | 后梁 Later Liang | 907—923 |
| | | 后唐 Later Tang | 923—936 |
| | | 后晋 Later Jin | 936—947 |
| | | 后汉 Later Han | 947—950 |
| | | 后周 Later Zhou | 951—960 |
| | 十国 Ten States 902—979 | 北汉 Northern Han | 951—979 |
| | | 吴 Wu | 902—937 |
| | | 吴越 Wuyue | 907—978 |
| | | 闽 Min | 909—945 |
| | | 南汉 Southern Han | 917—971 |
| | | 荆南(又称"南平") Jingnan (Nanping) | 924—963 |
| | | 楚 Chu | 927—951 |
| | | 南唐 Southern Tang | 937—975 |
| | | 前蜀 Former Shu | 907—925 |
| | | 后蜀 Later Shu | 934—965 |

续表 Continued Table

| | | |
|---|---|---|
| 宋<br>Song Dynasty 960—1279 | 北宋<br>Northern Song | 960—1127 |
| | 南宋<br>Southern Song | 1127—1279 |
| 辽<br>Liao (契丹 Qidan/Khitan) | 907—1125 | |
| 金 Jin | 1115—1234 | |
| 西夏 Xixia (Tangut) | 1038— 1227 | |
| 元 Yuan Dynasty | 1206—1368 | |
| 明 Ming Dynasty | 1368—1644 | |
| 清 Qing Dynasty | 1616—1911 | |
| 中华民国<br>Republic of China | 1912—1949 | |
| 中华人民共和国<br>People's Republic of China | 1949— | |

# 附录二
Appendix II

| 古籍名称中英文对照附录<br>Chinese-English Titles of Ancient Classics | | |
|---|---|---|
| 中文<br>Chinese Title | 拼音<br>Pin Yin | 英文<br>English Title |
| 《抱朴子》 | Baopuzi | Baopuzi |
| 《本草纲目》 | Bencao Gangmu | Compendium of Materia Medica |
| 《本草图经》 | Bencao Tujing | Illustrated Classic of Materia Medica |
| 《博物志》 | Bo Wu Zhi | Records of Diverse Matters |
| 《褚氏遗书》 | Chushi Yishu | Fragmentary Book of Master Chu |
| 《大观经史证类备急本草》 | Daguan Jingshi Zhenglei Beiji Bencao | Overview of the Classified Materia Medica from Historical Classics for Emergency |
| 《大唐西域记》 | Datang Xiyu Ji | Records of the Western Regions of the Great Tang Dynasty |
| 《大医精诚》 | Dayi Jingcheng | On the Absolute Sincerity of Great Doctors |
| 《帝王世纪》 | Diwang Shiji | The Ages of Emperors |
| 《滇南本草》 | Diannan Bencao | Materia Medica of South Yunnan |
| 《跌损妙方》 | Diesun Miaofang | The Effective Prescriptions for Trauma |
| 《东医宝鉴》 | Dongyi Baojian | Treasured Mirror of Oriental Medicine |

续表 Continued Table

| | | |
|---|---|---|
| 《读素问钞》 | Du Suwen Chao | Notes for Reading Plain Questions |
| 《范汪方》 | Fangwang Fang | Fan Wang's Prescriptions |
| 《风俗通义》 | Fengsu Tongyi | General Discussions of Customs |
| 《辅行诀》 | Fuxing Jue | Essentials of Formulas for Zang-fu Ailments |
| 《骨蒸病灸方》 | Guzhengbing Jiufang | Moxibustion Prescriptions for Steaming Bone Diseases |
| 《光州志》 | Guangzhou Zhi | Records of Guangzhou Prefecture |
| 《韩非子》 | Hanfeizi | Hanfeizi |
| 《寒温条辨》 | Hanwen Tiaobian | Detailed Analysis of Cold and Epidemic Febrile Diseases |
| 《和剂局方》 | Hejiju Fang | Formulary of the Bureau of Pharmacy |
| 《河南通志》 | Henan Tongzhi | General Records of the Henan Province |
| 《河图》 | He Tu | The Yellow River Map |
| 《怀庆府志》 | Huaiqingfu Zhi | The annals of Huaiqing Prefecture |
| 《淮南子》 | Huainanzi | Huainanzi |
| 《黄帝内经》 | Huangdi Neijing | Huangdi' s Internal Classic |
| 《黄庭经》 | Huangting Jing | Huangting's Classic |

续表 Continued Table

| | | |
|---|---|---|
| 《黄庭内景经》 | Huangting Neijing Jing | Inner Meditation Classic of the Huangting School |
| 《鸡峰备急方》 | Jifeng Beiji Fang | Jifeng Formulas for Emergency |
| 《鸡峰普济方》 | Jifeng Puji Fang | Jifeng Formulas for Universal Relief |
| 《纪效新书》 | Jixiao Xinshu | A Book on the Art of War |
| 《嘉佑本草》 | Jiayou Bencao | Materia Medica of the Jiayou Reign |
| 《甲乙经》 | Jiayi Jing | A-B Classic of Acupuncture and Moxibustion |
| 《解字》 | Jiezi | Elucidation of Characters |
| 《金匮要略》 | Jingui Yaolue | Synopsis of the Golden Chamber |
| 《金匮要略考注》 | Jingui Yaolue Kaozhu | Collected Commentaries on Synopsis of tthe Golden Chamber |
| 《金匮玉函要略辑义》 | Jingui Yuhan Yaolue Jiyi | A Collection of Annotations on Synopsis from the Golden Cabinet |
| 《经史证类备急本草》 | Jingshi Zhenglei Beiji Bencao | Classified Materia Medica from Historical Classics for Emergency |
| 《救荒本草》 | Jiuhuang Bencao | Materia Medica for Famine Relief |
| 《开宝重定本草》 | Kaibao Chongding Bencao | Revised Materia Medica of the Kaibao Reign |
| 《疗风气诸方》 | Liao Fengqi Zhufang | The Prescriptions for Treating Wind Diseases |

**续表** Continued Table

| | | |
|---|---|---|
| 《列子》 | Lie Zi | Liezi |
| 《灵枢》 | Ling Shu | Miraculous Pivot |
| 《洛书》 | Luo Shu | Lo Shu Square |
| 《吕氏春秋》 | Lüshi Chunqiu | Master Lü's Spring and Autumn Annals |
| 《脉经》 | Mai Jing | Pulse Classic |
| 《梦溪笔谈》 | Mengxi Bitan | Dream Creek Essays |
| 《难经》 | Nanjing | Classic of Difficulties |
| 《难经本义》 | Nanjing Benyi | The Original Meaning of the Classic of Difficulties |
| 《普济方》 | Puji Fang | Formulary of Universal Relief |
| 《千金方》 | Qianjin Fang | Prescriptions Worth a Thousand Gold Pieces |
| 《千金要方》 | Qianjin Yaofang | Important Prescriptions Worth a Thousand Gold Pieces |
| 《全生指迷方》 | Quansheng Zhimi Fang | Life-Saving Formulas for Differentiating Confusion |
| 《儒门事亲》 | Rumen Shiqin | Confucians' Duties to Parents |
| 《伤寒补亡论》 | Shanghan Buwang Lun | Supplement to What had been Lost from Treatise on Cold Damage |
| 《伤寒论》 | Shanghan Lun | Treatise on Cold Damage |

续表 Continued Table

| | | |
|---|---|---|
| 《伤寒论辑义》 | Shanghan Lun Jiyi | A Collection of Annonations to Treatise on Cold Damage Diseases |
| 《伤寒论考注》 | Shanghan Lun Kaozhu | Collected Commentaries on the Treatise on Cold Damage Diseases |
| 《伤寒杂病论》 | Shanghan Zabing Lun | Treatise on Cold Damage and Miscellaneous Diseases |
| 《商城县志》 | Shangcheng Xianzhi | Annals of Shangcheng County |
| 《尚书》 | Shang Shu | The Book of History |
| 《少林跌打损伤秘方》 | Shaolin Dieda Sunshang Mifang | Diesun Miaofang |
| 《少林武功医宗秘笈》 | Shaolin Wugong Yizong Miji | The Secret of Shaolin Martial Art and Classical Medicine |
| 《少林药局记》 | Shaolin Yaoju Ji | Record of Shaolin Pharmacy |
| 《神农本草》 | Shennong Bencao | Shennong's Classic of Materia Medica |
| 《神仙传》 | Shenxian Zhuan | Biography of the Immortals |
| 《圣惠选方》 | Shenghui Xuanfang | Holy Prescriptions for Universal Relief |
| 《圣济总录》 | Shengji Zonglu | Comprehensive Recording of Sage-like Benefit |
| 《十四经发挥》 | Shisijing Fahui | Elucidation on Fourteen Channels |
| 《食疗本草》 | Shiliao Bencao | Materia Medica for Dietotherapy |

续表 Continued Table

| | | |
|---|---|---|
| 《史记》 | Shiji | Records of the Historian |
| 《水经注》 | Shuijing Zhu | Commentary on the Waterways Classic |
| 《说文》 | Shuowen | Explanation of Script |
| 《说文解字》 | Shuowen Jiezi | Explanation of Script and Elucidation of Characters |
| 《嵩崖尊生全书》 | Songya Zunsheng Quanshu | Songya's Complete Treatise on Respecting Life |
| 《宋大诏令集》 | Song Dazhaoling Ji | The Collection of Emperor's Orders in the Song Dynasty |
| 《宋史》 | Song Shi | History of the Song Dynasty |
| 《素问》 | Su Wen | Plain Questions |
| 《素问识》 | Suwen Shi | Corrections of Plain Questions |
| 《太平惠民局方》 | Taiping Huiminju Fang | Formulary of the Taiping People's Welfare Bureau |
| 《太平圣惠方》 | Taiping Shenghui Fang | Taiping Holy Prescriptions for Universal Relief |
| 《汤液经》 | Tanye Jing | Classic of Decoctions |
| 《汤阴县志》 | Tangyin Xianzhi | Records of Tangyin County |
| 《铜人腧穴针灸图经》 | Tongren Shuxue Zhenjiu Tujing | Illustrated Manual of Acupoints of the Bronze Figure |
| 《图经》 | Tu Jing | Illustrated Classic |

续表 Continued Table

| | | |
|---|---|---|
| 《图经本草》 | Tujing Bencao | Illustrated Classic of Materia Medica |
| 《外台秘要》 | Waitai Miyao | Arcane Essentials from the Imperial Library |
| 《五十二病方》 | Wushier Bingfang | Fifty-Two Medical Formulas |
| 《洗冤集录》 | Xiyuan Jilu | Records for Washing Away of Wrong Cases |
| 《小儿药证直诀》 | Xiaoer Yaozheng Zhijue | Key to Medicines and Patterns of Children's Diseases |
| 《新刊补注铜人腧穴针灸图经》 | Xinkan Buzhu Tongren Shuxue Zhenjiu Tujing | New Compilation of Supplemental Annotations to Illustrated Manual of Acupoints of the Bronze Figure |
| 《新校正》 | Xin Jiaozheng | The Newly-Revised Medical Books |
| 《一统志》 | Yitong Zhi | General Geographical Records |
| 《伊尹汤液经法》 | Yiyin Tangye Jingfa | Canon of Yi Yin's Decoction |
| 《医史》 | Yishi | Biography of Medical Figures |
| 《医心方》 | Yixin Fang | Ishinpo |
| 《医学心悟》 | Yixue Xinwu | Comprehension of Medicine |
| 《医宗金鉴》 | Yizong Jinjian | Golden Mirror of the Medical Ancestors |
| 《易经》 | Yi Jing | The Book of Changes |

**续表** Continued Table

| | | |
|---|---|---|
| 《御药院方》 | Yüyao Yuanfang | Formulas collected by the Royal Medical Academy |
| 《战国策》 | Zhanguo Ce | Strategies of the Warring States |
| 《彰德府志》 | Zhangdefu Zhi | Records of Zhangde Prefrecture |
| 《折狱龟鉴》 | Zheyu Guijian | A Collection of Model Judicial Cases |
| 《针灸甲乙经》 | Zhenjiu Jiayi Jing | A-B Classic of Acupuncture and Moxibustion |
| 《诊家枢要》 | Zhenjia Shuyao | Essentials for Diagnosticians |
| 《植物名实图考》 | Zhiwu Mingshi Tukao | Illustrated Reference of Botanical Nomenclature |
| 《植物名实图考长编》 | Zhiwu Mingshi Tukao Changbian | Detailed Analysis of Illustrated Reference of Botanical Nomenclature |
| 《重广补注黄帝内经素问》 | Chongguang Buzhu Huangdi Neijing Suwen | Revised and Supplemental Annotations to Plain Questions of Huangdi's Internal Classic |
| 《周易》 | Zhouyi | The Book of Changes |
| 《诸病源候论》 | Zhubing Yuanhou Lun | Treatise on Causes and Manifestations of Various Diseases |
| 《庄子》 | Zhuangzi | Zhuangzi |